PHYSICS
IN THE
REAL WORLD

Keith Lockett

CAMBRIDGE
UNIVERSITY PRESS

Published by the Press Syndicate of the University of Cambridge
The Pitt Building, Trumpington Street, Cambridge CB2 1RP
40 West 20th Street, New York, NY 10011-4211, USA
10 Stamford Road, Oakleigh, Victoria 3166, Australia

First published 1990
Reprinted 1992

Printed in Great Britain by Scotprint Ltd, Musselburgh, Scotland

British Library cataloguing-in-publication data
Lockett, Keith
  Physics in the real world.
  1. Physics
  I. Title
  530

Library of Congress cataloging-in-publication data
Lockett, Keith
  Physics in the real world.
  1. Physics.   I. Title.
  QC21.2.L62 1989   530   88–30513

ISBN 0 521 36690 9

Contents

Introduction

This small book has two main purposes: it wants to show you that physics is inextricably part of our modern way of thinking and living, and it aims to give you practice in applying the basic physics that you learn in the classroom to real life situations. As far as I can make them, all the figures quoted are absolutely reliable and realistic. Some people who have seen it say that there is too much about war and weapons in it. That may be true, but at present, in the west, over half of all research physicists are working to design or develop weapons (and I imagine the proportion is even higher in the Soviet bloc). Thus any book that tries to look at the place of physics in the modern world must include a fair bit about the preparation for war.

I do hope that you will try the questions before turning to the back of the book to look up the answers. There is little to be gained from just reading my answers, and nothing to be lost from getting the answers wrong. No one minds getting a wrong result. There is only one kind of wrong answer that infuriates a physicist and that is serving up a fatuous number, like saying a man runs at 100 m s^{-1} or a rocket flies at 10 m s^{-1}. It is for this reason that my answers are all given in round figures only (I don't have a calculator). There are very few questions in the whole of physics where an answer to ± 10 per cent is not good enough. If you do use a calculator, round off all your answers to that precision, and take π as 3 and π^2 as 10. Please note that in many cases it is necessary to read the answers in order to benefit fully from the exercises. Generally, we only need an order-of-magnitude answer. To encourage this kind of thinking, the great Enrico Fermi used to ask his students, 'How many piano tuners are there in Chicago?'. He wanted his students to make reasonable guesses to get order-of-magnitude answers.

I have tried to write a book that is not stuffy and I hope the jokes are not too feeble because I think that physics is an enthralling subject, an exciting adventure of the mind. It is a subject not only for the study and the lab but also for all the experiences of living – doing the washing up, watering the lettuces and looking at pictures. It may well be that I have made mistakes or missed seeing all the implications of the problems. You could have more up-to-date information than I have and you too will probably think up questions as you walk about the streets or sit quietly at home. If you do, please write to me, tell me where I am wrong, what I have missed, and what you have discovered. My daughter has read this book and says that the tone is sexist in parts. If anyone is put off I do apologise most sincerely and I hope that the view of the physics will not be obscured by my deficiencies in writing. Writing a book like this is a continuous process. I sincerely hope that you will want to compile your own book. Make it a better one than this.

Keith Lockett
72 Awanui Street, New Plymouth, New Zealand

Readings

1   Acceleration due to gravity

An exercise on understanding basic principles

We learn about the way things fall from our earliest days. Your first scientific experiment was probably to drop a rattle over the side of your pram and carefully watch its fall. You were happy to do this for as long as anyone could be induced to pick it up for you again. Plants know about gravity and send their roots down and their shoots up. They can be fooled by putting them in a rotating basket, when they will send their shoots towards the centre. Animals know about the dangers of gravity and even young mice will not fall off the end of a table. Cuckoos exploit gravity in a clever way. The cuckoo lays its eggs singly in the nest of another species of bird. It arranges its timing so that the cuckoo's egg hatches first, and almost as soon as it can walk the hatchling proceeds to remove the other eggs from the nest. It spreads its immature wings and, walking backwards up the side of the nest, pushes the egg until it topples over the top of the nest. Of course, the egg often slips off the back of the cuckoo chick and great perseverance is needed to get rid of all the eggs in the nest. The effort is worth it, however, as the cuckoo now enjoys the undivided attention of its unwitting foster parents.

We now know that falling objects do not move with constant speed, but accelerate. Galileo was the first to make the point clearly, although it had been known before. It is surprising that the ancients did not know it, since we can learn it from common observations. You know that cricketers find it easy to catch a gentle lob but often drop one when fielding on the boundary (even professionals sometimes drop a skier). You also know that you will not be hurt if you jump from a metre-high wall, you may break a leg if you jump from 5 m, and you will certainly be killed if you fall from the top of a skyscraper. The ancients must have known this – indeed both the Romans and the Hebrews executed wrongdoers by throwing them off high cliffs. Their ways of thinking did not lead them to make general conclusions of this kind.

Galileo knew that all objects fall with the same acceleration. It does now seem that the charming story of him dropping different weights from the top of the Leaning Tower of Pisa is not a myth, although historians keep changing their minds. When I wrote an earlier draft of this chapter a year ago, I was told that the story had no basis in fact. Now I read that it is probably true. He is also supposed to have tied a series of weights to a long string with the distances between the weights in the ratio 1:3:5:7 . . . and so on. When the string was dropped, the weights hit the floor and the intervals between the noises they made were constant. The distances through which the weight fell were then in the ratio 1:4:9:16 . . . : a result that he had already obtained for his experiment of rolling a ball down a long slope.

Galileo also knew that the path of a projectile is a parabola. He even published tables of the range of artillery for different muzzle velocities. He worked out that for optimum range, the angle was 45°. These tables must have been quite useless because there was no way of finding the speed of the cannon balls, and also because they did not take air resistance into account. However, the development of artillery attracted (comparatively) as much attention and commercial enterprise then as the 'Star Wars' programme does now.

Questions

1.1 Someone is looking out of the top floor window of a skyscraper with a brick in his hand. At the same instant, someone else is looking out of the window of the floor below. She also holds a brick. If both bricks are dropped at the same instant, will the distance between them
(a) increase,
(b) stay the same,
(c) decrease?

1.2 You are standing at the top of a high cliff with a brick in each hand. You drop one brick and one second later you drop the other brick. How does the distance between the bricks change? Does it
(a) get shorter because the second brick is accelerating,
   or
(b) stay the same because the acceleration on both bricks is the same,
   or
(c) increase because the first brick is always moving faster than the second one?

1.3 If you have not done this already, answer the last question by sketching a v–t graph.

1.4 A child climbs to the top of a slide in a children's park. As she slides to the bottom we can say that
(a) her acceleration increases and her speed increases,
(b) her acceleration increases and her speed decreases,
(c) her acceleration decreases and her speed decreases,
(d) her acceleration decreases and her speed increases.
Which is correct, assuming that friction is negligible?

1.5 Which of the above is correct if friction is taken into account? You will have to analyse the forces acting on the child, and work out under what conditions friction is considerable.

1.6 In practice, is friction between a child and a slide very small? How do you know?

1.7 A ball is thrown vertically upwards with speed 20 m s^{-1}. How far does it go in 4 s?

1.8 What is the displacement of the ball in the previous question?

1.9 In 1966, the *Surveyor 1* spaceship landed on the Moon. Rocket motors held its speed of descent constant at 15 m s^{-1} from 12 m above the surface to 4 m up. The motors were then shut off. If the acceleration due to gravity on the Moon is 1.6 m s^{-2}, with what speed did the rocket hit the Moon's surface?

1.10 Not long ago, a television programme showed a man who could jump over cars driven at him at a speed of, say, 20 m s^{-1}. Assuming that the car was 1.5 m tall and that the man could jump a height of 1.8 m, was the film a fake?

1.11 In an emergency, you have a reaction time of about 0.7 s and your car has a maximum deceleration of the order of -7.5 m s^{-2}. How long would it take you to stop when travelling at 30 m s^{-1}? How far would you go in that time?

1.12 The first science fiction story seems to have been written by Kepler (one of the giants on whose shoulders Newton stood). He knew that the Moon rotates on its axis with the same period as it rotates round the Earth and therefore always presents the same face to us. (I remember being told as a boy that one thing we humans could never hope to see was the back of the moon.) Kepler imagined that there were two races of people on the Moon: the Subvolvans who always saw the Earth and the Prevolvans who never saw it. For these people, how many days were there in a year? What was the great disadvantage in living on the Moon?

1.13 You are walking down the street when an overhead power line snaps, and you are hit by the bare wire. If the line is 8 m above the ground and it takes 1 s for the automatic mechanism at the power station to shut off the current, are you killed?

1.14 Does your distance from the power station and the speed of the current in the wire come into it?

1.15 Why does a stream of water get thinner some way below the tap?

1.16 When I did the experiment with the hot water tap in the kitchen, I found that the rate of flow was about 150 ml in 2 s or 75 cm^3 s^{-1}. (It is more convenient to work this question in cm.) The dimensions of the stream were as shown. Work out the speed of flow at the top and bottom (v_0 and v respectively), and show that these figures are in accord with the formula $v^2 = v_0^2 + 2ad$. (Alternatively, the Bernouilli equation, $\frac{1}{2}\rho_1 v_1^2 = \frac{1}{2}\rho_2 v_2^2 - \rho_2 gh$, applies.)

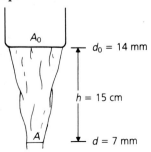

$d_0 = 14$ mm

$h = 15$ cm

$d = 7$ mm

1.17 A flea jumps off with a speed of 1 m s^{-1}. How high can it jump? (I suspect that the source of my data actually worked out this question backwards. I do not know how else you could measure the speed of a flea's take-off.)

1.18 A kangaroo can jump vertically 2.8 m (i.e. raise its centre of mass that distance). What is its take-off speed? (Deer can clear fences almost as high.)

1.19 If you wanted to repeat Galileo's experiment with the weights tied to a string (mentioned in the reading), would you hold the string with the small separations at the top or the bottom? Where must the lowest weight be?

2 Weightlessness

An exercise in understanding basic concepts

There are two basic ways in which you can be weightless. One way is to go in a space ship far out in space, so far from any heavenly body that its gravitational field is effectively zero; then you will be weightless. This state has only, so far, been achieved by science fiction characters. The nearest that real people will come to experiencing it will be on NASA's planned journey to put a man on Mars by the year 2000. It will be a long time before humans are able to leave the solar system, though. Unmanned space ships have been sent beyond it; *Voyager*, after visiting Jupiter and Saturn, is now moving ever further away, although it is still not beyond the orbit of Pluto.

The other way in which people become weightless is during a trip to the Moon or while orbiting the Earth. Then the only force acting on the space ship and its crew is gravity, because no force is needed to keep the craft circling the Earth. The force required is the centripetal force, and gravity supplies this. The situation is exactly the same as if you were in a lift and someone cut the steel rope. If you were standing on a weighing machine at the time, you would find that the machine registered zero. You (and everything in the lift) would appear to be weightless, although the force of gravity would still be acting in the usual way. In the early days of space travel, it was feared that astronauts might suffocate while they slept. Normally, the air we breathe out is heated by its passage through our lungs, expands and so becomes lighter than the surrounding cold air, and rises by convection. In a weightless environment there is no convection and it was thought that each sleeping astronaut would be enveloped in a cloud of his own exhaled air. In fact these fears were

groundless; the air purifiers sucked in the air and mixed it sufficiently.

You can try a similar experiment by putting a lighted candle in a large Kilner jar, sealing the lid and dropping it about one metre. If you catch the jar gently, you will find that the candle is extinguished. Another simple experiment is to fit a tin can with some strings (as shown here) and hang a weight from the strings. You drop the can, about a metre; the weight will only hit the bottom of the can when you catch it. While it was falling, the weight was effectively weightless.

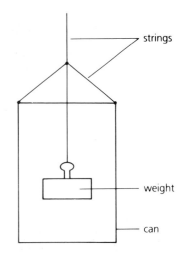

Another hazard of space flight was discovered after one of the early flights. It was found that some people sneezed a lot and that this was due to the minute hairs from electric shavers floating about in the weightless cabin. Now, the shavers are fitted with small vacuum cleaners to suck up the hairs, but most astronauts prefer to grow beards. (Another reason for having women astronauts?)

Questions

2.1 What is the control experiment for the 'candle in the Kilner jar' experiment?

2.2 What is the control experiment for the 'dropping tin can' experiment?

2.3 How do you know that no work is needed to keep a satellite orbiting the Earth?

2.4 How do you know that no work is needed to keep the Earth in orbit round the Sun?

2.5 In Jules Verne's novel '*A voyage to the Moon and a trip round it*, we read about a space ship (fired out of a cannon) going to the Moon. The crew notice that they gradually get lighter and at a point like X in the diagram they are completely weightless. What is wrong with that?

2.6 Under what (very unlikely) circumstances could you be weightless only at the point X?

2.7 The sketch below shows the approximately parabolic path taken by a KC-135 (Boeing 707) airplane while allowing astronauts in training to experience weightlessness. You will see that the astronauts undergo weightlessness (and periods of almost double weight) for long enough for experiments to be performed to test how well they keep their manual dexterity under these strange conditions. If at the top of the path the speed is 515 km h^{-1} (140 m s^{-1}) and the radius of curvature of the path is about 1600 m, confirm that the astronauts are indeed weightless then.

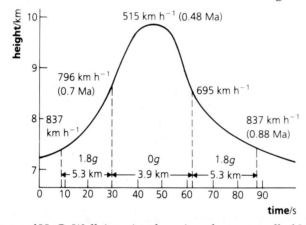

2.8 In one of H. G. Wells' stories there is a character called Mr Cavor who invents a substance which he names 'cavorite'. This has the property of shielding things from the effects of gravity. He makes a space ship and surrounds it with cavorite, apart from some shutters which open. When he wants to take off, he opens the shutter facing the Moon and the Moon's gravitational attraction pulls him off. He steers by opening other shutters facing the appropriate stars.

It is possible to shield against electrical effects, and both gravity and electricity follow an inverse-square law. So why do we think that it is unlikely that cavorite will ever be made?

2.9 Military men are said to want the discovery of substances with negative mass, on the supposition that a missile made of such a substance would rise up from the surface of the Earth and so end all their launching problems. Suppose that it were possible to make matter with negative mass, would it rise up from the Earth? (Incidentally, a group of men still have outstanding a multi-million dollar suit against the Mahareshi Yogi because of his failure to teach them to levitate as promised. There is a photograph in existence which allegedly shows grown men levitating; actually they are hopping in the lotus position, and very painful it must be.)

2.10 We know that two masses in empty space attract each other, according to Newton's law. What would happen to two spherical voids in a large lump of matter? Would they attract or repel each other?

2.11 A helicopter is used to lift live deer out of the bush. If a deer has mass 600 kg and the helicopter is rising at a constant 2 m s^{-1}, what is the tension in the rope?

2.12 Now suppose that the helicopter is rising with a constant acceleration of 2 m s^{-2}. What is the tension now?

2.13 On the planet Jupiter, the acceleration due to gravity is 25 m s^{-2}. If you can clear 1.6 m in a high jump on Earth, how high could you jump on Jupiter? (Treat this question simplistically. As it depends on suppositions, there is no point in being too pernickety.)

2.14 It is said that if and when astronauts reach Jupiter, they will not be able to stand up but will have to crawl on all fours. What do you think?

2.15 A locust (mass 3.0 g) takes off with a force of about 0.45 N applied at an angle of about 60°. Calculate its initial acceleration. If that acceleration acts over a distance of about 4 cm, calculate the locust's take-off speed, and how high and how far it can jump.

3 Plastic bullets

An exercise in using data

In parts of Britain, and elsewhere, plastic bullets are in frequent use to help control demonstrators and rowdies. Because they are very light for their size they are supposed to slow down very quickly after firing and so not be lethal. In fact, at least four children have been killed in Northern Ireland after having been hit in the head at close range. With the data given here, we will analyse their motion. They have a mass of 134 g, and they are fired with a muzzle velocity of 250 km h^{-1} (70 m s^{-1}). Their effective range is about 50 m. We then guess that they will stop completely in about 100 m.

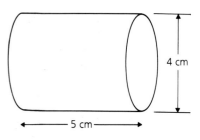

   We can then compare the effectiveness (or horribleness) of the bullet with that of another device for crowd control, the water cannon, and also with the elephant gun. We assume that the water cannon has a range of about 20 m at 45° and that the size of the jet is about 2 cm × 2 cm (I know it's circular but we only want rough figures and I hate π).

Questions

3.1 Use the data given to calculate the deceleration of the bullet.

3.2 Plastic bullets are not supposed to be used at distances less than 20 m. What is their speed at that distance? (Use your answer to the last question.)

3.3 To find whether the bullet can harm at that speed, calculate its k.e.

3.4 As I write, the Indian batsman Gavaskar is batting with his arm in plaster. It was broken when it was hit by a ball from an Australian fast bowler. Calculate the k.e. of a cricket ball, mass 160 g, moving at 30 m s^{-1}. Compare your answer with the previous one.

3.5 We can now calculate the force of air resistance on the bullet, using the formula $F = 0.5\rho CAv^2$. Here ρ is the density of air (1.3 kg m^{-3}), C is a factor related to the shape of the object (0.1 for a cylinder), A is the frontal area of the bullet, which you can calculate, and v is the speed of the bullet, in this case 70 m s^{-1}.

3.6 Now calculate the deceleration of the bullet, and compare it with the value you got in question **3.1**.

3.7 Even if they had the same energy, which would hurt more: a cricket ball or a plastic bullet?

3.8 If the range of a water cannon is 20 m when the jet is angled at 45°, calculate the speed of the water leaving the cannon.

3.9 Now, using Newton's second law in the form $F = $ d $(mv)/dt = v \, dm/dt$, calculate the rate at which water is emerging from the cannon and so the force of the water.

3.10 To compare the plastic bullet with the water jet, calculate the force the bullet exerts assuming that it stops after making a dent in your skin 2 cm deep. (Hint: use the formula $v^2 = 2ad$ to find the deceleration of the bullet when it strikes, and then find its force.) Assume you are hit when the bullet is travelling at 20 m s^{-1}.

3.11 A book of stories which I had as a boy told of a man who had an elephant gun with which he shot a charging rhinoceros and 'stopped it dead'. Can the story be true? Make the following reasonable assumptions: mass of rhino 500 kg, speed of rhino 5 m s^{-1}; mass of bullet = 0.1 kg, speed of bullet 400 m s^{-1} (this is a bit more than the speed of sound, 330 m s^{-1} – you never hear the one that gets you). Which has the greater momentum?

3.12 Now suppose that the gun recoils a distance of 1 cm in the hunter's shoulder. Assume that the mass of the gun is 4 kg. Calculate the force exerted by the gun in recoil.

3.13 Also used for crowd control are rubber bullets. Which is more likely to knock you over, a rubber bullet or a brass bullet of equal mass and moving at the same speed? Assume that they are not going fast enough to break the skin.

3.14 Which would do more damage to your body, a brass bullet or a rubber bullet?

3.15 Let us now estimate the effect of air resistance on an anti-tank shell. We are told that its muzzle velocity is 950 m s^{-1}, and that with an elevation of 17° its range is 10.5 km. Calculate the range assuming no air resistance, and compare this with the real figure.

3.16 The agreement is hopeless. To try to improve it, assume that the air resistance on the shell travelling at 900 m s^{-1} is about 400 N. This I calculated using the formula given earlier. If the mass of the shell is 20 kg, calculate the deceleration of the shell and so find how long it would take to stop. Compare this with the time of flight.

3.17 Similarly we have data for a naval gun. Here the muzzle velocity is 900 m s^{-1}, the angle of elevation 40° and the range 28 km. Repeat the exercise and say which case agrees better with the formula.

3.18 The case was reported recently of a young boy who got into an unattended petrol tanker. He opened the taps to let the petrol escape and then drove off. When the tanker was going at about 20 km h^{-1}, he put it into neutral and jumped from the cab. Assume that if the taps had been closed it would have gone at constant speed. With them open it must speed up, as it is losing mass and momentum is conserved. What do you say?

3.19 Many guns now are described as 'recoilless'. How is that possible?

3.20 We have data for the way in which a bullet loses speed due to air resistance. Unfortunately the speed is given against distance and not against time. So we shall have to box cannily.

Speed/m s^{-1}	823	660	508	391	325
Distance/m	0	225	450	675	900

Plot the graph and assume that it is a straight line between the given points. As $a = dv/dt = (dv/dx)(dx/dt)$, $a = v\,dv/dx$. Then for each of the four sections calculate dv/dx and multiply by v (taking the average value) to get the value of the acceleration, a.

Now make out a table of a against v and against v^2. Finally, plot the graph of a against v^2 and comment on the result.

4 ICBMs

An exercise in the practical applications of physics

ICBM stands for Inter-Continental Ballistic Missile, which means a weapon that can travel between continents with a range of up to 10 000 km. *Ballistic* means 'thrown' and comes from the Latin word *ballista* or catapult – not the kind that David used to slay Goliath but the type that hurled rocks and burning oil at city walls. This means that the rocket motors only work for the time it takes to get to height (the 'boost' phase) and for the time to turn it to a more or less horizontal path. The boost phase only lasts about two minutes. The rockets usually have three stages, discarding the first two.

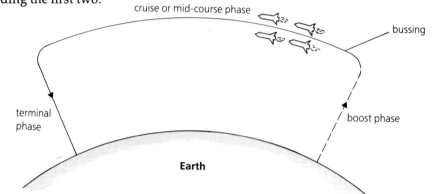

During the 'bussing' phase the missile acts as a bus, giving a lift to the fourteen or so MIRV (Multiple Independently Routed Vehicle) missiles. After that phase the missile splits up and the MIRVs, along with the decoys and radar jammers, proceed independently to their targets. For example, the Poseidon missile has a mass of about 30 000 kg, a length of 10 m and diameter 1.9 m. It has fourteen MIRVs, but their range is only 5000 km because the Poseidon is fired from a submarine when under water and it can get closer to its targets. Each submarine carries sixteen Poseidon missiles and so can deliver a total of 224 thermonuclear devices, each with a destructive power of 1 MT (that is a megatonne, equivalent to a million tonnes of TNT). One submarine carries more destructive power than all the bombers in the six years of the Second World War.

During the cruise or mid-course phase, the rocket motors are not working. When near its target, each MIRV is turned down to its target; each one is guided by inertial gyroscopes and gets directional fixes from the stars. Each missile can be directed to a different target during the terminal phase and may have some capability of evading opposing missiles. The maximum height can be up to 1000 km. I cannot discover why they go so high, as 200 km would have taken them well above the effects of the atmosphere.

Questions

4.1 Calculate the speed of the ICBM, assuming that it travels in a circular arc at a height of 600 km above the Earth (radius 6400 km). Take the mass of the Earth M as 6×10^{24} kg and the gravitational constant G as 6.7×10^{-11} N m^2 kg^{-2}.

4.2 Is there much error in taking the path as circular?

4.3 How long does it take a missile to travel the 8000 km from North Dakota to Moscow, or from Slerdvosk to New York?

4.4   How long will the (well-named) terminal phase take?

4.5   Why can you neglect the acceleration due to gravity in this calculation?

4.6   Calculate the average acceleration during the boost phase, assuming that it takes two minutes.

4.7   How will the maximum acceleration compare with the average? And when, during the boost phase, will the maximum occur?

4.8   Assume that the fuel consists entirely of hydrogen. (The nature of the fuel is a secret, but this will not be far out.) Calculate the efficiency of the whole business, assuming that a useful payload of 1000 kg is lifted to a height of 1200 km and that the value of the acceleration due to gravity hardly changes from its Earth value. Take the enthalpy of formation of water as 300 kJ mol^{-1}.

4.9   Why is no work done in the subsequent phases of the flight?

4.10   If you are whirling a ball on the end of a string around your head it will stay in a stable orbit. Suppose now that you pull on the string so as to shorten it. The ball will settle down into a new stable orbit. Will it go faster or slower? What law is operating here?

4.11   How does that law relate to Kepler's second law? (That is the one which says that planets circling the Sun sweep out equal areas in equal periods of time.)

4.12   What force is responsible for the change in speed in the new orbit?

4.13   In a synchrotron, electrons or protons are whirled round in a circular path. Every time they pass 'go' they get a pulse of energy to make them more energetic. If they are going fast enough relativistic conditions apply and they do not go any faster, but become more massive. In what way is their motion similar to that of an ICBM, or that of a planet in orbit round the Sun?

4.14   In the Brookhaven proton synchrotron, the radius of the path is 120 m and the energy of the protons at the end of their journey is 10 GeV (1.6×10^{-9} J). What is the magnetic field strength necessary to keep the protons in a circular path? Note: in this case relativistic conditions apply and we have to use the formula $E = p \times c$. Here E is the energy and p the momentum of the protons, with c the velocity of light (3×10^8 m s^{-1}).

4.15   You may not know any relativity formulae, but you can see that the formula given above looks right. How?

5 Some sporting controversies

This reading will look at several separate issues in sport that are in dispute or are the subject of continued research.

1 Ice skating

It is stated in several books that an ice skater does not move over ice but over a thin layer of water. Other writers dispute this, however.

It is well known that increasing pressure will cause ice to melt and this is called 'regelation'. This is the reason that glaciers can flow; under the great pressure of the weight of the glacier above, the melting point of ice is lowered. To demonstrate regelation, a block of ice is supported above the bench. A fine wire is attached to a mass, about 5 kg, at each end and is hung over the ice. Soon the wire will be seen to eat into the ice, and in about half an hour will pass right through it. The melted ice freezes again after the wire has passed through so the block is unchanged, although you can often see a fine line where the wire has been.

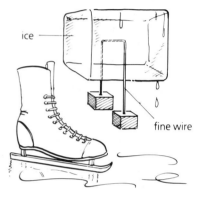

Why does ice melt if increased pressure is applied? This follows from the way in which water expands when it is frozen. (You know this is true because you have seen ice floating on water.) Hence an increase in pressure will assist melting. It is then said that regelation causes the ice to melt under the increased pressure of the skate.

In support of this idea, it is said to be impossible to skate in very cold weather, as the pressure of the skate blade can no longer melt the ice. Against the idea, you might think that young children should not be able to exert enough pressure to form ice and so should not be able to skate – but some of them certainly can. Now it is agreed that the pressure due to a skate may be large since the area of the skate blade is very small (the width may be less than a millimetre). There is, however, another consideration. The regelation experiment works much better with a copper wire than an iron one.

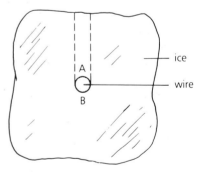

I have never been able to get an iron wire to cut right through the block before the ice melts. This is clearly due to the fact that copper has a higher coefficient of thermal conductivity than iron. To allow the water above the wire to turn back to ice, as at A in the diagram, heat energy has to be removed. This heat energy has to be conducted through the wire and delivered to the ice, as at B, so as to melt it. If the wire were a thermal insulator regelation would be impossible, at least in this experimental arrangement. Now if skating is possible only because of regelation, heat would have to be abstracted from the back of the blade to allow the ice to freeze again and conducted through the blade to the front to melt the ice. The blade of a skate is certainly made of steel and it is said that there would not be time for the heat to be conducted along its length, considering the speed at which the skate moves.

There is another consideration. If regelation depends on heat conduction then heat would be conducted better through a thick wire than through a thin one. Therefore the experiment ought to go equally well whatever the thickness. We know, however, that it will only work with thin wire.

Clearly there is room here for more experiments. My own views on the matter are divided, but I would observe that if the effect is *not* due to regelation, where do the lines come from which show the path of the skater over the ice?

2 The magic angle

Several books say, without qualification, that the greatest range for a projectile is obtained with an angle of elevation of 45°. Certainly no one throws the javelin, puts the shot or takes off in the long jump at anything like 45°, so other considerations must apply.

Firstly, the derivation of 45° assumes that air resistance is negligible and we know this is not so. Many records were set in the rarefied air of the Mexico Olympics, and Bob Beaman increased the long jump record by 0.5 m at one go. To take advantage of the decreased pressure at heights, long-distance guns fire at an elevation of about 60°.

Secondly, the derivation assumes that the firing and the landing are at the same height. This is surely not so for the shot, which is put from a height of 2 m or so, or even the long jump, where the centre of mass of the jumper is about 0.5 m above the landing place. If this factor is taken into account, the optimum angle is about 41°.

Thirdly, and most importantly, the derivation assumes that the initial velocity of the projectile does not depend on the angle of elevation. This is only true for guns; humans impart the maximum speed to a ball at about 35° elevation. We can throw a javelin much faster at an angle of about 30° than at 45°. This follows because we run horizontally before throwing and the javelin then has our horizontal speed. We should have almost to stop to throw a javelin at 45°.

3 Why dimples?

Why are golf balls dimpled but table tennis balls smooth?

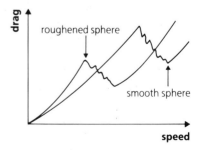

In the early days of golf, the balls were smooth. It was found by chance, that old scarred balls went further than new ones and now they are all dimpled. A swing that will drive a modern ball 220 m would send a smooth ball about 50 m and manufacturers spend a lot of money trying to improve the design of the dimples.

At high speeds, the boundary layer around the ball becomes turbulent for the roughened sphere before it does for the smooth one; a turbulent layer remains attached to the sphere longer and so produces a smaller wake. You can see this for yourself if you suspend the golf balls in turn in the blow of a powerful vacuum cleaner. A table tennis ball, however, goes slower and roughening increases the friction drag. This fascinating topic is covered fully in the book *Shape and flow* by Ascher Shapiro (Heinemann).

Questions

5.1 If you try the experiment of directing a blast of air at the golf balls, will not the balls be pushed sideways out of the air flow?

5.2 I read in a book on 'sports science' the following:

> Floodlights for illuminating sports grounds have to be high to avoid glare dazzling players under a high ball. Because of the inverse-square law, lamps of great brightness are required to produce adequate illumination at ground level.

What is wrong with that?

5.3 We often read in an account of a game that the goalkeeper made a 'reflex save' or that the fielder made a 'reflex catch'. Strictly speaking, these remarks are wrong. Why?

5.4 An Olympic long-jumper runs at approximately 10 m s^{-1} and takes off at 30°. Neglecting air resistance and assuming that all his k.e. is converted to p.e. in the jump, calculate how far he will jump. Compare your answer with the current long jump record of 8.9 m.

5.5 What is unrealistic about the previous question?

5.6 Competent long-jumpers give a 'hitch-kick' while in mid-air – that is, they appear to walk. What is the purpose of this?

5.7 An Olympic high-jumper runs to the bar at 7 m s^{-1}. Making the usual assumptions, find how high he can jump and compare your answer with the current record of 2.4 m.

5.8 For an adult male, the centre of mass is about 57 per cent of the total height above the ground and is about 2 cm below the navel.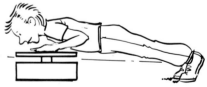
I made a rough determination of the position of my centre of mass as follows. I found that my mass is 80 kg. I then supported myself on my toes and on my hands in front of my face, resting on a balance. The balance then read 53 kg. If my hands were then 156 cm up from my toes, where was my centre of mass? If my total height is 176 cm, what proportion of my height is the height of my centre of mass?

5.9 A man of height 1.80 m and total mass 73 kg (assumed evenly distributed) and with a centre of mass at a height of 1.03 m raises both arms above his head. Where is now his centre of mass, assuming each arm is 0.66 m long and has mass 3.75 kg? When the arm is raised its centre of mass is 1.53 m above ground level, and it is 0.87 m above ground when the arm is lowered. Assume that all members have their centres of mass at the middle.

5.10 A hammer-thrower spins faster and faster, and the last revolution before release takes 0.5 s. If the wire holding the hammer is 1 m long and his arms are, effectively, $\frac{2}{3}$ m long, with what speed is the hammer released? The mass of the hammer is 7 kg, so find the force on the thrower's shoulders just before release. Could you sustain such a force?

5.11 The following data refer to a stroboscopic photograph of a diver taking off from a high board. By chance, a photograph was taken at the instant when the centre of mass of the diver was at its highest point. A photograph was taken every 0.2 s and the figures in the following table are the coordinates in metres of the diver's centre of mass.

x/m	0	0.42	0.74	1.11	1.50	1.89
y/m	3.45	3.24	2.70	2.04	1.14	0
t/s	0	0.2	0.4	0.6	0.8	1.0

Analyse separately the horizontal and vertical motions of the centre of mass of the diver and get a value for g, the acceleration due to gravity.

5.12 The diver referred to in the previous question was executing a somersault. Does that affect the previous result?

5.13 When a karate practitioner delivers a punch she stands with her feet apart, one almost behind the other. During the punch, as one hand goes forwards, the other goes back. Why is this an efficient way of doing it?

5.14 Karate training stresses the need for speed of movement of the striking hand. Why is that important?

5.15 Why do karate experts break a stack of thin planks rather than one thick one?

6 The effects of nuclear war

An exercise in understanding the applications of physics

The most obvious effect of a nuclear explosion is the mushroom cloud. In fact any big explosion will form a mushroom cloud but the best common source is (unfortunately) a nuclear detonation. For a 1 megatonne device detonated at a height of about 2 km, the history is as shown here.

The fireball, at a temperature of about ten million degrees, forms after about a millisecond and then hardly changes in size. It gradually decreases in brightness, until after about half a minute it is no longer luminous. Anyone who happened to be looking at the bomb from a distance of about 10 km would be blinded, at least temporarily. A person with her back to the explosion would not be much better off, since the X-rays and γ-rays would go straight through her head and still damage the eyes. Sailors who looked at the Christmas Island test explosions with their hands over their eyes could clearly see the bones of their hands. These rays all travel at the speed of light.

The blast wave travels out at roughly the speed of sound (330 m s^{-1}). When it hits the ground it is reflected in the same way that water waves are reflected in a ripple tank. After about 45 s, the reflected pressure wave joins up with the primary blast wave to form what is called the Mach front. All the while, the over-pressure decreases as the pressure wave spreads. Even after it has spread about 20 km, however, it is still capable of breaking windows. As far as humans are concerned the effects of radiation at these distances are irrelevant; if the heat doesn't burn you to ashes, the blast will blow you to bits.

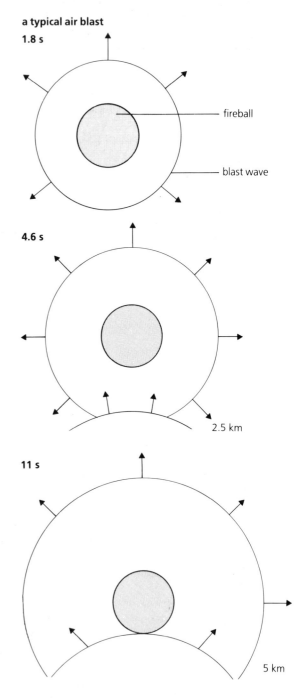

a typical air blast

1.8 s

fireball

blast wave

4.6 s

2.5 km

11 s

5 km

The fireball soon begins to rise, pulling a trail of dust and cloud with it. It expands slightly, until its pressure equals that of the surroundings. As it rises, it cools and some water particles condense out. When it reaches the inversion layer (where the temperature begins to go up slightly) it can no longer rise and so can only expand outwards, being still hotter than its surroundings. It continues getting hotter due to the nuclear reactions still taking place inside. If the inversion layer is not very pronounced, the mushroom cloud can break through and rise higher still, into the stratosphere (this happened at Hiroshima). There is normally an inversion layer at a height of about 10 000 m, and this is where the mushroom cloud forms.

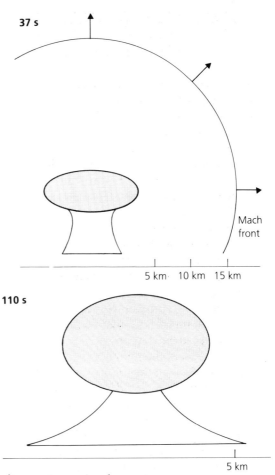

In Canterbury, New Zealand, there is often an inversion layer at a height of about 1000 m. This occurs when cold air from the sea drifts inland, under the hot air from the Canterbury plains, sliding off the Southern Alps. Similarly, there are inversion layers in Los Angeles, which is situated on a plain between the San Gabriel Mountains and the sea.

There is a horrible photograph from Hiroshima. A soldier had just climbed down from an observation tower and he leant his rifle against the tower. The photograph shows the silhouette of the soldier, the rifle and the ladder burnt into the walls of the tower. The blast wave then blew the soldier (now killed) to nothing. All that remains of the man is his shadow.

Another effect of an atomic explosion (and one that came as a complete surprise) is the electromagnetic pulse. The prompt, instantaneous γ-rays can strip electrons from air molecules over a wide area. The electrons travel radially in the Earth's magnetic field, in the opposite direction to the charged ions. These charged particles then cause electrical surges in exposed power lines and, especially, in switchgear. During a hydrogen bomb test over Johnston Island (in mid-Pacific), the street lights in Honolulu (1200 km away) were put out as the safety cut-outs were tripped under the large currents flowing.

A uranium bomb has the general layout shown here. A subcritical mass of uranium-235 has a spherical shape and is surrounded by an explosive charge. When the explosive charge is fired, the uranium is compressed all round to make a critical mass. (A 90 kT bomb – one with the destructive power of 90 kilotonnes of TNT – would have a mass of uranium of about 5.5 kg which, after the compression, would have a volume of about 180 cm^3, which is about as big as your fist.) At the same time, a neutron source is shot in by another explosion and this starts the chain reaction. A uranium bomb was dropped on Hiroshima. A plutonium bomb, which works on the same principle, was used on Nagasaki. The hydrogen bomb is similar except that at the centre is the deuterium or tritium, or a mixture of the two. This explodes spontaneously if the temperature is high enough (about 10^7 K) and this is provided by the explosion of the uranium (or more likely plutonium) bomb.

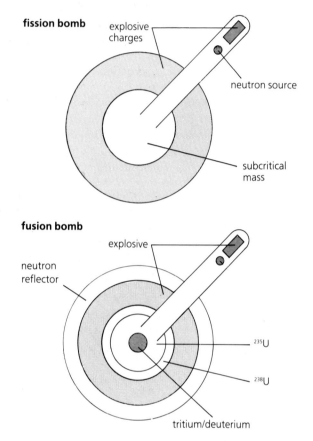

Questions

6.1 Open coal fires are now forbidden in Christchurch, New Zealand, and in many other places. Why?

6.2 As you come in to land at Los Angeles airport, you often see a layer of reddish-brown smog stretching (seemingly) all over the city. What is this?

6.3 In the case of the Japanese soldier at Hiroshima, why was he first killed by the heat wave and then blown away by the blast wave?

6.4 A woman living in Hiroshima happened to be wearing a white kimono with a pattern of black flowers on it when the bomb fell. After the explosion, this pattern was found to have been burnt on to her skin. What caused this?

6.5 The pipelines across Alaska are laid on permafrost, that is, land that is permanently frozen. What could happen if the pipeline burst and black oil spread over the permafrost? (Think of your answer to the previous question.)

6.6 Why is it painful to walk across the beach in those places (such as

Taranaki, New Zealand) where the sand is black?

6.7 How long did it take the electromagnetic pulse to travel the 1200 km from Johnston Island to Honolulu?

6.8 One consequence (a relatively minor one) of a nuclear holocaust is that all over the world transistor and other radios would be knocked out. None of the standard methods of communication would remain (assuming that there were still any survivors wanting to communicate). How could radios be protected?

6.9 What other means of communication would still be available?

6.10 One pleasant consequence of the hydrogen bomb tests conducted in the atmosphere over Johnston Island was that people in Hawaii could see (for the first time) the aurora. This was due to the interaction between the charged radioactive particles (constituting an electric current) and the Earth's magnetic field, which caused the particles to spiral round the magnetic field lines. What basic physical principle accounts for the spiral motion?

6.11 Granted that the radioactive particles spiralled round the field lines of the Earth's magnetic field, why is light emitted?

6.12 Some books state that the absorption of radioactive rays depends only on the mass of material between the source and detector – in other words, that all substances are equally good at absorbing radiation (on a mass basis). Consider the data given here for the absorption of γ-rays.

Substance	Lead	Steel	Concrete	Soil	Wood
Thickness/cm	1.8	2.8	10	14	25
Density/g cm^{-3}	11.4	7.8	2.4	0.8	0.6

The *thickness* quoted in the table is that needed to reduce the intensity of the γ-rays by half. The density figures are taken from tables except that for soil, which I measured.

Do these numbers confirm the suggestion that all substances absorb γ-rays equally, on a total mass basis? Suggest a reason for your answer.

6.13 This table gives similar figures for the absorption of β-rays, except that in this case it gives the thickness of substance needed to cut out the radiation completely.

Substance	Lead	Steel	Concrete	Soil	Wood	Air
Thickness/mm	0.8	1.5	5	7	16	10 000

Again determine if the relationship holds. In addition, you will need the density of air, which is 1.3×10^{-3} g cm^{-3}.

6.14 What is meant by the term 'subcritical'?

6.15 From the figures given, calculate the density of uranium. Compare this with the figure given in reference books of 19 050 kg m^{-3}.

6.16 After the explosions in Japan, it is reported that Einstein said that he wished he had been a plumber. What did he mean?

6.17 In a hydrogen bomb, the hydrogen is surrounded by the uranium (or plutonium). Why is it done this way? Why not put the hydrogen on the outside?

7 Galileo at Arcetri

A comprehension exercise

On Wednesday 22 June 1633 Galileo, then aged 70, was led into the great hall of the Dominican convent of Santa Maria spora Minerva in the centre of Rome. Clad in the white shirt of penitence, he was made to kneel down while sentence was passed. He had been examined by the Inquisition and shown the instruments of torture. He was found guilty of supporting Copernican views, which were condemned: 'The proposition that the Sun is the centre of the world and does not move is absurd and false philosophically and formally heretical because it is expressly contrary to Holy Scripture.' Galileo affirmed forcefully that he was a good Catholic and this was agreed. He expected to be imprisoned but was allowed to retire to his villa at Arcetri, near Florence, under perpetual house arrest. There he performed some of his most crucial experiments and wrote his crowning glory, *The discourses on two new sciences*. The book could not be printed in Italy and appeared in Protestant Leiden in 1638. Galileo knew that the suppression of his work would be followed by the end of the scientific movement in Italy. Galileo's assistants Torricelli and Viviani continued his work, but after them we hear of no Italian scientist until Volta and Galvani. John Milton noticed the decline when he wrote of his visit to 'the famous Galileo, grown old, a prisoner of the Inquisition'. It was this, he said, that 'damped the glory of Italian wits'.

Galileo's spirit was not broken but he was resigned to isolation, his letters being opened and his visitors questioned. To a friend he wrote, 'I do not hope for any relief and that is because I have committed no crime. I might hope for and obtain pardon, if I had erred'. Indomitably he worked on, and perhaps because of this isolation he was able to produce the *Discourses*, which collated and summed up all his long life's work on mechanics. Even today, Italian schoolchildren read this book as an example of the best argumentative prose in their language. We can still profit from his discoveries and here we will look at a few of them.

1 Perhaps most importantly, Galileo established the experimental method. He insisted that where there was doubt an experiment was the only arbiter: not argument, not authority, but experiment. Galileo used the word 'cimento' or 'ordeal' where we should use 'experiment' and this expresses the idea – re-presented in our own times by Popper – that scientific experiments must be crucial, they must be devastating. At the same time, Galileo stressed the need for mathematical analysis. He wrote: 'We cannot understand it [science] if we do not first learn the language. It is written in the mathematical language.' The two new sciences about which Galileo wrote his *Discourses* were what he called 'Coherence and resistance to fracture' and 'Uniform, accelerated and violent or projected motions'. The first forms the basis of much of engineering, while the second is the groundwork of mechanics. We now turn to these.

2 Galileo knew that a suction pump (a device of great importance in his time) would not lift water much above 11 m. He assumed that this was because the water column was then broken by tensile forces, just as a long wire will break if too much weight is hung from it. This led him to state that the strength of a bar in tension does not depend on the length of the bar and is proportional to the cross-sectional area. He thus came close to defining the concepts of stress and strain. He saw that the idea of stress (force per unit area) has the same definition as that of pressure. We might have expected him to say then, from his method of arguing by analogy, that the height of the mercury column of a barometer depends on its cross-sectional area. He did not do this, and it was left to his assistant Torricelli to show that the height of the barometer does not depend on the area of the tube. This is puzzling, since Galileo knew that air has weight and was, in fact, the first person to measure the weight of a bottle of air.

Instead Galileo considered the strength of objects built to different scales. The sketch is a copy of one of Galileo's, comparing a normal femur (below) with the form it would need to support an animal three times bigger in each dimension. He knew that a larger machine will not be as strong as a smaller one of the same design. He expressed this as the 'square–cube' law: the weight of an object increases as the cube of the dimensions, but the cross-sectional area to carry the load increases only as the square. This result has important applications in biology as well as engineering.

3 Galileo's experiments on accelerated motion are the basis of all our studies in mechanics. How well are they borne out in practice? We will look at three of his most crucial experiments.

(a) Galileo stated that a ball will roll down a slope from a constant height in a time that is independent of the angle of the slope. I took a piece of angle aluminium 2 m long, and covered the inner surfaces with smooth sticky tape. I raised one end different heights above the bench and measured the times for a steel ball-bearing, 2.54 cm in diameter, to roll down, but always releasing it from the same height – 11.2 cm – above the bench.

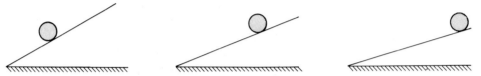

These were the results:

Height/cm	11.2	21.0	34.5	44.5
Time/s	3.29	1.68	1.18	0.97
	3.27	1.79	1.37	1.06
	3.26	1.81	1.14	0.87
Average time/s	3.26	1.76	1.24	0.97

Clearly the times are very different and it is difficult to see how they could be found to be the same, unless Galileo only used very steep runs. Clearly, too, Galileo was reaching towards the idea of conservation of energy, not to be fully expressed until 200 years later.

(b) The most important of these experiments measured the times for a ball to cover different distances down the same slope. In Galileo's words,

> A piece of wooden moulding 12 metres long, half a metre wide and three finger-breadths thick, had cut on its edge a channel one finger in breadth, very smooth and polished. A hard smooth bronze ball was rolled along it. Having placed this board in a sloping position, by lifting one end a metre or two above the other [I have converted Galileo's units into modern ones], we rolled the ball along the channel, noting the time of descent. We repeated this till the deviation between two observations never exceeded one-tenth of a pulse-beat. We now rolled the ball only one-quarter the length of the channel, and having measured the time of descent, we found it precisely one-half of the former. Next we tried other distances . . .

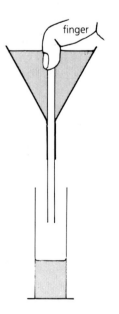

Galileo used a water clock to measure the time of descent: he weighed the amount of water that came out of a can as a thin jet.

When I repeated Galileo's experiment, I used a funnel and tube and stopped and released the water flow with my finger. Instead of weighing the water, I used a measuring cylinder to get the volume. The rest of the apparatus was as in the previous experiment. My results are as follows:

Distance d/cm	25	50	100	150	200
Time t/ml	5	8	15	18	21
	6	8	15.5	16.5	21
	6	9	13	18	20
	6	9	14	18	20.5
Average t/ml	5.75	8.5	14.4	17.7	20.6

These figures will be analysed later, but they give a pretty good straight line and we have great confidence in Galileo's claims.

(c) If we analyse Galileo's rolling ball experiment in the light of more recent physics, we use the law of conservation of energy and see how well our assumption of no frictional losses is borne out in practice.

The p.e. lost is mgh, the translational k.e. gained is $\frac{1}{2}mv^2$ and the rotational k.e. gained is $\frac{1}{2}I\omega^2$. For a sphere, $I = \frac{2}{5}mr^2$ and the rotational speed $\omega = v/a$, where a is the radius of rotation, in this case equal to $r/\sqrt{2}$. Putting all this together, I get this:

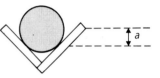

$$mgh = \frac{1}{2}mv^2 + \frac{1}{2}\frac{2}{5}\,mv^2$$

yielding $gh = 0.9\,v^2$. The speed of the ball at the bottom of the slope, v, is independent of the mass of the ball and its radius.

I then used a set of ball-bearings and measured the times for them to roll 2 m down a slope raised at one end a height of 0.1 m. These are the results:

Diameter of ball/cm	Time/s			Average time/s
0.5	6.64	6.76	6.39	6.60
1.0	6.36	6.37	6.35	6.36
1.18	6.11	6.01	6.17	6.10
1.29	4.87	4.82	4.72	4.80
2.54	4.15	4.00	4.02	4.06

We see that the times are by no means constant: in general, the larger the ball the shorter the time. When we put in the figures, we get 1.0 for gh; for $\frac{1}{2}v^2$, taking the best case, average speed $= 0.5$ m s^{-1}, speed at bottom of slope $= 1$ m s^{-1}. So the value on the right-hand side is 0.9 m^2 s^{-2}. About one-tenth of the p.e. goes into frictional losses, in the best case. For smaller balls, more energy is lost to frictional heating. Now Galileo could not measure the speed of a ball dropped vertically, so he 'diluted gravity' and let the ball roll down a slope. Galileo used a rolling ball experiment to deduce a result that was only concerned with translational energy, falling. As we have seen, the rotational energy is almost as big as the potential energy.

The question is then: was Galileo lucky or was he a bit of a rogue? You will have to read about the character of this most fascinating of men to decide for yourself. I think the best book for this is *The crime of Galileo* by Giorgio de Santillana (Mercury Books).

Questions

7.1 Take the figures given for the distance d and the time t for a ball rolling down a fixed slope (measured as ml of water) and plot d against t^2.

7.2 I used the same 2 m track but propped it up at different heights and measured the times for the ball to roll down, using a stopwatch.

Height/cm	11.2	19.4	25.2	36.6
Time/s	3.71	2.70	2.56	1.87
	3.74	2.88	2.47	1.93
	3.91	2.73	2.48	1.91
Average time/s	3.79	2.77	2.50	1.90

7.3 Why do babies have to be well wrapped up?

7.4 What special dangers did baby dinosaurs run, assuming them to have been 'cold-blooded'?

7.5 Other things being equal, do you buy large or small oranges?

7.6 Apart from taste, are other things equal for oranges?

7.7 Why is it easy to make a model aeroplane fly?

7.8 The energy stored in a bent bow is given by $E = \frac{1}{2}F \times d$, where F is the force needed to stretch the bow and d is the extension. Considering that we usually say that *work = force × distance*, why is there the $\frac{1}{2}$ in the formula?

7.9 What is the connection between this formula and the energy stored in a charged capacitor?

7.10 For a typical bow, a force of 350 N is needed to pull the arrow back a distance of 0.6 m. How much energy is stored in the bow?

7.11 In practice, almost all the energy in the bent bow is given to the arrow. With what speed would an arrow of mass 100 g leave the bow?

7.12 The strongest archer of ancient myth was Odysseus; while he was missing (believed dead) many suitors came for the hand of his wife Penelope. She agreed to marry anyone who could bend Odysseus's bow. No one could do this because it was pre-tensioned i.e. it was bent backwards by 60 cm, the same amount it could be pulled in the usual direction. How much energy would be stored in the bow in this condition if the required force is the same, 350 N?

7.13 Besides Galileo, many other scientists tried to make pumps that would work at depths greater than 10 m. Why was there great pressure to do this?

7.14   The best-known kind of modelling clay has the trade name 'Plasticine'. What is the significance of this name?

8 The end of the world

A comprehension exercise

It is now generally agreed that life on Earth will end with the destruction of the Earth about 4 billion years hence. Of course, there may be some more localised catastrophe that ends all life before then. A best-seller in America, *The late planet Earth* by Hal Lindsay, detailed several of these. Some slight change in the power output of the Sun, either an increase or decrease, could upset the delicate balance of the climate and make the Earth uninhabitable. Or there could be a change in the stream of charged particles from the Sun that we call the 'solar wind'. This could cause a change in the magnetic field around the Earth and so alter the shield that protects us from particles from space, the cosmic rays which are mostly energetic protons. A nearby star could explode and douse us in lethal radiation. A black hole could wander into our solar system and upset the orbits of the planets. However, fates like these are not considered likely. After all, the Earth has been circling the Sun for some 4.5 billion years and has escaped all these hazards so far. Much more likely is it that a nuclear holocaust will end everything (but perhaps we can begin to hope that fear is starting to recede).

Nevertheless, in 4 billion years or so, the Sun will have burnt up much of its hydrogen fuel. It will turn into a 'red giant' star that will boil off all the Earth's atmosphere and vaporise the inner planets, and possibly the Earth itself. Then the Sun will have to burn the less efficient fuel helium, and when that is gone the other heavier and still less efficient elements until iron is reached. Then with all its fuel gone there will be no force from its radiation to balance the force of gravity, and the Sun will collapse to about the size of the Earth. It will become a 'black dwarf' with a density of about 1 billion kg per cubic metre (10^9 kg m^{-3}). Gradually all the other stars in the galaxy will do the same.

This is the 'heat death' that has been predicted ever since the second law of thermodynamics was set out in the last century. The law predicts that all energy sources will become degraded – in other words, that entropy will increase. Entropy means, roughly, the amount of disorder in any system. In a lump of coal, consisting almost entirely of carbon atoms in a well-ordered state, there is a great deal of order (and so little entropy). When the coal is burnt, it combines with oxygen to form carbon dioxide which goes up the chimney and is spread all over the town. It now has virtually no order: its entropy has increased.

When a baby grows in its mother's womb it gains order and so might seem to disprove the second law. It only grows because it gets food from its mother, however. She has consumed food to give nourishment to her baby. This food loses more order than the baby gains. The food gains more entropy than the baby loses. In the same way during the long record of evolutionary growth from a single-celled creature 3.5 billion years ago to human beings today, there has been a great increase in order. But that has been at the expense of all the food all these creatures have eaten. This has lost more order, because all digestion is bound to be inefficient. The way that humans have evolved in accordance with the second law has been amply demonstrated by Ilya Prigogine, who was given the Nobel prize for his efforts (although not all his ideas are universally accepted).

Some stars will end their lives by exploding as 'supernovae', blowing themselves to pieces, emitting great energy and releasing the heavy elements they have been making in their solar furnaces. All the heavy elements on the Earth have come from some supernova which exploded long ago. As Sir James Jeans said, 'our bodies are formed from the ashes of long-dead stars'. Our Sun is a second-generation star, formed from others that have lived out their lives.

Eventually all the stars will burn themselves out, even the ones that are now being formed from the clouds of hydrogen that are still swirling about, particularly near the centre of the galaxy. According to one view, that will be the end: dead lumps of dense matter will go on expanding for ever and ever. The cosmos is said to be 'open'.

There is another view, however. We know that the galaxies are all expanding away from each other and we think that the rate of expansion is decreasing as the force of gravity pulls the galaxies together. It could be that the force of gravity is strong enough to stop the expansion of the universe eventually and start pulling the galaxies together again. Whether this will happen depends on the total mass of all the galaxies. Now we know pretty well what the mass of a galaxy is, and it might seem an easy thing to multiply that by the number of galaxies to get the total mass of the cosmos. If that is done it turns out that the sum of all the matter in the cosmos is not massive enough. The force of gravity is not enough to stop the expansion of the galaxies. However, there is a great deal of matter in the galaxies which we cannot see directly, whose presence we have to infer by other means. The present consensus is that the amount of matter in the universe is enough to halt the expansion. In this picture, the cosmos is said to be 'closed'. The cosmos will start to contract, slowly at first but with increasing speed. Any stars still shining will be seen to be emitting light shifted towards the blue end of the spectrum. All the galaxies will rush towards each other in the 'Big Crunch' – like the 'Big Bang' in reverse. This is the total annihilation, the end of all space, time and matter; nothing is left. Everything is destroyed by the enormous power of gravity. This whole business is part of an intense theoretical and experimental effort. According to the popular 'inflationary theory' of the Big Bang, due to Alan Guth, the total mass of the universe is precisely matched so that the expansive and contractive forces exactly balance.

There is still another view. Some argue that something will cause the Big Crunch to stop at some incredibly high value of the density, causing the universe to bounce back out again in another Big Bang. This is the 'oscillating' universe. After all, we know there has been one Big Bang;

why not a whole series of them?

At the present all this is speculation, and it would seem that there is no way of knowing anything about the universe before the Big Bang, just as there is no way of knowing whether it was wrecked Rolls-Royces or wrecked Minis that were melted down to make the steel for your new car. Nevertheless some theoreticians believe that answers to these questions, and to many more, will be found. As Thorsten Veblen said, 'the only outcome of any piece of scientific research is to raise two problems where one existed before.'

It is intriguing to note that while the estimates of the total mass of everything in the cosmos are poised precisely between those that imply that the cosmos is closed and those implying it is open, so equally are the measurements of the expansion of the universe. It is known that the galaxies are expanding. It is also presumed that the rate of expansion is decreasing, but it is not yet known with sufficient precision whether that rate of decrease is enough to allow us to say that, at some time in the future, the expansion will stop and be followed by a contraction. Truly we live in one of the most fascinating of all times.

Questions

8.1 We say that as the Sun burns its hydrogen fuel its energy is degraded, that is, reduced to a less useful form. But is the energy lost, then?

8.2 Why do stars like the Sun collapse when all their fuel is burnt?

8.3 What has been the ultimate source of the energy that has fuelled the evolutionary rise of humans from single-celled creatures?

8.4 What is one source of some of the invisible matter in the universe?

8.5 I originally wrote ' . . . the cosmos is not heavy enough . . . ' and changed it to ' . . . the cosmos is not massive enough . . . '. Why?

8.6 At the Big Bang, the force of the explosion was very precisely balanced against the force of gravity. Why could there have been no life on Earth if the force of gravity had been a little stronger?

8.7 Conversely, why could there have been no life on Earth if the force of gravity had been a little weaker?

8.8 The Earth is in a stable orbit that is just right for living things. What would happen if the output of the Sun were increased slightly and the Earth got hotter? (It is obvious what would happen if the Earth got colder; the next ice age, which we are now told is overdue, would come more quickly.)

8.9 The first part of the previous question is badly expressed. Put it in a better form.

8.10 When a star contracts to form a black dwarf, it begins to spin faster. Why?

8.11 Could a black dwarf spin so fast as to burst apart?

8.12 How do we know the masses of the galaxies?

8.13 Why do we think there is dark matter in each galaxy that we cannot detect directly?

8.14 If life on Earth is endangered by a nuclear war, most damage would be caused by blast. We have data for the over-pressure against distance for both an air burst and a ground burst. An air burst is one in which the fireball, radius about 1 km, does not reach the ground. Thus an air burst is detonated at a height of more than 1 km. The data are:

Over-pressure P/kPa	83	35	13.8	6.9
Air burst: distance d/km	4	7	12	10
Ground burst: distance d/km	3.3	5	8	13

To find out if these figures mean anything, we assume that there is a relationship of the form $P = Cd^n$, where C and n are constants. When we take logs we get $\log P = \log C + n \log d$ (strictly, these should be natural logs, to base e, but we can use logs to base 10 as the two kinds of logs only differ by a constant). Tabulate the data and plot the graphs.

8.15 What are the values for the slopes? Comment on them.

8.16 Compare the two graphs.

9 Newton's mistake and Einstein's blunder

Both Newton and Einstein were recognised in their own times as men of outstanding abilities, the greatest intelligences of their generations: among the greatest of all time. Since their deaths, our admiration of both has grown. Both had one quality which we value even more than their piercing intelligence, however: both had insight, an instinctive understanding of the workings of nature. So that although both expressed their findings in mathematical terms (and in Newton's case, at least, invented the mathematics) these findings related directly to the way the universe works. Both were profoundly religious men, even if they did not express it in conventional terms. Their delight in the subtlety and beauty of their discoveries made them believe that there must be some over-riding purpose in life and that so intricate a creation could not be blind chance. Newton staunchly believed that in studying the workings of the cosmos, he was learning about the nature of God. The last few years of Einstein's work were devoted to the problem of 'whether God had any option in making the universe as He did'.

Newton's greatest discovery was his Law of universal gravitation: that every particle in the universe attracts every other particle with a force proportional to their masses and varying inversely as the square of their separation:

$$F = -GMm/d^2$$

Newton had amazing success with the law, predicting the force holding the Moon in its circular orbit. (It is supposed that the origin of the story about Newton seeing an apple fall is that he also saw the Moon at the same time and wondered if the same force acted on both.) Newton was also able to account for the tides (and even the very high tides in the Gulf of Tonkin) and for the equatorial bulge of the Earth.

Newton's problem was: if all the stars attract each other (and there is no reason to suppose they don't), why have they not all pulled themselves together into one big heap? Newton believed that the universe was not rotating. He therefore had to assume that it was infinite, with all the conceptual difficulties that caused. He also thought that an infinite universe was evidence for a God of infinite power. If there are no stars outside the circle, they will all pull themselves into the centre.

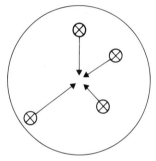

Einstein's solution to the same problem (although in his case it referred to galaxies rather than stars) was to assume an extra term in the Law of gravitation which provided a repulsion, so

$$F = -GMm/d^2 + G'Mmd$$

(Einstein did not write it this way, he used the language of tensor calculus, but the meaning is the same.) In the new term, the force is proportional to the separation and gets bigger the greater the distance apart. The new constant G' is very small, so the new term becomes significant only at very great distances. It must not be thought that Einstein just dreamed up this new term. It came out naturally as a kind of constant of integration in his general theory of relativity.

We now know that the extra term is not needed (Einstein called it 'my greatest blunder'). The galaxies do not all attract each other into one enormous pile because they are all expanding away from each other and have been ever since the Big Bang some 15 billion years ago.

The Hubble space telescope is the most interesting of a dozen or so scientific experiments awaiting the recommissioning of the American space shuttle so that large loads can be put into orbit. The telescope will be put into a circular orbit 500 km above the Earth's surface and is expected to last initially for 15 years, but it can be repaired and upgraded in further shuttle missions. It will be powered by solar panels generating a maximum of 4.6 kW. The main mirror will be 2.4 m in diameter and there will be five different detectors. One camera will be especially for faint objects and the other will be for wide-field views of planets (presumably this is for public relations purposes). There will be two spectrometers, one for faint objects and one for high resolution, and one high-speed photometer. Conditions for viewing will be such that the angular resolution will be 0.1 seconds of arc, ten times better than is possible on Earth and equivalent to being able to see a house on the Moon.

Questions

9.1   Newton did not write his second law as $F = ma$ because that is not always true. In what circumstances doesn't $F = ma$ work?

9.2   How does the way Newton gave us his law get round that difficulty?

9.3   This question tries to put you in Newton's shoes (a very good place to be). Suppose (as Newton believed) that all the stars were in one large galaxy, and suppose (as was beyond Newton's power to measure) that this galaxy is rotating. How does that solve Newton's problem?

9.4   But if the whole galaxy were rotating, how would it be possible to tell? There would be no fixed reference point. Does not the theory of relativity tell us that it is impossible to detect absolute motion?

9.5   Both Newton and Einstein were thinking in terms of a stationary universe. Suppose that all the galaxies were at rest, in equilibrium under their common forces of gravitation. Suppose too that the law of gravitation includes both the attractive and the repulsive terms. Now consider that something upsets that delicate equilibrium: suppose that two galaxies move a little further apart. What will happen to the force of gravity?

9.6   Conversely, what would happen to two galaxies (in equilibrium) if some upset caused them to move a little closer together?

9.7   So why is Einstein's extra term not needed?

9.8   What experimental evidence is there that the galaxies are all receding?

9.9   Do we think any less of Newton or Einstein for being wrong?

9.10 Why is it necessary to put the Hubble space telescope into orbit round the Earth?

9.11 Is the Hubble space telescope in a geostationary orbit? Take the gravitational constant as 6.7×10^{-11} N kg^{-2} m^2, the mass of the Earth as 6×10^{24} kg and its radius as 6400 km, and calculate the period of the telescope if it is to be 500 km above the Earth.

9.12 It is hoped that the telescope will be able to detect galaxies that are 15 billion light-years from Earth. What is the significance of this figure?

9.13   What is the purpose of its faint-object spectrometer?

9.14   Creationists are people who believe that the universe was created about 10 000 years ago and has not changed substantially since. They have a great problem with the story of Joshua, who on one occasion caused the Sun to stop in its orbit. If the Sun can be stopped it must mean that it is circling a stationary (whatever that may mean) Earth. To get round this difficulty creationists say that since, according to Einstein, all motion is relative – there is no way of telling whether the Earth circles the Sun or the Sun circles the Earth. What do you say?

10   The space shuttle

An exercise in the use of data

The space shuttle is a re-usable space craft that is put into low Earth orbit to deliver civil or military goods in space. It is propelled upward by three liquid-fuel rocket motors in its tail and two solid-fuel booster rockets. Most of the liquid fuel is carried in the large cylindrical fuel tank, which is discarded and lost. It is thought that the *Challenger* orbiter was lost because of a leak in one of the O-rings circling this fuel tank. The O-rings are made of rubber and are believed to have lost their resiliency in a sudden frost in the night before the take-off. Frosts do occur as far south as Florida and are a regular hazard for the orange crop. It was not thought that the O-rings could be damaged in this way. Fuel leaked from the gap and ignited.

The orbiter vehicle itself only carries enough fuel for manoeuvring and for slowing the descent. It is about the size of a Boeing 737 and normally carries a crew of three, with four others to handle the payload or perform scientific experiments. It is usually launched from Cape Canaveral in Florida, and can also land there. If the landing is likely to be hazardous (and the shuttle lands like a glider, with no second chance) it is directed to the Edwards Air Force Base, which is in the desert and has an enormous runway. In that case it is carried piggy-back on a special 747 to Cape Canaveral to be made ready for another launch. Two minutes into its orbital mission, the solid-fuel boosters fall off, and are recoverable for future use. The liquid-fuel motors fire for another six minutes, lifting it to a height of 90 km. At this height its speed is nearly right (but too big) for stable orbit.

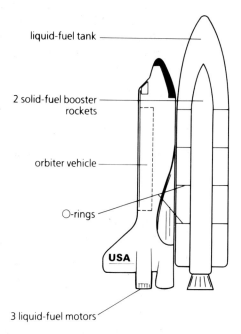

liquid-fuel tank

2 solid-fuel booster rockets

orbiter vehicle

O-rings

USA

3 liquid-fuel motors

The liquid-fuel tank drops off and the orbiter coasts to a height of
185 km, where it goes into a nearly circular orbit.

With the data below, we are going to calculate the total thrust and the
acceleration, speed and height after two minutes of flight (when the
solid-fuel boosters have burnt out and fallen away and when a quarter
of the liquid fuel has been burnt).

Mass of orbiter vehicle = 68 t.
Mass of liquid-fuel tank = 35 t; mass of fuel = 703 t; total = 738 t.
Mass of each solid-fuel booster = 82 t; mass of fuel = 588 t;
total = 670 t.
Thrust of each of three liquid-fuel motors = 1.67 MN (million
newtons).
Thrust of each of two rocket boosters = 11.8 MN.

Questions

10.1 Calculate the total thrust and the total mass (at take-off), and so
find the initial acceleration a.

10.2 Using your well-known kinematic equations, find the speed
after two minutes and the height at that time (assuming constant
acceleration). Compare your answers with the published figures
of speed = 1390 m s^{-1} and height 45.6 km.

10.3 What is the reason for the discrepancy?

10.4 Re-calculate; find the acceleration after two minutes, assuming
that the thrust has gone up to 31 MN and that the mass has been
reduced by the loss of the two solid-fuel booster rockets and the
use of a quarter of the liquid fuel.

10.5 Take this value of the acceleration with the first value, find the
average and again calculate the speed and height reached.

10.6 What on earth has gone wrong now?

10.7 Find the acceleration after one minute, assuming that the thrust
is 30 MN and that the mass is the initial mass less half the solid
fuel and one-eighth of the liquid. Then plot a graph of
acceleration against time, measure the area under it for each 30 s
interval and so find the total increase in speed.

10.8 Why is this fortuitous?

10.9 To find the height risen, you will have to repeat the whole
business. Plot a graph of speed against time, and estimate the
distance travelled from the area under the curve.

10.10 Why is your answer low?

10.11 The Boeing 747 that is used to take the orbiter back from
Edwards Air Force Base to Cape Canaveral for another launch
has two extra rudders, one on each end of the tailplane. Why?

10.12 The Boeing is also used to carry the orbiters aloft so that the crews can be trained in landing techniques. Why is this so important?

10.13 When an orbiter is getting ready to break out of its stable orbit round the Earth prior to landing, it is turned round to face backwards and its rockets fired. For this burn near the end of the first flight of the *Columbia* orbiter:

Mass of craft = 100 tonnes.

Thrust of each rocket motor = 6000 lb (total = 54 000 N).

Loss of speed = 300 feet s^{-1} = 90 m s^{-1} in a time of 160 s.

Use the data to find the loss of speed and compare this with the quoted value.

10.14 For that same first orbital flight of the *Columbia*, we are told that it went 1 074 000 miles (1 720 000 km), travelling round the Earth 137 times in 53 hours 10 min (191 500 s) at an average height of 150 miles (240 km). If the radius of the Earth is 6400 km, its mass 6×10^{24} kg and the gravitational constant $G = 6.7 \times 10^{-11}$ units, compare the centripetal and gravitational accelerations of the craft.

10.15 The liquid-fuel tank contains 604 t of liquid oxygen and 102 t of liquid hydrogen. So what?

11 Earth satellites

An exercise on understanding satellite motion

Satellites that are used to relay television programmes and telephone messages stay in a stable orbit for many years. They have to be replaced when their batteries run down or when they can no longer be recharged from electricity produced by their photocells. The satellite must be put into orbit with exactly the speed to match its height above the Earth or, more correctly, its distance from the centre of the Earth. In the stable situation the centripetal force, needed to keep anything in a circular orbit, mv^2/r, is provided by the force of gravity between the satellite (m) and the earth (M), GMm/r^2. Cancelling gives us

$$v^2 = \frac{GM}{r}$$

We see that the smaller the radius r, the faster the satellite must travel.

Alternatively, we could have used the other formula for centripetal force,

$$F = m\omega^2 r$$

Putting this with the gravitational force formula, we get

$$\omega^2 = \frac{GM}{r^3}$$

and since $\omega = 2\pi/T$ (T being the period of the satellite), we finally finish up with

$$T^2 \propto r^3$$

which is Kepler's third law.

We now come to the point of the whole business. Suppose that an Earth satellite is in a stable orbit, circling the Earth and losing very little kinetic energy. Suppose now that it meets a cloud of dust, the debris from some cosmic cataclysm. This will slow the satellite and it will fall into a lower orbit. But in the lower orbit, it has to go faster. How can slowing it down increase its speed? This is called the 'satellite paradox'.

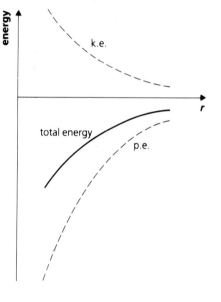

The answer is, of course, found from the law of conservation of energy. When the satellite falls into the lower orbit, it is nearer the Earth and so has lost gravitational p.e. (or, as in the diagram, it has less negative p.e.). In fact, we can show that the loss in p.e. is twice the gain in k.e. So when the satellite drops down into a lower orbit it has lost energy and this is a more stable state. The amount of the gravitational p.e. is given by GMm/r; we have seen that this equals mv^2, and this is twice the k.e. ($\frac{1}{2}mv^2$). We can put the transaction in the form of an equation:

loss in gravitational p.e. = gain in k.e. + energy lost to dust etc

The sketch graphs here show the gravitational p.e., which is negative because work must be done to lift the satellite from the surface of the Earth (or, more correctly, from the centre of the Earth). The k.e. must be always positive, because the velocity is squared. The total energy is still negative because the value of the p.e. is twice that of the k.e.

The same thing happens to an electron circling the nucleus of an atom. In this case, it does not encounter dust (there isn't any) but it can change into a higher or lower orbit with the absorption or emission of a photon. In this case it trades electrical p.e. for the increased k.e. in the lower orbit and the energy is converted into light energy as a photon; the energy equation is:

loss in electrical p.e. = gain in k.e. + light energy emitted ($E = hf$)

where h is Planck's constant and f is the frequency of the emitted photon. Alternatively, when the atom is excited by heat or by receiving light energy of exactly the correct amount, the electron can jump into a higher orbit which is stable.

Many space ships are accelerated towards their objective, by the 'slingshot effect'. It might seem unreal that the force of gravity can speed up space craft but *Voyager* was speeded up by passing close to Jupiter while en route to Saturn. To understand this, consider an analogy.

You are playing centre forward in a soccer game. You run towards the goal as a centre comes in from the wing. You meet the ball perfectly and head a brilliant goal. The ball bounces elastically off your head and you say that there has been no change in its speed; its k.e. is the same. The goalkeeper, on the other hand, says that you were running at the ball and so speeded it up and that was why he could not stop it – the ball gained momentum and you lost an equal amount. Because you are so much more massive than the ball, you did not notice your loss in velocity but the ball travelled appreciably faster.

The same happened to *Voyager* as it passed behind Jupiter (if it had passed in front, it would have been slowed down). We can be sure that there was no change in total k.e. as *Voyager* passed near Jupiter (this is where the analogy with heading the ball breaks down). We will work out *Voyager*'s increase in speed, using the following data:

Mass of *Voyager* = 825 kg.
Mass of Jupiter = 1.3×10^{27} kg.
Speed of *Voyager* (at that time) = 1.0×10^4 m s^{-1}.
Speed of Jupiter = 1.3×10^4 m s^{-1}.

We shall use the convention that V_{VCB} means the velocity of *Voyager* in the common frame of reference before the encounter. Similarly, V_{JSA} means the speed of Jupiter in the Sun's frame of reference after the meeting.

in the Sun's frame of reference

$\bar{V}_{VSA} = \bar{V}_{JSA} + \bar{V}_{VCA}$
$= (1.31 + 1.65) \times 10^4$
$= 2.8 \times 10^4$ m s^{-1}

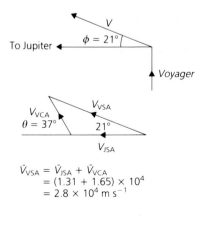

in the frame of reference of the centre of Jupiter and *Voyager*

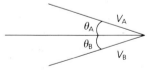

$$\frac{\text{speed of Jupiter}}{\text{speed of Voyager}} = \frac{825}{1.88 \times 10^{27}} \to 0$$

The speed of *Voyager* is unchanged in this frame of reference and $\theta_A = \theta_B$

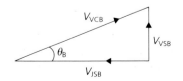

Hence the speed of *Voyager* is increased by a factor of 2.8 and its k.e. by nearly 8 times. The result of *Voyager*'s near visit to Jupiter allowed some beautiful pictures of its moons to be taken and a new, tiny, one to be discovered. The four main moons, discovered by Galileo, are each about the size of the planet Mercury.

Questions

11.1 When working out the speeds and periods of satellites, why does the mass of the satellite not come into it?

11.2 What would happen to a satellite that was lifted up to a certain height and then given a horizontal velocity too great for that height?

11.3 Think about a roundabout in a children's park; this consists of a pole with a set of rings hanging from chains at the top. The chains are fixed to a circle of metal which can rotate freely. A child runs towards the pole and grabs hold of one of the rings. What happens, assuming that the circle of metal at the top of the pole can turn without friction?

11.4 What happens if, with the child swinging freely round the pole, the circle of metal at the top suddenly jams and the top of the chain is fixed?

11.5 How could you demonstrate this in the lab?

11.6 Why is the k.e. of the satellite (and the electron) always positive?

11.7 How do we know from the motion of the planets that Kepler's third law is confirmed? (You would need a table of data to get numerical confirmation.)

11.8 Why do we not consider other forms of energy when talking about satellites in orbit and electrons circling protons?

11.9 Suppose someone says to you, 'It is rubbish to talk about electrons circling the nucleus of an atom. That's all old hat. We now talk about electron clouds and the probability function – the chance of finding an electron in a certain place.' What do you say?

11.10 The Russian anti-satellite system is incredibly antiquated. An obsolete missile launcher fires a missile into a stable orbit a little lower than its target and a little behind it. When it gets closest, a swarm of pellets is fired, in the hope that one will hit the satellite. Why is the weapon put into orbit behind its target?

11.11 Why is this system so hopeless? (It is years behind the American system.)

11.12 One of the very latest American surveillance satellites is the Teal Ruby. This has i.r. detectors that are so sensitive that they will find the body of an ICBM soon after launch, as well as cruise missiles coasting. All previous i.r. detectors could only find the heat from rocket and jet engines. Its life is about a year, compared to that of similar Russian satellites which are active for only about two months. This is why the Russians have so many launches, and so many dead satellites that are taken by the credulous for UFOs when they are burnt up in the atmosphere. The Teal Ruby is in circular orbit at a height of 740 km. If the mass of the Earth is 6×10^{24} kg, its radius 6400 km and the gravitational constant G is 6.7×10^{-11} N m^2 kg^{-2}, calculate the speed of the satellite.

11.13 If the mass of the craft is, near enough, 1000 kg, calculate its k.e.

11.14 How much work must be expended in raising the satellite to its working height? You may assume that the acceleration due to gravity on Earth has the same value at the height of the satellite.

11.15 Are we allowed to use this simple formula for the p.e. of the craft if we are only interested in 10 per cent accuracy?

11.16 Surely the k.e. of a satellite is equal and opposite to half the p.e., but the answers given here contradict that. What's wrong?

11.17 Referring to the slingshot effect, why, for an increase in speed, must the football be in front of you but *Voyager* pass behind Jupiter?

11.18 How do you know that there was no net energy change when *Voyager* and Jupiter interacted?

11.19 Some people think it is wrong to muck about with the orbits of the planets in this way. What do you think?

11.20 The moon Io is 3.5×10^8 m from Jupiter and makes a circuit round it in 1.77 days. If the constant $G = 6.7 \times 10^{-11}$ units, what is the mass of Jupiter?

12 Moon rocket

An exercise in handling data

In this reading we look at the motion of a three-stage Moon rocket at different stages of its mission. In doing so we shall see that a stepwise approach is needed – there is no complete solution to the problem.

Various sources give very different values for the data, which in any case were different for the various missions. Typical data for the *Saturn V* Moon rocket system is as follows:

Stage	Unit	Length/m	Total mass/kg	Total thrust/N
First	*Saturn* Ic	42	2 106 000	33 750 000
Second	*Saturn* II	25	450 000	5 200 000
Third	*Saturn* IVb	19	103 500	900 000
Command module		4	5 800	–
Service module		7	25 500	93 000
Lunar excursion module		7	16 500	15 750
Total take-off mass			2 708 300	
Mass after dropping first stage			602 300	

Questions

12.1 Calculate the acceleration of the system on take-off.

12.2 Calculate the acceleration at the end of the first-stage burn, assuming that the acceleration due to gravity has hardly changed during the 2½ minute flight.

12.3 Assume that the mean acceleration is the average of these two values and so calculate the speed of the rocket after 2.5 minutes.

12.4 Compare this value with the published figure of 2400 m s^{-1}, and explain the discrepancy.

12.5 Calculate the acceleration of the rocket just after the first stage is dropped and the second stage is ignited, and comment on your result.

After the third stage has finished its first burn, that is after about 15 minutes, the craft does one orbit of the Earth. Another burn of the third stage sends it on its way to the Moon; this burn takes five minutes and raises the speed to 12 000 m s^{-1}. The three remaining modules coast to the Moon, with engines off. The command module stays in orbit round the Moon, with the service module: this has rockets for mid-course correction, retro fire to go into Moon orbit and thrust for the return to Earth. The lunar excursion module consists of a descent stage with one variable motor for the descent to the Moon and an ascent stage with one constant-thrust motor for the ascent to the waiting service module. The descent stage is left on the Moon and, once the crew are back in the command module, the ascent stage is dumped and presumably goes on circling the Moon as an artificial satellite. The service module motor fires, taking the remainder of the craft out of its lunar parking orbit and back to Earth.

During the trip to the Moon the rocket decelerates, due to the gravitational pull of the Earth. We can find an expression for this negative acceleration, as follows.

We have $F = ma$ and $F = GMm/d^2$, where M is the mass of the Earth, m is the mass of the Moon rocket, G is the gravitational constant and d is the distance from the centre of the Moon. Hence

$$a = \frac{GM}{d^2}$$

or, cross-multiplying,

$$ad^2 = GM = \text{constant}$$

We can check on this relationship using data supplied by NASA. They set out the speed of the craft against the distance from the centre of the Earth, thus:

Distance d/km	Speed/m s^{-1}	
26 306	5374	
29 030	5102	ten minutes (600 s) later
54 356	3633	
56 386	3560	600 s later

12.6 For each pair of readings, work out the average distance d and the acceleration a. Then compute ad^2 and compare with the value for the surface of the Earth, 6400 km from the centre.

On the way back, of course, the speed increases continuously and by the time the craft reaches the Earth's atmosphere its speed is about 8000 m s^{-1}. While the craft is decelerating in the Earth's atmosphere it is out of radio contact with the Earth for a period of about five minutes. When any object travels faster than about 15 Mach (15 times the speed of sound under the conditions prevailing) it ionises the air around it. We say that a plasma has been formed. The craft is moving so fast that it compresses and heats the air in front of it and around it to such a high temperature that the air molecules lose their electrons and become ions, which form a layer around the craft. The ionised layer is a conducting layer and so will not let radio waves (or any other electromagnetic waves) through. This might seem to be a bind; in fact, it is very useful. The kinetic energy of the space ship that is used to ionise the air molecules would otherwise have appeared as heat energy, and the problem of heating is bad enough already. When the space ship is going at about 25 Mach, its outside temperature gets to about 12 000 K, in places. It has been calculated that if energy was not used in ionising the air, then the temperature would have reached 25 000 K.

The problem of over-heating was severe on the Moon craft, but was much worse on the space shuttles due to their much greater mass. The front of a space shuttle is covered in tiles which have a very high specific heat to absorb heat energy and are also poor conductors of heat. Unfortunately, under the extreme conditions of space heating, the tiles have tended to come unstuck.

12.7 How do we know that electrical conductors will not transmit radio waves?

12.8 Why does a car radio always sound worse underneath a bridge?

12.9 Why are some bridges worse than others?

12.10 For that matter, why does a car radio have an aerial at all, when an ordinary transistor does not?

12.11 Why is there no loss of radio contact with the crew on the outward journey?

13 Gullibility

An exercise to encourage a properly sceptical attitude

Our age is characterised by the enormous number of people who proclaim the most bizarre beliefs. There are people about who think the Earth is flat, that the Sun goes round the Earth, that UFOs from outside the solar system are visiting us and that the Earth was created less than 10 000 years ago. Such people join up with other similar enthusiasts to hold meetings and to confirm their beliefs. Some of these people believe that they can send their 'astral' bodies through great distances and through brick walls. We do not question their ability to send their brains through brick walls. In support of these ideas, one believer relates how his cat was meowing pitifully in his absence; when he sent his astral body into the room, he says, the cat stopped meowing! Most remarkable of all, there are even science graduates who hold the most far-out beliefs. There are at least ten men with science degrees in New Zealand who do not think that the age of the Earth is measured in billions of years; they think it is less than a hundred centuries.

Typical of these strange groups is the Flat Earth Society of America. It boasts that it has 200 members who are science graduates. The president of the society, Charles K. Johnson, is vehement about scientific dishonesty. Writing in the *Flat Earth News*, he says that conventional scientists are 'liars' and 'demented dope fiends'. Space travel is a 'carnie game'. When shown a photograph of the Earth from space with the remark that it certainly looked like a sphere he replied, 'yes, it would to the untrained eye'. He says that the U.S. government will one day officially proclaim that the Earth is flat. Most flat-earthers believe that the Earth is a circle, with the North Pole at the centre; all around the outer edge is a circular wall, 50 m high. The Equator is a circle roughly half-way in. Others think that the Earth is a rectangle, because the Bible talks about the 'four corners of the Earth'. They all think that the Sun, Moon and planets circle the Earth in the region of the Equator at a height of about 900 km, that is, below the 'firmament'. It is great fun arguing with these people, but you can never hope to win because they will not admit any argument that contradicts their beliefs. All scientists, however, know that their picture of the world is fallible and likely to be changed as further discoveries are made. The essential of any theory is that it should be, in Sir Karl Popper's phrase, 'falsifiable' – open to disproof.

> Sir Karl Popper
> Never told a whopper.
> He knows he's liable
> To be falsifiable.

Or, as Don Cupitt has put it, 'science is grounded on a firm foundation of doubt'. Flat-earthers can never be beaten in argument because they know that they can never possibly be wrong. To the scientist, the fact that they cannot be wrong is their greatest weakness.

There is in America a growing number of people who think that the Sun goes round the Earth in the Tychonian system, invented by the great Danish astronomer Tycho Brahe (although a few still cling to the theory of Ptolemy). In the Tychonian scheme the Sun and the inner planets, Mercury and Venus, go round the Earth while all the other planets go round the Sun. Many of these believers belong to the Bible Science Association, which has accepted this theory. It publishes the *Bulletin of the Tychonian Society*. At least two members of this society were trained as astronomers and are now computer scientists by trade. They think that the Copernican theory with the Sun at the centre is a 'Satanic counterfeit', a ploy to discredit the Bible. John Hampden described the Copernican theory as 'that Satanic device of a round and revolving globe, which sets Scripture, reason and facts at defiance'. A qualified engineer, R. G. Elmendorf, has a standing offer of $1000 to anyone who can prove that the Earth moves (as he will not say what he will accept as proof, it is quite impossible to win the money).

A third modern aberration which enjoys great esteem is astrology, the belief that the arrangement of the planets at the instant of someone's birth influences (in some way, never explained) his or her future life. Astrologers make little attempt to give reasons for their beliefs; they merely claim that throughout history their methods have worked. Unfortunately for them, the times of the year for the different signs of the Zodiac are now about twenty days out from their originals, set some two thousand years ago. To get out of this one astrologers now say that all dates are 'notional', with no relationship to the positions of the heavenly bodies. The greatest weakness of all such predictions is that they are always correct – they are so vague as to be universal.

Questions

13.1 Above a flat Earth, the gravitational field lines are parallel and the field strength is constant. Above a spherical Earth, the field lines diverge and the strength of the field obeys an inverse-square law. How high above the Earth would you have to go if you want to discriminate between the two theories (assuming you can measure field strength with a precision of 5 per cent)?

13.2 Show that the Copernican theory and the Tychonian theory give equally good accounts of the way that the distance between the Earth and Jupiter varies as the Earth goes round the Sun. Note: because Jupiter takes about 11.5 years to go round the Sun (on both theories) we can consider it to be motionless in its orbit – in six months it will only have moved by 15°.

13.3 If you had a radar set to measure the distance of the planets, how could you show, from measurements on Venus, that the Tychonian system was invalid?

13.4 Assume that the Earth is fixed in space (whatever that may mean) and that the Sun circles it at a distance of 1.5×10^{11} m. Calculate the time for the Sun to make one orbit of the Earth (one year). Take the mass of the Earth as 6×10^{24} kg and the gravitational constant as 6.7×10^{-11} N m^2 kg^{-2}.

13.5 How would the Tychonians answer these points? (Remember it is impossible for them to be wrong.)

13.6 Assume that astrological influences work because of the effect of the force of gravity. Compare the gravitational effect of Mars on a newborn baby (the correct term is neonate) with that of the midwife who delivered it. (Mass of midwife = 80 kg. Mass of baby = 4 kg. Midwife–baby distance = 0.5 m. Mass of Mars = 6.4×10^{23} kg. Earth–Mars distance = 2.2×10^{11} m. Gravitational constant $G = 6.67 \times 10^{-11}$ N m^2 kg^{-2}.)

13.7 What would an astrologer say to these figures?

13.8 Suppose that the Sun does orbit a stationary Earth (in some suitable frame of reference). Calculate the period for one rotation of the Sun round the Earth, given that the mass of the Earth is 6×10^{24} kg, and that the Earth–Sun distance is 1.5×10^{11} m.

13.9 To be fair to those who believe that the Sun rotates round the Earth, we ought to take their figure for the Earth–Sun distance, that is, that it is less than the height of the firmament, 900 km. Calculate the time for one rotation of the Sun round the Earth.

13.10 Henry Morris, the director of the Institute for Creation Research (and a retired professor), believes that everyone now living on Earth is descended from Adam and Eve, who lived about 6000 years ago. He works it out this way. Since accurate records have been kept, the population of the Earth has grown at a nearly constant rate of about 0.33 per century. We know that the population of the Earth in 1800 was about 1 billion. If you work backwards from that date with the known rate of increase, you get to the number 2 (Adam and Eve) in 4300 B.C. So he says that the Earth is 4300 + 1987 years old. To test his results, plot a graph of the date from −4300 to 2000 on the x-axis against the numbers from 2 to a billion on the y-axis, using a logarithmic scale for this axis. (A log scale is used because Morris assumes a constant growth rate from 2 to a billion.) From your graph read off the population of the Earth in 2500 B.C., when the Great Pyramid was built. Assume that one-tenth of the population of the world lived in Egypt. Comment on your result.

14 Credulity

An exercise in assessing information

In the last reading, we looked at some of the bizarre beliefs which are flourishing these days. There are so many that we had better look at a few more. Strange as these examples are, the strangest thing about them is that they are all vouched for by the 'best' authorities on the subject. Allan Hynek, for example, who is generally recognised as the leading 'expert' on UFOs, has never denounced any of the outrageous tales which will be recounted here.

The most obvious thing about UFOs is their ability to zoom about the sky. We are told (by the credulous) that they can turn in their own length while travelling at the speed of a jet plane, or faster. Some people tell us that they have been taken for a joy ride by the kindly disposed extra-terrestrials, who beckoned them aboard with smiles and courtly gestures.

Some UFO buffs believe that the Earth is hollow. This is so that they may have an answer to the question 'where do UFOs go at night and when they are not flying about the stratosphere?' They think that the central cavity has a radius about half that of the Earth, with tunnels leading down from the North and South Poles (they have movable flaps over them during the day). This is not the most stupid idea on these lines. Even further out than the flat-earthers are those who say that the Earth is spherical but that we live on the inside of a hollow sphere.

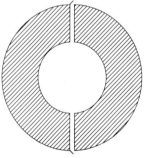

In the 1960s the best evidence for UFOs came from radar 'sightings'. These are now very rare, however, except in a few areas; one of these is the district around Wellington, New Zealand, which because of the surrounding hills is notorious for spurious radar signals. One of the difficulties is that some radar signals are very weak, especially when the beam passes through cloud. More important are the cases of spurious echoes from temperature inversions in the lower atmosphere. As atmospheric conditions vary, it is quite possible for a false 'blip' to appear for a moment, vanish and then reappear soon after. This might give the impression that the craft has travelled, say, 40 km in 20 s, corresponding to a speed of 7200 km h^{-1}. Nowadays the computers attached to the radar systems at large airports are programmed to disregard anything flying at a speed greater than 5000 km h^{-1}. Another recent development that greatly reduces false sightings is that large aeroplanes are now fitted with transponders. When the 'plane detects a radar signal, the transponder sends back a signal indicating the height and flight number. As a result of all these changes there are very few claims of radar detection of UFOs. The only notable recent case was of an Air New Zealand pilot who wrote a book about a UFO which he said was detected partly as a result of readings from the Wellington radar. We now know that the visual sightings were the lights from Japanese squid boats and the radar signals were from Wellington's over-eager system.

People who believe in extra-sensory perception (ESP), clairvoyance, remote viewing and out-of-body experiences all claim that these effects act just as well over long distances as short – that the intensity of the effect is independent of distance. This is unlikely, because it contravenes the inverse-square law. Some of these psychics argue that the effects are unique and do not have to obey an inverse-square law. That only shows up how little physics they know. The inverse-square laws enjoy enormous prestige, not just because they are always confirmed by the most careful experiments but because they follow from our basic assumptions about the nature of space. Consider a small point charge of electricity q at the centre of a sphere. The flux of electricity will spread out uniformly in all directions and will be distributed over an area equal to $4\pi r^2$. The flux of electricity from a charge q equals q/ε and so the flux density (or electric field strength) due to the charge is $q/4\pi\varepsilon r^2$ and this is the inverse-square law.

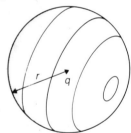

surface area = $4\pi r^2$

Thus we have a law of power to the minus two because we live in a world of three dimensions. Psychics claim to have a law of power zero, and so presumably dwell in a one-dimensional world. The connection between the power of the law and the number of dimensions of our world was known to Immanuel Kant (1724–1804), so it ought to be accepted now.

There seems to be no limit to the number of quack diets and quack foods about these days (tasteless garlic, chlorophyll and buckets of water are all cited as cures for every ill). It is generally easy to tell the quack from the genuine by the language of the advertisement. One special diet promised to help remove from 5 to 10 kg from your body in only seven days and to 'flush your system of impurities'. Another give-away is a boast (put out by a woman who claims to be a qualified dietician) that 'the foods eaten burn more calories than they give the body in calorific value'. Some of these diets also claim to cure non-existent diseases. 'Severe gastro-intestinal toxicity', 'over-stimulation of the lymphatic system' and 'spasticity throughout the large intestine' sound bad enough. They are beyond the reach of orthodox medicine but any quack can cure them with a packet of tablets made from 'natural sources'.

It is interesting that at a time when medicine can at last supply remedies that are scientifically proven, there should be a revival of faith healing. Fifty years ago, doctors' work was largely limited to diagnosis and prognosis (predicting the outcome of the illness); there were very few useful treatments. Within the last half-century, the prevention of killer diseases like diphtheria, smallpox and poliomyelitis has become routine and others, such as tuberculosis, can now be cured. Yet there has at the same time come a resurgence of 'alternative medicine'.

Among the strangest of these 'cures' are those that are grouped together as 'homoeopathy'. This method depends on the 'principle' that 'like cures like'. So that to cure, say, pneumonia the patient is given substances which are claimed to produce the symptoms of pneumonia. All these substances are easily obtained; for example, the standard cure for appendicitis is charcoal and chalk and that for diabetes is sodium bicarbonate and iron rust. Prescribing can be difficult; one homoeopath claimed to be able to produce a thousand symptoms in healthy people by administering doses of common salt.

With simple remedies like these one would expect that the treatment would be inexpensive, but in fact it costs more than that from doctors. The cost arises from the second main distinguishing feature of homoeopathy, and that is the 'principle' that the potency of a cure increases as it is diluted. No homoeopath would think of giving a medicine diluted less than a billion times, and for a cure dilutions of 1 in 10^{60} are desirable. In between dilutions, the liquids have to be shaken and the bottles banged on the bench in a ritual way; all this takes a lot of time and effort, which clearly must be reflected in the cost. Homoeopaths believe that although there are no molecules of the medicine remaining in the bottle after dilution, the liquid 'remembers' them in some (undisclosed) way. Banging the bottle is supposed to help this 'remembering'.

Questions

14.1 Calculate the acceleration on a person in a space ship which is travelling at aircraft speed (say 200 m s^{-1}) and which turns in its own length (say in a circle of radius 10 m).

14.2 Could a human survive such an acceleration?

14.3 Could an extra-terrestrial?

14.4 Think about waves on a string. What is analogous to radar beams being reflected from a temperature inversion?

14.5 And what is analogous in the realm of light waves in air?

14.6 Why are we not surprised to read that radar waves are attenuated when they pass through clouds?

14.7 Why do a plane's transponders send to Earth information about its height?

14.8 Name three examples of numerical values which would be very different if the Earth were hollow (as in the first diagram).

14.9 Why can no diet 'consume more calories than it gives to the body'?

14.10 Why are homoeopathic dilutions greater than about 1 in 10^{24} unreasonable, even in homoeopathic terms?

14.11 Homoeopathic medicines are most valued when the dilution is as great as 1 part in 10^{60}. If 1 drop of the medicine were diluted in 10^{60} drops of water, what would be the volume of the water? If this volume of water were in the form of a cube, what would be the length of its side?

14.12 Use kinetic theory to explain why the basis of homoeopathic prescribing, that a liquid can 'remember' the shape of medicine molecules that are no longer there, is unlikely to be true.

14.13 What easy practical test could you do to test these claims?

14.14 Explain why banging the medicine bottle is unlikely to help a homoeopathic liquid 'remember' departed molecules.

14.15 If we lived in a two-dimensional universe, how would the strength of a magnetic field decrease with distance? Would there even by magnetic fields?

14.16 An advertisement for a branded garlic preparation (garlic with the taste removed) claims that it can 'rejuvenate the nervous system, kill bacteria, purify the blood, tune up the lymphatic system, make you look younger and feel better'. Which of these claims is open to objective testing?

15 The risks from radiation

We want to assess the risk we run from the natural background radiation. To do this, we shall first consider some other sources of risk so as to have something to compare it with.

We first look at accidental deaths (including car deaths) – those that could kill any of us, the penalty of living in a sophisticated western society. In New Zealand, the number of accidental deaths per million per year is 476, so the individual risk is 4.76×10^{-4} per year (in the United States, the figure is slightly larger, 5.96×10^{-4} chances per year). As there are 8780 hours in a year, the chance of anyone being killed in an accident in the next hour is $0.000\,476/8780 = 5.1 \times 10^{-8}$. We may take the average life expectancy as 70 years and so the lifetime accident risk is $4.76 \times 10^{-4} \times 70 = 3.3 \times 10^{-2}$, or about 1 in 30. The relative risk is the lifetime risk times the average life lost, $0.033 \times 35 = 1$ year. So the average person loses about 1 year of life due to accidents. In both the United States and New Zealand, the death rate due to car accidents is the same, about 250 per million per year. In New Zealand there are about 350 suicides per year, that is about 100 per million of the population.

Let us now look at deaths due to smoking cigarettes. In New Zealand, in a population of about 3.2 million, 1050 people die each year of lung cancer; that is 0.0033 chances per year. In the United States, the data for heavy smokers (people who smoke more than one pack a day) is available. There, 75 000 heavy smokers out of 22 million die each year. So the individual risk per year is 75 000/22 000 000 or 0.0034, the same as in New Zealand. Assuming that a smoker starts at age 20 and so goes at it for 50 years, then the lifetime risk is $50 \times 0.0034 = 0.17$ and the relative risk is $25 \times 0.0034 = 4.2$ years. If we add in the risks due to heart disease, emphysema and so forth to those of lung cancer, this figure is doubled to about 9 years. Such a person smokes $20 \times 365 \times 50 = 365\ 000$ cigarettes in his or her lifetime and loses $9 \times 365 \times 24 \times 20 = 4\ 700\ 000$ minutes of life; hence each cigarette cuts short a person's life by the ratio of these two figures, i.e. 13 minutes. There seems to be a definite danger to 'passive smokers', non-smokers who live in the same house as a heavy smoker, but no one can yet put a figure to the risk.

In New Zealand we all receive a radiation dose (background radiation) of about 17 millisieverts (mSv) each year. It is known that an immediate dose of 90 Sv is fatal and severe illness is caused by about 22 Sv. In Hiroshima and Nagasaki, the 24 000 people who were cared for are estimated to have received an average dose of 17 Sv; 81 of these died of leukaemia, compared with 20 cases in a comparable group of people not exposed to the bombs. In this illness, there is generally a latent period of 5 years after exposure to radiation with no deaths, then a high-risk time of 20 years, after which you are pretty safe; you have escaped. Since we are continually receiving the background radiation we are continually at risk. For the Japanese victims, the risk per year was $61/20 = 3.05$ cancers per year and the individual risk was $3.05/24\ 000 = 1.25 \times 10^{-4}$. We now assume that the risk due to radiation is proportional to the size of the dose, hence the individual risk per sievert received is $1.25 \times 10^{-4}/17 = 8.4 \times 10^{6}$. Now this figure is for deaths due to leukaemia; for all causes of radiation-induced deaths, we must multiply by 6. For us in New Zealand, with an average dose of 17 mSv per year in 20 years, we get 0.34 Sv. The individual risk is then $0.34 \times 6 \times 8.4 \times 10^{-6}$. As we are at risk for 20 years from that dose, our lifetime risk is $20 \times 1.5 \times 10^{-5} = 3 \times 10^{-4}$. This is approximately 600 times smaller than the risk due to heavy smoking and about half that due to accidents. If you live in a brick-lined house, you get an extra 5 mSv per year, due to radiation from the trace elements in the brick. Similarly, a granite house will give you a bigger dose still. Your risk hardly rises if you live right outside a nuclear power station; in the United States, regulations say that you must get no more than an extra 1 mSv per year from the plant. This is the same risk as that from smoking one cigarette each year.

Since the Soviets are still somewhat secretive, it is impossible to estimate the danger to the people who lived near the Chernobyl nuclear power station. We do know that people in Sweden (in the direct line of the fall-out) received an extra year's dose in a few days. Some Russians, living much nearer, must have received several years' dose in a very short time.

We do not yet have enough information to work out the risks due to drug taking. It is known that marihuana is now the second most valuable crop grown in the United States ($17 billion a year) and that 40 million people in that country have tried it. We do not know if the drug has shortened lives to any extent. In America, 17 million people have tried cocaine and 4 million have used heroin, but the deaths and damage they may have caused have not yet shown up in the statistics.

Questions

15.1 Ivan Illich has estimated that people who drive cars travel at an average speed of about 8 km per hour. Work it out this way: assume you drive 20 000 km per year and that the car costs 10p per km to run. How long would you have to work to raise that much money? How many hours do you have to work per km?

15.2 What can we, tentatively, deduce from the fact that the death rate for all smokers in New Zealand is roughly the same as that for heavy smokers in America?

15.3 We made two simplifications in our estimate of the deaths due to cigarette smoking. What were they?

15.4 Would these simplifications have increased or decreased our estimates of the risk?

15.5 How much more likely is a heavy smoker to die from his or her cigarettes than from the ordinary risks of daily living?

15.6 What proportion of the population die in car accidents?

15.7 As you get older, your life expectancy rises. For example, when you are 20 years old your life expectancy is 46 (total 66), but at 30 you are expected to live another 38 years (total 68) and at 60 years old you are expected to have another 14 years to go (total 74). Why is this?

15.8 There has been no detectable increase in the proportion of deformities and abnormalities among the children born to the survivors of Hiroshima and Nagasaki. What does that tell you?

15.9 If we are surrounded by harmful radiations throughout our lives, why are there not more deformed babies born? (As it is, about 1 per cent of all babies born suffer from a genetic or chromosomal defect.)

15.10 There seem to be two ways in which radiation affects the human body. It can have a primary effect, knocking an electron out of a hydrogen atom which can then affect the DNA in our cells. Alternatively, a secondary effect is produced when the electron hits a water molecule and knocks out the hydroxyl group. Which of these do you think would cause most harm?

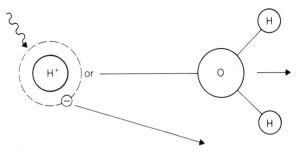

15.11 There are four main kinds of damage to a DNA molecule:

(a) severing a single strand,
(b) severing both strands,
(c) cutting one of the linking bases,
(d) making a chemical cross-link.

Which of these do you think would be easiest for the body to repair?

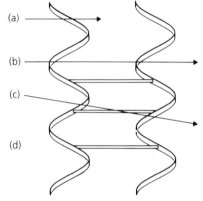

16 Isolation transformers

An isolation transformer should always be used with electrical equipment that is liable to give a shock. Such a device will always protect against a lethal shock, although I have had a tingle when one was in place. In normal circuits, there is only one wire from the generator to your home. The return is made through the earth. Thick copper rods are sunk into the earth at the power station and at your home (yours is probably outside the kitchen door). In some parts of the world, the resistance of the earth is so high that a return wire is needed. (This is the case in the U.K. Here one side of the supply mains – the 'neutral' lead – is earthed at the sub-station and not at individual houses.) When you switch on the light, one side of the filament is connected to the 230 V line, the

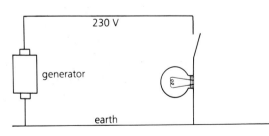

other side is connected to earth. If you touch a live wire, you complete the circuit and whether the shock you get will be lethal or not will depend on your resistance. To prevent the current from flowing through you, an isolation transformer is inserted. This has an equal number of turns in both its primary and secondary windings, so the voltage is unchanged at 230 V. Only the primary coil has one end earthed, however, so that if you touch a live wire you do not complete a circuit. It is just like touching only one terminal of a high-tension battery.

isolation transformer

A similar arrangement is used in cars. There is only one wire to most switches and lamps. In this case, the return is made through the metal chassis of the car. If you look under the bonnet of your car, you will see that one side of the battery is connected directly to the chassis, usually through a thick braided wire.

Which side of the battery is earthed is a matter of taste. In my wife's car it is the negative side of the battery that is earthed. Of course, lamps and electromagnets work equally well whichever way the current flows. If the battery were reversed it would be easy enough to reverse the leads to the ammeter, the dynamo and the few other components that have a definite polarity. Experts say, however, that having the negative side earthed reduces corrosion and rusting due to electrolytic action. It does not seem to have worked very well for my wife, as all the four doors of her car have rusted from the inside. One of my previous cars had the positive side of the battery earthed as that was supposed to reduce rusting. The sills and boot of that car were a mass of rusting from the inside, with the first hint of trouble the dreaded bubbles of rust. I expect that we shall soon be advised to do away with d.c. in cars and have a.c. generators in order to prevent rusting.

Some devices are now being marketed as 'doubly insulated' with the story that an isolation transformer is not necessary. My electric lawn-mower makes such a claim. This means that there are two layers of insulation applied in such a way that if one became faulty, the other would still insulate the user from the live conductor. I have no faith in this and always wear my gumboots while using the mower to cut the lawn.

Questions

16.1 What kinds of electrical device always need an isolation transformer?

16.2 How is it possible to kill yourself even if an isolation transformer is fitted?

16.3 Do the transformers we use in the lab act as isolation transformers?

16.4 Why do electrified railway lines have only one overhead wire while trolley buses have two overhead wires? In the same way, trams had only one overhead wire; why?

16.5 I recently read in a physics book, 'She was wearing gumboots and so no electricity could flow through her.' What's wrong with this?

16.6 By far the most lethal piece of electrical equipment in the home is the television set. This has a transformer inside to give about 20 000 V to accelerate the electrons towards the screen. Why could this not be made safe by having the transformer 'floating' (that is, with neither side earthed)?

16.7 I had trouble starting my car one cold morning. At the garage, they removed the 12 V coil (transformer) and put in a 6 V one. Why did that work?

16.8 They also had to put a ballast resistor in the primary circuit. What was the reason for that?

16.9 We may compare the action of a transformer with that of the hydraulic brake system of a car. In the transformer, we have a small voltage and a big current in the primary and the opposite in the secondary. In the hydraulic system we have a small force working through a big distance at the foot pedal (master cylinder) and a big force moving through a small distance at the brake pad (slave cylinder). In these two systems, what is the analogous quantity that stays the same?

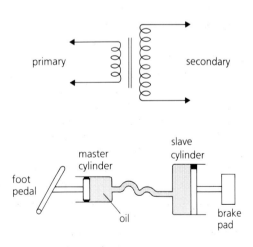

16.10 You have come across a drawer full of old transformers. How can you tell the primary from the secondary, just by looking at it?

16.11 Does that work for an isolation transformer?

16.12 The transformer outside my house serves about 30 houses. Assuming that the average demand from each house is no more than 3 kW and that the transformer is 99 per cent efficient, how much heat must the device dissipate?

16.13 What does that tell you about the shape of the transformer?

17 The Mitsubishi Lancer

An exercise in handling data

My car is a Mitsubishi Lancer (eight years old, but still running sweetly). I recently used it for an experiment in data analysis. I drove along a long, straight, flat road with three passengers. I took it up to about 90 km h^{-1}, put it into neutral and then let it coast to a slow speed. As the speed fell off, one passenger read the speedometer, another called out the time and the third recorded the readings. I watched the road. The results are shown here (I have converted the speeds into a more civilised unit, m s^{-1}).

v/m s^{-1}	23.6	22.2	20.8	19.4	18.0	16.6	15.3	13.9	12.5	11.1	9.7	8.3
t/s	0	1.3	3.19	7.51	13.3	18.4	22.2	26.7	31.6	37.3	39.2	47.1

It is an interesting exercise in basic mechanics to derive the formula for the force of air friction on an object moving at constant speed.

Think about a cylinder of cross-sectional area A, moving with speed V in a medium (air) of density ρ. The volume of air swept out per second is Av. Then in one second the cylinder collides with air particles of mass ρAV. The change in momentum in that time $(2MV) = 2\rho AVV = 2\rho AV^2$. There will be some effect due to streamlining so it is necessary to put a constant C_D in front also; for historical reasons, it is usual to put another constant, ½, in front. Then the formula is

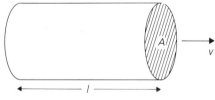

$$F = \tfrac{1}{2}C_D\rho AV^2$$

Questions _____

17.1 Plot a speed–time graph of the data.

17.2 What does it mean?

17.3 We expect the air resistance to depend on the speed of the car, as we have shown it to be proportional to the (speed)^2. Hence work out the acceleration for each time period. We ought really to take the tangents to the v–t graph but that is too wearisome. Instead, work out the change in speed Δv (it is constant in this case) and also the change in t (Δt) for each time interval and so get the acceleration a. Work out also v^2 and then plot the graph of v^2 against a.

17.4 And what does that signify?

17.5 A driver is keen to preserve her car's brake pads. As she is driving along, she sees a traffic light ahead turn red and knows she will have to stop. Should she apply the brakes immediately and then coast to a stop, or should she take her foot off the gas, allow the engine to cause a deceleration and then brake just before the stop sign?

17.6 This question has nothing to do with the previous ones except that it is about cars. In normal running (average speeds), does a piston of a car move further vertically or horizontally? Consider a car moving at 80 km h^{-1}, with the engine rev speed of 6000 r.p.m. and a piston stroke of 10 cm.

17.7 Following on from the above, which is greater, the average horizontal speed of the piston or the maximum vertical speed? (Assume that it moves with s.h.m.)

17.8 You think up this brilliant idea: to save cars having to carry petrol about with them, it is arranged that they suck petrol from a trough running along the side of the road (through telescopic tubes). Assuming that the car has a fuel consumption of 10 km per litre, how wide should the tube be?

17.9 An experimental Leyland bus had a large flywheel to store energy during braking and release it during running. It was made of plastic and glass fibre. As it had most of its mass on the rim we shall assume that all the mass was on the outside of a circle of radius 20 cm. If the total mass was 25 kg, calculate its rotational inertia.

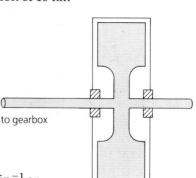

to gearbox

17.10 If the maximum rotational speed was 16 000 rev min^{-1} or 1600 rad s^{-1}, calculate the maximum energy stored in the flywheel.

17.11 We are told that that is equivalent to a 16 tonne bus travelling at 48 km h^{-1} or 13 m s^{-1}. Do these two figures for the k.e. agree? What is their significance?

17.12 We are also told that the bearings were so good that it takes 50 minutes for the flywheel to stop when running freely. So work out, in turn, the angular acceleration in stopping, the frictional torque and the angle turned through in stopping from 1600 rad s^{-1} in the 50 minutes, and so find the work done by the frictional torque.

17.13 A friend uses her car to tow a caravan. In the handbook for her car she read that the 'downweight' of the caravan (that is, the downward force exerted on the car by the caravan) should not exceed 50 kg (500 N). She put some bathroom scales between the towbar and the fitting on the car and the indication was off the scale, more than 2000 N. She therefore quickly transferred some weighty items from the front of the caravan to the back. When she drove the car she found that the caravan swayed more but with a longer period of oscillation. Explain.

17.14 The brochure for the new Mazda 121 makes much of the effort that has gone into achieving a smooth air flow, and claims that the drag factor at $C_D = 0.36$ is the lowest of any small car. Use the formula

$$F = \frac{1}{2}C_D\rho Av^2$$

to calculate the frictional drag on the car when the speed is 130 km h^{-1} (36 m s^{-1}). The frontal area of the car A is about 2.7 m^2 and the density of the medium (air) is $\rho = 1.3$ kg m^{-3}.

17.15 Then work out the power developed by the car at that speed and compare it with the figure in the brochure of 43.4 kW.

17.16 When the car starts from rest, there will be no air resistance. Hence calculate the initial acceleration of the car, given that its mass is 715 kg. What have you neglected?

17.17 The brochure also says that the maximum torque of the engine is 105 N m at 3500 r.p.m. Calculate the power developed from these figures.

18 Firewalking

An exercise on the difference between temperature and heat energy

There has recently been a return of the craze for 'firewalking'. People are willing to pay large sums to be taught the secret of safely walking over white-hot coals. They are enjoined to undertake a period of spiritual purification beforehand. They are given an uplifting address by the charismatic teacher, then taken out to see the fire lit. The claim that it is 'over a thousand degrees' seems fair. The fire seems very hot – much hotter than it really is and for a very interesting reason. We are used to heat sources that are very small, like point sources. We assume that the heat intensity falls off as the square of the distance. So that if you hold your hand over a fire and note the hotness, it will be four times as hot at half the distance. But firewalkers have a large rectangular fire and the inverse-square law does not operate. In fact, the heat flux is constant – the temperature does not increase the closer you get to the fire. (This is only strictly true, of course, if the fire is infinitely big and has a parallel heat flux. It will be nearly so if you do not go more than a metre or so above the kind of fires that firewalkers use.)

The fire is left to get to an overall temperature and the audience is given another uplifting talk, stressing the need for purity and determination. Then outside, off with the shoes and everyone follows the leader over the glowing coals. The secret is to be quick, usually no more than a second. Much attention is given to the preparation of the fire. The red-hot embers are like fluffy pieces of charcoal. They are certainly hot, but because they are so light they contain very little heat energy. Thus when the bare foot touches the coal, very little heat energy is transferred. After a person has skipped across, black footmarks are clearly visible in the coals where they have been cooled by the passing feet. In a moment the marks vanish as the embers warm up when heat flows in from the interior of the coal. Many people do get small blisters on their feet, but do not notice them as they are on a 'high'. One unfortunate woman believed the words of her teacher implicitly. She stood on the coals for over five seconds and had to be rushed to hospital with third-degree burns. The teacher said that her faith had endured only for a few seconds and then Satan took over.

There is, then, no secret about firewalking. It is a straightforward demonstration of many basic ideas in physics. In a similar way, we know that if we take some jam tarts from the oven and, wishing to sample our delicious cooking, eat them straight away we burn our tongues not on the pastry but on the jam. When the tart touches the tongue, heat energy is transferred from the hot tart to the cold ($37° C$) tongue. The jam has much more heat energy than the pastry and so the pastry has less heat to give up to the tongue. We say that the jam has a higher heat energy capacity (or specific heat capacity) than the pastry. This is presumably because the jam contains more water than the pastry, and water has the highest heat capacity of all common substances (4.2 kJ per kg per °C). The same effect is noticeable when eating quiche; there is a marked difference in the apparent temperatures of the pastry and the vegetables.

Another analogy is provided by the discharge of an electroscope. If you touch a charged electroscope, the leaf falls to zero. This is because when you touch it, you share the charge on it. You and the electroscope have the same potential. As your capacitance is so much greater than that of the electroscope, you retain so much more of the charge. So it is not strictly true to say that the electroscope is totally discharged, only that the charge it keeps is too small to measure. In the same way, if you step on a red-hot coal you share its heat energy; you get most of it, the coal retains little of the energy and it goes black, a sign of a lowered temperature.

Questions

18.1   How do you know that the pastry and vegetables of a quiche are in fact at the same temperature?

18.2 Why is a hot-water bottle so delightful on cold winter's nights?

18.3 Why do you not burn your hand inside an oven at 300 °C?

18.4 But why do you burn it on a metal tray taken from that same oven?

18.5 In Fiji, the firewalkers perform on pumice after going into a cataleptic trance. Why is pumice especially suitable?

18.6 If you ever attend a firewalker's performance, you can say to him, 'I see you walking on coals which are at a temperature of over 1000 °C; would you please now stand for a couple of seconds on this portable electric hot-plate which is at 300 °C (and which by a strange coincidence I just happen to have with me)?' What would happen to the firewalker?

18.7 Now calculate the quantity of heat that would be transferred to the teacher's feet in the two seconds. Assume that it is a 1 kw element and that the plate has mass 0.5 kg and specific heat capacity of 0.1 kcal $kg^{-1} C^{-1}$.

18.8 Why does all the heat flow from the hot-plate into the standing feet?

18.9 In the Middle Ages, defenders of castles used to pour boiling oil on the attackers. Oil has a specific heat capacity only half that of water and a boiling point less than double that of water. So why did they go to all the trouble and expense of using oil? The figures are as follows:

	Specific heat capacity/$J\ kg^{-1}\ K^{-1}$	Boiling point/K
Oil	1970	570
Water	4190	373

18.10 Estimate the area of the bottom of your shoe; if your mass is 60 kg, calculate the pressure on your foot when you are standing on one leg. Soldiers who have to walk across minefields are provided with inflatable overshoes, 50 cm × 20 cm; what pressure do they exert? Finally, when you are running across a bed of white-hot charcoal, what pressure do you exert? What is the significance of this?

18.11 You have a steaming hot cup of coffee and you are in a hurry to drink it. Do you pour in the cold milk first and then wait a bit, or do you wait first and then pour in the milk? Think up a reason for adding the milk immediately.

18.12 Now think of a reason for letting the coffee cool first and then adding the milk.

18.13 Newton's interests were in gravitation and light. How did he come to discover his law of cooling?

18.14 About a century ago James Joule performed a whole series of experiments which led to the enunciation of the Law of conservation of energy (Joule was the son of a wealthy brewer and could devote a lot of time to experimental work). In his most famous experiment he allowed two masses, each 14 kg, to fall 20 times through 2 m. What was the total amount of p.e. lost?

18.15 If all that energy were converted into heat energy, what rise in temperature could Joule expect in the 7 kg of water that he used? (The specific heat capacity of water is 4200 J kg^{-1} K^{-1}. Remember that the magnitude of a kelvin is the same as that of a degree Celsius.)

18.16 One of the experiments performed by Joule while on his honeymoon in Switzerland was to measure the difference in temperature of the water at the top and bottom of a waterfall. If the waterfall was 100 m high, what is the maximum temperature difference that Joule could expect?

18.17 What kind of gravitational field is analogous to the heat flux from a firewalker's fire?

18.18 And what kind of light flux similarly?

18.19 In the year 1275, Marco Polo crossed the Pamir Mountains at a height of 4000 m. He wrote, 'Moreover I tell you . . . because of the great intensity of cold . . . things are not able to be cooked so well as down below.' What do we now think is the explanation of Marco Polo's observation? Do we think less of him for being wrong in the matter?

19   The Fokker Friendship

An exercise in data interpretation

The Fokker Friendship has been the standard aircraft for domestic services in many countries. It has been built for twenty years but will soon be superseded by an improved version, the Fokker 50. At the time it first came out, the British firm of Handley Page produced the Herald aircraft. The two planes are almost indistinguishable; they had the same engines, were almost the same size and carried the same number of passengers. Yet the Herald was a failure and only a few were made, while the Friendship has been one of the most successful planes ever built.

The two engines are Rolls-Royce 'Dart' type of 1835 h.p., and they are prop-jets, that is, jet engines in which the drive shaft is connected to a four-bladed propeller and very little thrust comes from the jet exhaust. This system is more efficient at lower speeds but does not give as much thrust as a pure jet. It is thus better for smaller, slower aircraft. The system will be modified to drive the next generation of larger, faster and much more fuel-efficient Boeing jets, the Boeing 7J7 aircraft. These will have two 'unducted' fan engines driving two contra-rotating propellers, one with eight blades and the other with ten. These are like the fan-jets which power the big jetliners but without the outer casing; the propeller becomes the unducted fan.

On a recent Friendship flight, I took along one of my home-made accelerometers. This one consists of a short pendulum hung in front of a circular scale, marked in degrees. As soon as the plane began to move along the runway a friend in the next seat called out every other second, I then read off the angle of the pendulum and called it out and he recorded the angle. (The other passengers thought we were nuts.) We did this for the 35 seconds it took for the plane to reach the speed known as V_2, which is the speed at which the pilot pulls back on the control column and the plane will take off. In jet aircraft, this process is called 'rotation'. (Incidentally, V_1 is the decision speed; if anything goes wrong before that speed is reached, there is still enough runway left for the take-off to be aborted. After V_1 is reached the take-off must be continued, even on one engine.)

The table shows the angle of the pendulum θ for each time interval and also the acceleration, calculated from $a = g \tan \theta$. The area under this graph is V_2 and the pilot told me that for the plane loaded to 17 700 kg total mass and for the current runway conditions, V_2 was 95 knots or 48 m s^{-1}.

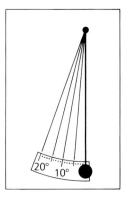

t/s	2	4	6	8	10	12	14	16	18	20	22	24	26	28	30	32	34
θ/°	10	12	10	10	8	8	8	7	7	7	6	6	6	5	5	5	5
a/m s^{-2}	1.8	2.1	1.8	1.8	1.4	1.4	1.4	1.2	1.2	1.2	1.05	1.05	1.05	0.88	0.88	0.88	0.88

We see that the average acceleration over this time is about 1.3 m s^{-2} and this, using $\Delta V = a \, \Delta t$, gives V_2 as 45 m s^{-1}. (The satisfying agreement between these two values must be good luck, it is difficult enough to read the accelerometer at the best of times.) The graph below shows the acceleration plotted against time.

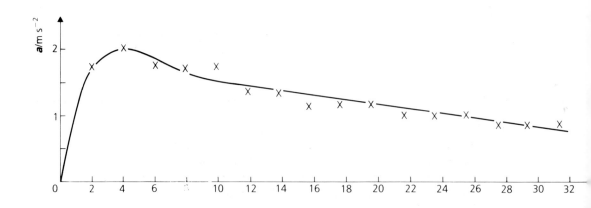

I should have preferred to take a v–t graph for the rush along the runway, but that is not possible as aircraft airspeed meters only start at about 50 knots. I still dream of doing it by having a posse of observers stationed along the side of the runway at regular intervals, each armed with a stopwatch. They would record the instant the plane reaches them. The reason for the lack of sensitivity at low speeds is that on the Friendship (and other planes), the airspeed is still measured by the Pitot tube system, as used in First World War fighters. The difference in pressure in the tubes is proportional to the air speed.

When the aeroplane banks while turning, the lift of the wings has to overcome the weight of the craft and also provide the centripetal acceleration to permit motion in a circle. The weight of the plane is mg and the centripetal force is mv^2/r. Hence

$$v^2/r = g \tan \theta$$

The diagram shows the graphs used by pilots. The pilot knows his airspeed (still in the bizarre units of knots) and wishes to read off the angle of turn for the given radius of turn (here given in thousands of feet). Some typical data are given here for the speed of 200 knots.

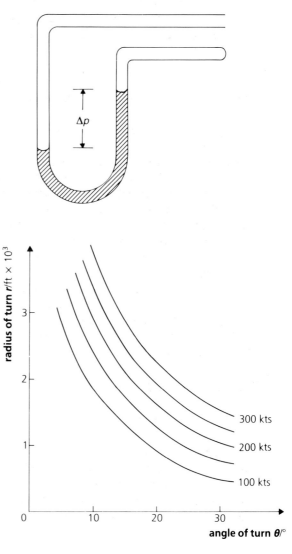

radius/× 1000 ft	35	20	13	10	7.5
$\theta/°$	6	10	15	20	25
$\tan \theta$	0.0945	0.176	0.268	0.364	0.466

Questions

19.1 Using the acceleration–time graph, read off the speed at the end of 4 s as the area under the graph. Calculate the thrust of the engines as $F = ma$. Then calculate the power developed as *power = thrust × speed*. Compare this with the total take-off power of the Dart engines, given as 3670 h.p. (1 h.p. = 750 watts).

19.2 Repeat the exercise for the first 8 s of the trip along the runway.

19.3 Why is it pointless to try this at V_2, after 35 s?

19.4 Why was it not possible for me to take acceleration readings beyond 35 s?

19.5 How do you justify the formula for tan θ quoted above?

19.6 For the data given, plot the graph of $1/r$ against tan θ.

19.7 Why does the Pitot tube speedometer have two tubes, since the air only presses on one?

19.8 Why does the acceleration of the Friendship increase at first and then decrease?

19.9 Chinese civil aircraft use altimeters that are calibrated in mm of mercury. On what principle does this scale depend?

Atmospheric pressure varies with height according to the table below. Plot a graph of this relationship.

Height/km	0	1	2	3	4	5	6	7	8	9	10
Pressure/kPa	101	90	80	70	62	54	48	41	36	31	26

19.10 What are the advantages and disadvantages of this peculiar method of measuring height? Consider the change in pressure for a change in height of 300 m (1000 feet) at the height at which aeroplanes fly, and compare this with typical changes in atmospheric pressure at sea level (which are of the order of several kilopascals).

19.11 The Seastar is a two-engined flying boat made by the Julius Dornier company. The engines are mounted in tandem, on top of the wings; this keeps them out of the spray of sea water, but has one grave disadvantage when acceleration is desired. What is it?

20 | Helicopters

An exercise on rotation

Helicopters are now very much part of our modern way
of life. They are used for linking city centres with
peripheral airports, for fighting fires with 'monsoon'
buckets, for catching deer in the bush, for rescuing the
drowning from capsized boats, for top-dressing crops
and for lifting mountain huts (in sections) to
inaccessible locations. These varied tasks are only
possible because of the helicopter's unique ability to fly
slowly and, indeed, hover almost stationary.
Helicopters get their lift and forward thrust from a
single propeller (or rotor). This means that the axis of
the propeller must point forward. We can then resolve
this upward force into the horizontal component (equal
to the drag force, at constant speed) and the vertical
component (equal to the weight). Indeed, when
helicopters are moving at their fastest they often take
up a nose-down position, to increase the horizontal
component.

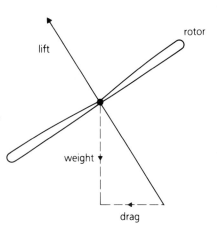

Helicopters also have a small propeller at the back.
This is to stop the helicopter going round in circles.
Consider a helicopter mounted on friction-free
bearings through its centre of mass. Suppose that the
rear propeller is not going and that the main one is
started up. Then the body of the machine would rotate
in the opposite direction to the rotor. As the body has
very much more rotational inertia (still called 'moment
of inertia' in older books) than the rotor, the body
would begin to turn very much more slowly than the
propeller. We know this from the Law of conservation
of angular momentum: the $I\omega$ of the body must equal
the $I\omega$ of the propeller.

Now when a helicopter is flying it is, effectively,
pivoted about its centre of mass. The problem in
designing high-speed helicopters is that the advancing
tip of the rotor goes much faster through the air than
the retreating tip. The amount of lift given by a wing or
rotor blade depends very much on its speed relative to
the air. Thus the two blades of the helicopter would
give very different amounts of lift. This effect is avoided
by making the angle of attack of the retreating blade
very much greater than the angle of the advancing
blade: the greater the angle of the blade, the greater the
lift. You will have noticed that when birds come in to
land and are flying slowly, their wings are at a bigger
angle than normal.

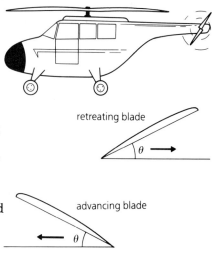

retreating blade

advancing blade

There is a limit to the angle of attack: if it is too big, the wing stalls and lift is lost. There is also a mechanical problem in making a helicopter blade that is strong enough to support the weight of the machine and yet which must be at virtually 0° to the horizontal while advancing and at about 20° to the horizontal while retreating.

To prevent the body turning, the small propeller at the back provides a contrary torque. It is put some way back so that the force it gives may be as small as possible (*torque = force × distance*). Of course, if the distance is made too big, the tail boom will be too heavy. It is the designer's job to settle these conflicting claims. It might seem that no torque would be needed to drive the main rotor. After all, it is turning at constant speed and torque is given by $T = I\alpha$, where α is the angular acceleration $d\omega/dt$, so the angular acceleration here is zero. The torque on the main rotor arises as the equal and opposite reaction to the work done in pushing the air aside as it rotates, in an analogous way to the force needed to drive a car forward at constant speed against the frictional force present.

Questions

20.1 What way would the small rotor tend to tilt the helicopter?

20.2 If the main rotor blade of an Iroquois helicopter (diameter 14.62 m) is rotating at 324 r.p.m., what is the speed of a point on the tip? And what are the speeds of the advancing and retreating tips if the machine is moving forward at its cruising speed of 62 m s^{-1} (140 m.p.h.)?

20.3 What is the significance of these figures?

20.4 A helicopter is used to lift a deer, mass 600 kg, out of the bush. Work out the tension in the rope supporting the animal if the helicopter is rising (a) at a constant speed of 3 m s^{-1}, and (b) with acceleration of 3 m s^{-2}.

20.5 A crew member of such a helicopter has a tranquillising gun. The helicopter is travelling with a horizontal speed of 10 m s^{-1} and the deer is running away from the helicopter at a speed of 3 m s^{-1}. How should the gun be aimed: straight at the animal, in front of it or behind it?

20.6 At the time I am writing this (mid-1987) the world speed record for a helicopter is held by a modified Westland Lynx. This speed is 216 kts (yes, they still use knots) and I make that 110 m s^{-1}. The only other pieces of data so far released are that the speed of the advancing rotor blade is 0.97 Mach and that the retreating blade has an angle of incidence of 21°. If 0.97 Mach is 320 m s^{-1}, what is the speed of the advancing rotor relative to the helicopter, and what is the speed of the retreating rotor tip through the air?

20.7 What is the significance of these figures?

20.8 When a star nears the end of its life, it explodes and then contracts into a tiny volume. Assuming that only a small proportion of its mass is lost, what happens to its rate of rotation?

20.9 A child is sitting on a roundabout in a children's park. The roundabout is given a spin and the child starts to walk towards the centre of the machine. What will happen to its speed of rotation?

20.10 Now suppose that the child has mass 25 kg and that the roundabout has radius 4 m and mass 80 kg (evenly distributed). Would the movement of the child make any appreciable difference? (For a circle, $I = mr^2/2$.)

20.11 Now suppose there are two children on the roundabout, which is standing still. Child P throws the ball directly to child Q. Suppose now that the roundabout is given a turn to the right and child P again throws the ball. Will the ball go directly to Q, or to the right of Q (as we see it), or to the left?

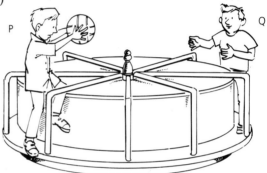

20.12 We have seen that it is difficult to increase the top speed of helicopters. One ingenious way of combining high speed with vertical take-off is the tilt-rotor craft Osprey, built by Bell-Boeing.

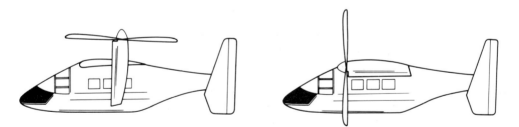

The two engines are on the ends of the wings. For take-off and hovering the engines are set vertically and the craft behaves like a helicopter. For forward flight, the engines are horizontal and the rotors act like propellers. When the plane is taking off there is no forward motion, so we can assume that the wings contribute nothing to its support. We assume that the rotors give three times as much thrust in the hovering mode, when there are large angles of attack on the rotors, as in forward flight. Compare the power given by each engine, 6000 h.p., with that calculated from the thrust and the top speed, 275 kts (130 m s^{-1}). The mass of the craft is 48 000 lb (22 000 kg). Take 1 h.p. as ¾ kW.

21 Lightning strikes

An exercise in understanding basic ideas

Electrical storms occur many times a day throughout the whole world
and several aeroplanes must be hit by lightning every day, but there is
no case recorded of a plane being downed by lightning. Aircraft are
made of metal and so the fuselage constitutes what we call a Faraday
cage (presumably the same applies to the modern composite materials
now coming into use, I take it that they contain enough carbon fibres to
make conducting surfaces). Faraday showed that if you charged a
hollow sphere, then all the charge stayed on the outside of the sphere.
This fact had been known earlier to Cavendish, who used it as evidence
for an inverse-square law of electricity. Faraday also showed that the
sphere does not have to be continuous; one made of chicken wire will
work just as well. In the same way, lightning does not penetrate the
small windows of an aeroplane. This is analogous to the way it is
possible to float a boat made of wire mesh on water, when surface
tension keeps the water out. When aeroplanes land, they are earthed so
that any charge they have picked up is discharged. If this is not done, it
is possible for a spark to jump from the plane to the earthed nozzle of
the refuelling pipe. It happened once, with a massive explosion.

The Science Museum in Boston, Massachusetts, has the original Van
de Graaff generator, restored to working order after its use in
experiments on artificial lightning. There, several times a day, a science
teacher puts on a fascinating display. He gets inside a large Faraday
cage and from it controls the Van de Graaff generator, which provides a
potential of over one million volts. Sparks several metres long jump
from the generator to the outside of the cage but the operator inside is
quite safe. It is also shown how sparks jump from the source to a
pointed object at a much lower voltage than from the generator to a flat
surface. A pointed lightning conductor discharges a thunder cloud
before a large voltage has built up.

A striking example of the need for lightning conductors is shown in
the celebrated painting by Canaletto of the Doge setting out for the
yearly ceremony of marrying the city of Venice to the sea. This shows
one face of the Campanile (bell tower) completely torn away following a
lightning strike. Benjamin Franklin, who invented lightning
conductors, must surely have been the luckiest scientist ever. His
experiment of flying a kite in an electrical storm was foolhardy in the
extreme. It was a miracle that when the lightning flash ran down the
kite string it jumped from the key at the bottom to earth. A German
scientist who tried to repeat the experiment was electrocuted.

The effect of a massive electric shock is often that of 'fibrillation'.
When the heart is pumping ordinarily about a dozen events must
happen in the right sequence and at the right times. Thus the valves
must open and the muscles must contract in proper order. In a
fibrillating heart the correct rhythmic sequence is lost and the heart is
said to look like 'a bag of squiggling worms'. It is beating weakly and

incapable of pumping blood. Death occurs in minutes. A defibrillator is a device that administers a massive shock to the heart; it stops all the electrical messages getting through to it and gives it a chance to start again with everything in the proper sequence. Not long ago, I saw a defibrillator being used in a television play, in an attempt to resuscitate a dying man. A shock was supposedly administered and one of the characters, a doctor, looking at the dials said after a pause, 'capacitors recharged', meaning that another shock could be given.

Defibrillation is one of the beneficial uses of severe electric shocks. The other one, apparently going out of fashion, is to give mentally ill people a shock. It is supposed to cure them. In the bad old days, insane patients were put in a snake pit and the bites were supposed to have the same effect.

The way charge builds up in thunder clouds is not fully understood (at least by me). It appears that in a thunder cloud, water droplets break up into two parts. The smaller part has a positive charge and rises, by convection, in the cloud. The larger part of the drop has an equal negative charge and falls, by gravity, to the bottom of the cloud. The bottom of the thunder cloud may be at -10 °C, the top at -20 °C. The bottom of the cloud acquires a negative potential and this is greater than the normal negative potential on the Earth's surface. Underneath the cloud the normal field reverses. Before the main thunderflash a leader jumps to Earth, ionising the air as it jumps from raindrop to raindrop. The main stroke then runs down this path to Earth.

It is quite safe to shelter in houses or within an angle of 45° formed by telephone and power lines. It is not safe to shelter under trees (though cows tend to do so). This is because the spark can jump from a lower branch to the Earth.

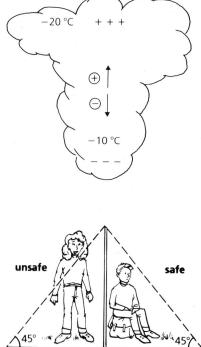

Questions

21.1 It has been observed that if a cow takes shelter under a tree in an electrical storm, then it is more likely to be killed if it is standing along a radius to the tree than if it was standing sideways on to the tree. Why is this? (Consider the tree to be at a potential of 1 000 000 V after the strike. Draw in a set of equipotentials round the tree trunk. Then put in a cow in the radial direction and a cow in the sideways direction.)

21.2 Suppose that the head of the cow in the radial position is at a potential of 600 000 V and its tail at 200 000 V. Suppose that the cow is 2 m long. What is the electric field between head and tail?

21.3 A typical thunder cloud may be at a potential of 10^8 V and the thunder strike may give a charge transfer of 20 coulomb. Assuming that the cloud acts as a parallel-plate capacitor, calculate the energy in the discharge.

21.4 If that energy could be harnessed, how long would it keep an average home supplied?

21.5 Is it reasonable to treat a thunder cloud as a parallel-plate capacitor?

21.6 If a thunder cloud may be taken as a parallel-plate capacitor of dimensions 4 km by 2 km and it is 0.5 km above the Earth's surface, what is its capacitance? Take the permittivity of free space as 9×10^{-12} F m^{-1}.

21.7 How does that value compare with the capacitance calculated from the data in the third question?

21.8 We may take the lightning strike as lasting 1 ms (1×10^{-3} s). What then is the average current in the strike?

21.9 The base of a typical thunder cloud is about 1 km up. How fast does the lightning strike? I have a book which gives the speed as one-sixth of the speed of light; do you think this is correct?

21.10 For a lightning discharge from cloud to Earth an electric field of about 330 000 V m^{-1} is necessary. This is the breakdown field for wet air. What is the maximum height of the bottom of a cloud at a potential of 10^8 V?

21.11 What causes the thunder?

21.12 Is it true that lightning 'never strikes in the same place twice'?

21.13 Two thunder clouds coalesce and join up to make one large cloud. What is the same as before and what is different?

21.14 In a typical defibrillator, a 16 μF capacitor is charged to about 6000 V and is then discharged in about 2 ms. Calculate the charge passed, the energy of the shock and the average current in the discharge.

21.15 It is now possible to get small-sized capacitors with large capacity. The large capacity is achieved by having an insulating material that can be very thin and also have very large permittivity. They are called Supercaps, and they are used to provide a back-up supply in computers in case there is a power cut. (It would be disastrous if a program were lost.) Such a capacitor has a capacity of 1 farad and can be charged to 5 V. What charge does it hold, and how much energy is stored?

21.16 Assuming that such a capacitor can be completely discharged, for how long could it supply 6 mW of power? Would the mains power be restored in that time?

21.17 In a full-sized Van de Graaff generator, 120 μC of charge is raised to a potential of 8 MV each second. What is the current carried up the rubber band, and what is the power developed? Would such a discharge through you be lethal?

22   Washing up

When you are doing the washing up, you sometimes get a soap (or more likely detergent) film across the mouth of the cup. Glad of any excuse to stop, you position yourself in the best way (that is, with your back to the light) and you see a marvellous set of interference fringes across the film.

The fringes are caused by the interference of light reflected back to your eyes from the front and back surfaces of the film. This gives an especially sharp set of fringes, because the bottom of the cup prevents direct light reaching your eye. Light transmitted through the film also gives fringes after two reflections in the film. These fringes are the opposite of the reflected fringes and tend to cancel them. So if you can eliminate the transmitted fringes, the reflected ones are extra clear. The fringes formed by light reflected from an oil slick are also without the transmitted fringe set but these do not have such regular colours.

The cup fringes consist of a set of parallel coloured bands of unequal thickness. Generally, green and red are at the bottom with yellow and blue higher up. As you hold the cup, the water gradually drains from the film and the whole fringe pattern falls. The thickness of the film is just right for the particular coloured light to interfere constructively. We should expect that for constructive interference the extra distance travelled by one light ray, $2t$, would equal an integral number of wavelengths, $n\lambda$.

Unfortunately, there is a cleverly hidden snag. We can see how it

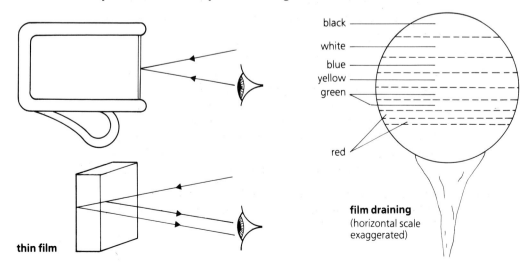

black
white
blue
yellow
green
red

film draining
(horizontal scale exaggerated)

thin film

gums up the works by observing what happens to the fringes just before the film breaks. The film continually gets thinner as the water drains away, and just before it breaks we can say that the film is essentially of zero thickness. We would thus expect the film to be bright there. In fact, the film goes 'black' just before it breaks. Indeed the blackness is not like that of a black paint but a total absence of colour, what John Milton called 'darkness visible'. The film reflects no light and is completely transparent. To account for this we have to assume that one of the interfering rays suffered a phase change on reflection of π or 180°. That puts the rays out of step and gives destruction where we would naturally have expected addition. The formula now becomes

$$2t = (n + \tfrac{1}{2})$$

since a phase change of π is equivalent to a path difference of $\lambda/2$.

We might have expected this if we had remembered that when a pulse on a string is reflected at a fixed wall it comes back upside down – it has suffered a phase change of π. The wave is reflected and is upside down in accordance with Newton's third law. If the string tends to pull the wall up, the wall will tend to pull the string down. As you would expect, the effect was first noticed by Isaac Newton. He did the experiment now called 'Newton's rings'.

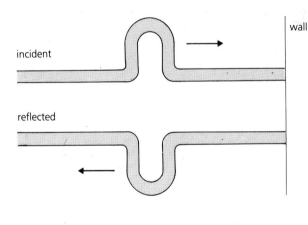

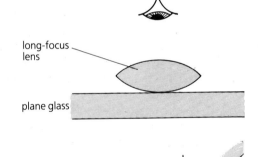

Newton put a long-focus lens on a plane sheet of glass and observed interference fringes in the thin air space between the lens and the plane sheet. Where the lens and glass sheet touch, at the centre of the set of interference rings, you would expect to see a bright spot because the two interfering rays have travelled the same distance. In fact, we always see a dark spot at the centre of the ring system seen in reflection. Newton said that this was because the ray that was reflected at the denser medium had suffered a phase change of π.

Most of the colours of animals and plants come from selective absorption of colour in the pigments. However, we know that the colour of the 'eye' in a peacock's plumage, the glow of butterflies' wings and the beautiful green sheen in the neck of a mallard duck are due to constructive interference. Unfortunately I cannot set a question on these instances as I can find no source for the refractive indexes of these materials. The case of the butterfly wing is particularly interesting, for often it appears to change colour as it flies past. This is because as the angle of incidence changes, so does the optical path length in the interference film.

The colours in some beetles and wasps and in mother-of-pearl have a different cause. Photographs taken with a scanning electron microscope show sets of closely spaced ribs which act as diffraction gratings in reflection. I presume that in these cases also, the colour changes with the angle of incidence. It is now possible to buy cuff links and ear studs that work on this principle.

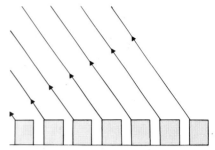

One of the snags with most present radar systems is that they are capable of tracking only one plane at a time as the large reflecting bowl has to be aimed at its target. They also depend on fallible electric motors to steer the bowl. An answer to this problem is to use 'phased array radar'. In a square array, a set of 1792 aerials (antennae) are set out to act as a kind of two-dimensional diffraction grating, like the pegs on a board for drying wet beakers in the chemistry lab. A pulse of electromagnetic energy is sent out and then the aerials are set to receive any reflected signal. To change the direction of search, a phase delay is inserted between the signals from adjacent aerials. This device is capable of tracking many aircraft at once as it is only necessary to switch from one phase delay to another. It is also possible to gauge the size of the aeroplane by sending very short pulses, shorter even than the length of the plane, and get two reflections, one from the front and the other from the back.

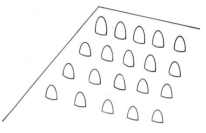

Questions

22.1 Why do we never see interference fringes in a thick sheet of glass, like a window pane?

22.2 What optical effect can you see clearly in a pane of glass?

22.3 If you use a laser beam as your light source, will you see interference fringes in a thick slab of glass?

22.4 The use of these interference fringes is of great importance in getting perfectly flat surfaces. How does that work?

22.5 What will you see if you look down on two strips of glass specially ground flat and separated by a thin piece of paper at one end? The light must come from over your shoulder.

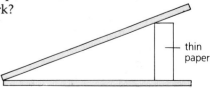

thin paper

22.6 It is possible to do the Newton's rings experiment with transmitted light (though the fringes are very faint). What would you see at the centre?

22.7 One use for this interference is to cut out unwanted reflections from the surface of lenses, a process called blooming. If you look closely at the surface of a good-quality lens you will see that it has a yellow or blue sheen; this sheen is the bloom. It is the same use of English as when we say that a pretty girl is blooming (though she may not cut out unwanted reflections). What is the minimum thickness of bloom that will cut out the reflected ray of wavelength $\lambda = 600$ nm (6×10^{-7} m)? Assume that the bloom has a refractive index of 1.4, and first calculate the wavelength of the light in the bloom. Then use the formula $2t = (n+\frac{1}{2})\lambda$ – we want destructive interference but there is the phase change of π at *both* the surfaces, air–bloom and bloom–glass.

22.8 It is sometimes necessary to cover the pictures in an art gallery with a sheet of glass. When that is done, there can often be unwanted reflections from the front of the glass and to prevent these a non-reflective coating is applied. How thick should such a coating be if it is to be of calcium fluoride (refractive index 1.4) laid on sheet glass (refractive index 1.6) and is to eliminate reflections of wavelength (in air) 550 nm (1 nm = 10^{-9} m)?

22.9 In the previous question, the reflected light never enters the glass. Why then are we given its refractive index?

22.10 The non-reflective glass in question **22.8** often has a purple hue. Why? What can be done about it?

22.11 Another important use for this principle is in the splitting of light in TV transmission (that is, if you think TV important). The white light of the TV image has to be split into the three primary colours and the three signals transmitted separately. The three colours are then combined in the TV receiver.

In the camera, the white light is first reflected from a mirror which only reflects the red light. The remainder then goes to a mirror which reflects only the green light. What is left is then the blue light. (In fact, the reflection usually takes place at an angle of 45° but that would make our calculation a bit too difficult, so we shall assume that the reflection occurs normally.)

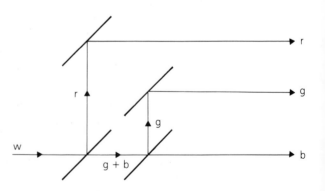

What layer of thickness of film will cause constructive interference for red light of wavelength 650 nm (6.5×10^{-7} m)? This time we want the formula $2t = (n + \frac{1}{2})\lambda$. Again put $n = 1$ to find the minimum thickness, and assume that the refractive index of the film is 1.5.

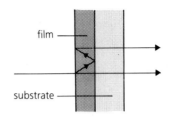

(In practice the different mirrors reflect different percentages of the three different colours. Compensating absorbers have to be put in to equalise the three beams to the original intensity proportions.)

22.12 Why do we always want the thinnest film?

22.13 What is the line spacing on a pair of ear-rings which act as reflective diffraction gratings, if they show the blue colour ($\lambda = 400$ nm) when seen almost head-on, say at 10°? You may assume first-order diffraction.

22.14 What colour would you see if you looked at an angle of 30° to the same ear-rings?

22.15 How do you know that the colours in the animals we have been talking about – peacocks, mallards and beetles – are not due to selective absorption?

22.16 At the school sports, two loudspeakers were used to warn competitors. One student said that from where she was sitting, she never heard her event called. Is this possible? Assume that the sound had wavelength $\lambda = 1$ m, that the speakers were 5 m apart and that the girl was sitting 50 m from them.

Calculate the distance of the first node from the centre line and so find if the sound could be destroyed for both ears, assumed 10 cm apart. Then carry out the same analysis for high-frequency sound, say $\lambda = 0.2$ m. Comment on your results.

22.17 In a phased array radar system, the aerials are 7 cm apart and the frequency in use is 300×10^8 Hz. Calculate the wavelength of this radiation, and so find the direction of the target.

22.18 If the far end of a Slinky spring is tied to a metre length of string whose other end is fixed and you initiate a pulse down the spring, what happens to the reflected pulse? What has that to do with the interference of light in thin films?

23 Waves at the seaside

An exercise on common observations

Waves of any kind travel at the same speed in a given medium. They do not get tired and slow down. Waves at the shore are called shallow-water waves; their wavelength is much greater than the depth and their speed does not depend on the wavelength. If you throw a stone into a pond, the pulse of disturbance travels at constant speed. When a wave moves from one medium to another, its speed usually changes; in particular, when a wave moves from deep to shallow water, its speed decreases markedly. We notice that when we are bathing, the waves that are at chest depth have a speed of about 1 m s^{-1} but the little ripples at the water's edge have a speed of about one-tenth as much.

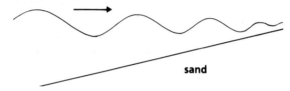

I remember this by saying that in shallow water, the sand is close and so there will be a lot of friction; in deep water, the sand is far enough away for there to be no friction. That is a good way of remembering, but unfortunately it is not the true explanation, which is rather too complicated for comfort.

The one thing that is the same for waves in deep and shallow water is the frequency; after all, any waves that start in deep water can only finish up in shallow water, there is nowhere else for them to go. As we have the formula $v = f\lambda$, we know that if the speed gets less then so does the wavelength. We have all noticed this, too. In chest-deep water I reckon the wavelength is often about 10 m; on the same day, the wavelength at the water's edge will be about 1 m. This allows us to explain the reason for the wave breaking.

Where the water is deep, the wave goes faster – so much so that the wave over-balances and breaks. When the wave has broken it is no longer what physicists call a wave. For the main characteristic of a wave is that the water particles do not move in the direction of the wave, but only move up and down. We know this if we are swimming out beyond the breakers. If you then lie on your back you will move vertically as the wave passes. In fact, there is often a slight movement towards the shore as the wave approaches and a backwards motion as it passes, but there is no net motion in any direction. (When a sea wave has broken that is no longer true, the water particles definitely move.) The only thing that does move in the direction of the wave is the energy transferred up the beach to scour out the dunes.

A body surfer can avail himself of this energy transfer (I am not being sexist when I write 'himself', I never see female body surfers). The body surfer is propelled along because the water is always rising up as the wave moves along. He would slide down the wave front but it is always moving along.

The speed of the waves is also independent of their amplitude (height) or their frequency. You appreciate this if you are attending a concert in a place like the Hollywood Bowl or the Bowl of Brooklands at New Plymouth. As a poor scientist, you will be sitting at the back but the music sounds as clear as if you were in the front row (although it may be softer, usually a blessing). This means that the loud notes (big amplitude) arrive at your ear with the soft notes (small amplitude) and the high notes (big frequency) at the same time as the low notes (small frequency). If this were not so, the music would arrive at your ear even more jumbled up than it does now. It is possible that there could be some distortion in the sound waves if there were a marked temperature difference between hearer and orchestra. In Hollywood, that is more than compensated by the locals' civilised practice of taking suppers and bottles of chilled wine to the symphony concerts.

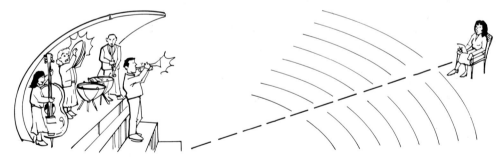

The same principle applies to light waves. During the start of an eclipse of the Sun, the light waves are cut off at the same time as the heat rays (smaller frequency); they travel at the same speed. When the Sun's rays are diminished in amplitude when going through a cloud, there is no gap when they do not reach us at all. Light waves of different amplitude travel at the same speed. To be strictly accurate, waves in deep water do have a difference in speed for a difference in wavelength. In the north Atlantic, waves with a wavelength of 50 m travel at about 32 km h^{-1} and those with a wavelength of 100 m travel at about 45 km h^{-1}. This phenomenon only applies to deep-water waves and does not affect the account of waves on the shore as given earlier. We call this dispersion; a more obvious example is the dispersion of white light when it enters a glass prism.

The 'white' light is a mixture of a range of wavelengths. In the glass, the refractive index (and so the velocity) changes by about 1 per cent across the visible spectrum. For most glasses, the natural frequency of vibration of the molecules, f_0, is in the ultra-violet. Hence ultra-violet light is almost totally absorbed by glass. The electric field of the electromagnetic radiation will cause the electrons in the glass molecules to vibrate. If the frequencies agree, the vibrations will have bigger amplitudes and more energy will be absorbed by the glass. Blue light is nearer the resonance position than red is, and it is slowed more by the glass.

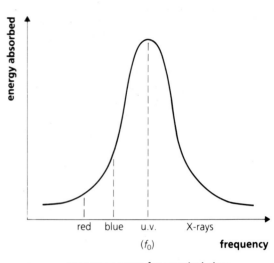

resonance curve for a typical glass

Questions

23.1 If a wave continues moving in the same medium, what does change?

23.2 Calculate the speed of a sea wave if its wavelength is 10 m and the period between one wave and the next is 8 s.

23.3 Surfers know that waves do not come at a constant rate, they often have to wait a long time for one. What is the other consequence of a long wait?

23.4 Surfers believe that every seventh wave is a big one. How would scientists describe that, and is there any truth in it?

23.5 At some beaches the shoreline is curved and surfers can clamber over rocks to save a long paddle out to deep water. The idea is that they then get a long ride into shore without a lot of wasted effort. This is a good idea, but it is not likely to work in practice. Why?

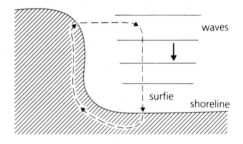

23.6 The idea does seem to work at the Lion Rock at Piha, north of Auckland in New Zealand. The rock stands out into the bay and divides the bay into two parts. Surfers walk out over the rocks along the path shown, and enter deep water with relatively little effort. They can then surf into the shore. Why does this work there?

23.7 When a surfer is paddling out to deep water, the waves go straight past him. What principle is acting here?

23.8 You are a competent life saver. You are walking along the beach when you see a swimmer in difficulties. To get there as quickly as possible, which path do you take?

23.9 What has this to do with one of the general laws of physics?

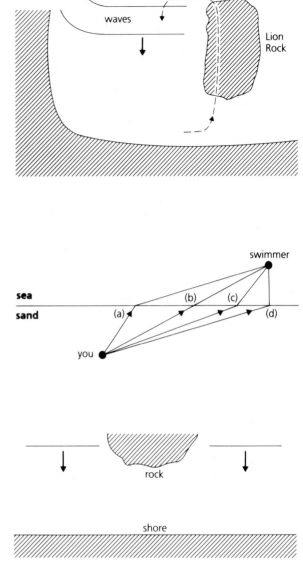

23.10 At Back Bay, New Plymouth, New Zealand, a rock sticks out from the shoreline and is surrounded by water. What is the shape of the waves as they go past the rock?

23.11 Would you expect X-rays to be absorbed by glass?

23.12 How do you know that the green material of plants, chlorophyll, has a molecule that has numerous resonances in the red and blue parts of the visible spectrum?

23.13 Also present in most plants is the pigment carotene, which is responsible for the red and yellow colours of, for example, tulips and carrots. Carotene is much more stable than chlorophyll, so why do the leaves of trees turn yellow in autumn?

23.14 The pigment melanin, present in the skin, absorbs all visible radiation, but the absorption varies inversely with the wavelength. Why is this essential for our health?

24 Nuclear winter

An exercise in the interpretation of information

The phrase 'nuclear winter' signifies the likely state of the world if a major nuclear war broke out. The first important study of the possibilities was made by the TTAPS group (so called from the initials of the surnames of the five authors). In 1986 a confirming study was announced by the British group SCOPE (Scientific Committee On the Problems of the Environment). They used a much more sophisticated three-dimensional model of the Earth's atmosphere to predict the effects of vast amounts of soot and smoke being released after quite a small nuclear confrontation. They worked out the effect of a few hundred megatonnes of bombs being exploded on a hundred cities across the northern hemisphere. This would release about 45 million tonnes of pure carbon into the atmosphere (although there could well be more if the fires were so severe that there was incomplete combustion).

The initial effects of the bombs would have been to kill 750 million people and injure another billion, with virtually no medical services to tend them. The most important long-term effect would be the immediate world-wide lowering of the temperature, possibly by as much as 20 to 40 °C. This would kill almost all the food crops in the whole world. The normal fluctuations in the average temperature, from year to year, are no more than 1 °C. In the target zone, it would be totally dark at mid-day for more than a week.

One matter that is still in dispute is the effect that a nuclear holocaust would have on the southern hemisphere, assuming that no bombs were dropped there. Normally there is little mixing of the air between the two hemispheres. This is because of the existence of the so-called Hadley 'cells', which are actually circulating air masses. At the Equator, the hot air rises, moves towards the poles (and speeds up, can you see why?) and then falls to Earth as it is cooled. These Hadley cells are quite stable and prevent air from flowing from one hemisphere to another. There are other Hadley cells further from the Equator too. In a nuclear winter there would be no Hadley cells on either side of the Equator, and air would be able to mix across it. What is in doubt is how much mixing would occur.

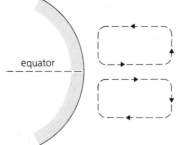

It is uncertain whether the southern hemisphere could supply food to any survivors in the northern hemisphere. In the south, there are only three countries with any sizable food surpluses: Australia, Argentina and New Zealand. Of these, Australia has most food to spare but the climate there is so precarious at the best of times that it is doubtful if it could help after a nuclear war.

The report of the TTAPS group makes fascinating reading as it draws evidence from a wide variety of sources, including the climates of other planets and the effects of volcanic eruptions in the past. For example, the eruption of Mount Tambora in the East Indies in 1816 was responsible for the 'year without summer'. The United States had snow and ice in August (mid-summer), there were world-wide crop failures and cholera epidemics caused by the mass starvation. Lord Byron commemorated the event in a poem 'Darkness', part of which reads:

> The bright sun was extinguished and the stars
> Did wander darkling in the eternal space,
> Rayless and pathless, and the icy earth
> Swung blind and blackening in the moonless air.
> Morn came and went and came and brought no day.
> All Earth was but one thought and that was death.

This tragedy was caused by an event which lowered the average temperature by no more than 0.6 °C.

The TTAPS work was a pioneer effort and has been revised by later workers. The TTAPS model assumed that the effect of winds was negligible, that the oceans had no effect and that there were no differences due to the seasons. A 1987 study by Covey, Thompson and Schneider removes these restrictions and uses a more sophisticated three-dimensional computer model. In general, they confirm the TTAPS results but with slightly less serious effects. For example, they predict that, in mid-latitudes, the temperature fall for the same explosion occurring in July would be half that predicted by the first model. In a summer war, temperature falls in the range of 10–15 °C would be quite enough to destroy all harvests. The main cause of uncertainty is that we still do not know how high smoke would rise after a nuclear war. The point at issue is whether it would go higher than the level of most of the water vapour in the atmosphere.

This subject is especially fascinating because there are good reasons for suspecting that a major nuclear war could also cause a *rise* in temperature. A megatonne bomb could send up to a million tonnes of water vapour into the air. A large-scale conflict could increase the amount of water vapour in the atmosphere by half. This water vapour would quickly freeze to form a blanket of ice crystals and these could have a very pronounced 'greenhouse effect'. Methane, formed during the burning of cities, could add to the effect. In a greenhouse, the shorter-wavelength ultra violet radiation passes through the glass and is absorbed by the plants and soil. These in turn emit longer-wave radiation, which cannot pass through the glass. (For an explanation, see the resonance curve for the absorption of energy given in Reading 23.) It could also be that some of the smoke particles could coagulate together in the cloud and further increase the heating below. There is still a great deal to be learnt and we can only hope we don't find out the hard way.

Questions

24.1 A typical graph for the temperature in the northern hemisphere against the time after the explosions is shown below. This is for the so-called 'baseline' attack. The computer programmers settle for a probable number of missiles, call this the baseline and then work out the effects for other numbers of weapons compared to the standard. Also shown is the projected effect of a more severe war, in which 5000 megatonnes of explosives were detonated (this by no means exhausts the world's arsenals). The graph shows the ambient temperature (the average temperature for that place) as 13 °C.

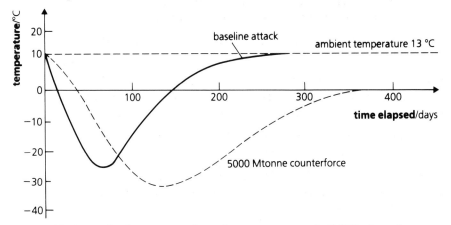

Estimate for how many days the temperature is 5 °C below the ambient temperature, assuming the baseline condition. Obviously, no great precision is possible. Note that with the more severe exchange, the temperature is expected to stay below freezing for over a year.

24.2 The graph below attempts to show the predictions of the temperatures at different latitudes. The different lines are for different periods after the war. We see that in the southern hemisphere there is a gradual recovery to normal. However, it is predicted that in the war zone the temperature would rise considerably a year after the explosions. Suggest a possible reason for this.

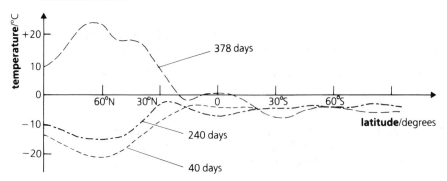

24.3 We have data for the temperature against time for both the northern and southern hemisphere. Plot the graphs and comment on them.

Time/months after explosion	1	2	4	9	10	12
Temperature/°C below ambient:						
Northern hemisphere			−43	−23		−3
Southern hemisphere	−31	−16			−6	

24.4 There are very good grounds for expecting that a nuclear winter would cause the end of monsoons. Why would this be?

24.5 One of the relatively harmless predictions is for greatly increased erosion in the northern hemisphere. Why?

24.6 More serious would be the vast increase in violent storms. What would cause them?

24.7 It is foreseen that some Pacific islanders might well survive in their remote homes. However they are not predicted to survive a return to their old hunter–gatherer life style. Why is that?

24.8 What would be the effect on the Earth's overall temperature if it lost its atmosphere?

24.9 What does the fact that the Earth's atmosphere has a 'greenhouse effect' tell us about the transmission of heat rays through the atmosphere?

24.10 Soot (carbon particles) absorbs sunlight, whereas soil dust tends to reflect sunlight. Explain why soot would have the greater effect in reducing the temperature.

24.11 Water clouds rarely form high in the stratosphere (above 12 km). Explain why soot in the stratosphere has an effect that is likely to persist for months.

24.12 The models predict general changes in the weather patterns – in particular, that there would be an increase in offshore winds. Why?

24.13 Would the nuclear winter be more prolonged if the bulk of the smoke generated rose above the level of most of the water vapour in the atmosphere?

24.14 The structure of a greenhouse ensures that the inside gets hotter. Does that mean that more energy flows into it than flows out?

24.15 What happens to the wavelength and energy of the infra-red photons entering the greenhouse, compared with those radiated from the soil and plants?

24.16 At present there seems to be a marked loss in ozone in the atmosphere, especially at the poles. This is under active investigation. Why is it a cause for concern?

Supplementary questions

1 Manipulation of numbers

S1.1 If it takes five minutes to boil a hen's egg, mass = 50 g, how long will it take to boil an ostrich's egg, mass = 5 kg? Make any simplifying assumptions you find useful.

S1.2 A compact disc has a track 4.5 km long. If the indentation is 0.4 μm long, how many bits of information are stored?

S1.3 In his delightful book *The flamingo's smile* Stephen J. Gould discusses whether large dinosaurs were warm-blooded or not. He notes that even though without any physiological mechanism for maintaining constant temperature (such as we have), they may have been effectively warm-blooded. What did he mean?

S1.4 Gould then reports some experiments on reptiles. A tiny alligator, mass 50 g, when placed in the sun heated up by 1 °C every minute and a half; a large alligator, 13 kg, had a temperature rise of 1 °C in 7.5 minutes. For how long do you predict that a 10 tonne dinosaur would need to sit in the sun for the same temperature rise? Assume a relationship of the form $T = kM^n$, and find the value of n from these figures.

S1.5 Why is the value of n not the ⅓ that you assumed in question **S1.1**?

S1.6 Most aerial photographs are taken with a scale of 1:20 000. The picture as printed is usually 23 cm square. What area of ground would one picture cover?

S1.7 The world records for men for various distances are given in this table.

Distance x/m	50	60	100	200
Time t/s	5.5	6.5	9.9	19.5

Are these figures consistent with a model of someone running with constant acceleration for T seconds and thereafter running with constant speed V? Note: $V = aT$, so $x = V(t - \frac{1}{2}T)$.

S1.8 We have the data for the way the braking coefficient for disc brakes changes with the speed of the car. The speed is given in m.p.h. but there is no need to change it. At what speed would the brakes fail, according to the data?

Speed/m.p.h.	30	38	46	56	61
Braking coefficient	0.5	0.4	0.31	0.24	0.2

S1.9 Measurements taken by means of a satellite in geosynchronous orbit by NASA indicate that Africa and South America are separating at a rate of approximately 1.5 cm a year (about the rate at which your fingernails grow). A certain island in the South Atlantic is about 27 million years old; estimate its distance from the Mid-Atlantic Ridge.

2 Straight line mechanics

S2.1 In Acapulco, professional divers dive from a rock 36 m above the sea level (compared with 10 m for the highest boards in diving competitions). Assuming that air friction is negligible how long does a dive last, and with what speed do divers hit the water? (This is a very dangerous stunt. There are rocks below and the inlet is very shallow, and divers have to wait for an incoming wave to give enough depth of water.)

S2.2 What effect would air resistance have on your answers to question **S2.1**? Do you think that air resistance would be very significant?

S2.3 A child is given a helium-filled balloon. What happens to the balloon when the tot suddenly starts to run?

S2.4 An old book says that parachutists land with a speed of 7 m s^{-1}. What height of scaffolding would parachutists in training have to use to simulate a jump?

S2.5 Why is question **S2.4** now outmoded?

S2.6 The record for a dragstrip racer covering a standing quarter of a mile (say 400 m) is currently 5.63 s. Assuming constant acceleration, calculate the average acceleration and the final speed.

S2.7 How would the acceleration differ from the average throughout the trip? Compare your final speed with the quoted value of 402 km h^{-1} (112 m s^{-1}).

S2.8 The regulations for this sport insist that all cars use parachutes for braking after the run. Why?

S2.9 The squirting cucumber (*Ecballium elaterium*) is a fruit with a most extraordinary method of dispersing its seeds. It is about as big as a plum, and it has a thick, thorny skin. Pressure is allowed to build up inside; when it has reached about 6 atmospheres, the fruit breaks away from its stalk and shoots off, like a rocket, firing its seeds backwards. Measurements show that it leaves at an angle of 50° to the ground with a speed of about 10 m s^{-1}. Making the usual simplifying assumptions, calculate the range of the fruit.

S2.10 The actual range is about 12 m. Account for the discrepancy.

S2.11 A rugby footballer, mass 120 kg, is running due north at a speed of 6 m s^{-1}. He is tackled by an opponent, mass 90 kg, running towards the south-east at 8 m s^{-1}. Make a scale drawing of the momentum vectors and so find the combined speed immediately after the tackle.

S2.12 A yacht is moving at constant speed. If the force on the keel is 80 N and the sail is set at an angle of 50° to the centre line, what is the frictional force, and what is the driving force on the sail? Make the usual simplifying assumptions.

S2.13 A book on baseball says that the record pitch speed was achieved by a ball that covered the 18.4 m from mound to batter in 0.51 s. It also says that the ball left the pitcher's hand at 90 m.p.h. (40 m s^{-1}). Making the gross assumption that these figures are correct and that the ball suffered constant deceleration in flight, calculate the speed with which it arrived at the batter.

S2.14 In many parts of the underdeveloped world, bicycles are adapted as sources of mechanical energy. For example, two men in Malawi were able to lift, by pedalling, 4300 litres of water per hour through a rise of 9 m. What power did each man develop? Comment on your answer.

S2.15 A child throws a ball into the air. If the force of friction is negligible, which of these drawings best shows the direction of the force on the ball?

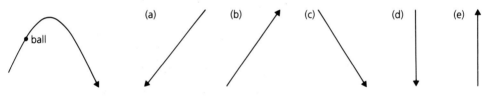

S2.16 If friction may not be neglected, which of these drawings best shows the friction F and the weight W?

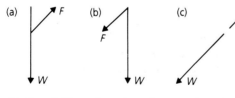

S2.17 A Hercules aircraft is used to drop sacks of flour to starving villagers in Africa. The sacks are pushed out of the back of the low-flying plane. A villager stands at the side of the flight path; to him, which sketch best shows the path of the sack, and why? Neglect the effect of air friction.

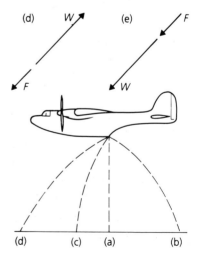

(a) Because the plane flies on after the sack is dropped;

(b) because the sack is pushed backwards;

(c) because the sacks move forward with the horizontal speed of the plane;

(d) because the sacks hit the ground at a glancing angle.

S2.18 Assume that the plane is at a height of 50 m. Calculate the time it takes for a sack to hit the ground and the speed with which it lands. If the speed of the plane is 100 m s^{-1}, is (c) or (d) in the previous question the more realistic?

S2.19 What happens to the sacks when they hit the ground?

S2.20 What would be the effect of air friction?

S2.21 A champion skier can achieve a downhill speed of 130 km h^{-1}. At this speed, calculate the force of friction on a 80 kg person, if the slope angle is 40°. Why couldn't you do this calculation at the same angle before full speed is reached?

S2.22 A 'hot-dogging' skier (one who does somersaults and twists in mid-air) goes much slower. What is the minimum speed that will allow a somersault of radius 3 m?

S2.23 A special ski wax has been developed for use by cross-country skiers. It has a low coefficient of sliding friction, but a high coefficient of static friction. What is the point of that?

S2.24 Your tennis service is delivered horizontally from a height of 2.4 m. It just clears the net, which is 60 cm high and 8 m away from you. How fast was the service?

S2.25 Your pathetic service is returned at a speed of 27 m s^{-1}. If the mass of a tennis ball is 60 g and the ball and racket are in contact for 0.030 s, with what force did your opponent hit the ball?

S2.26 A golf ball is in contact with the club head for a much shorter time (how do you know this?), in fact for about 0.5 ms. What force does a professional exert on the ball, if its mass is 100 g and its speed off the club is 50 m s^{-1}?

S2.27 A car (driven by a drunk) was recently found on a beach by the police, having been driven over a cliff. The car was 24 m out from the bottom of the cliff and this was 20 m high. How fast was the car going at the top? Was the speed limit broken? With what speed did the car hit the sand?

The next ten questions are about the DC10 airliner. Use the following data:

    take-off mass = 2.5×10^5 kg;

    total take-off thrust of three engines = 6.72×10^6 N;

    speed at take-off (rotation) = 88.5 m s^{-1};

    length of runway for take-off = 2.9 km.

S2.28 For the run along the runway, find the average acceleration and the time to rotation.

S2.29 Calculate the maximum acceleration, using $F = ma$.

There is great discrepancy here, and this is because air friction is zero at the instant the plane begins to move but is considerable at take-off. We have found that the average acceleration is half the maximum, implying zero acceleration at rotation, and we know that this is not so: the plane is still accelerating after take-off. The answer lies in the fact that flaps are used for the take-off. They give more lift at low speeds but incur the penalty of more drag. After take-off they are retracted, and the plane is going fast enough to continue to accelerate. Thus, when the plane starts to move, the net thrust will be less than the quoted value. The last time that I flew in a DC10, I measured the acceleration as the plane started to move (using a home-made accelerometer) as 1.7 m s^{-2}.

S2.30 Using that figure for the initial acceleration and our calculated value for the average acceleration, find the acceleration at rotation, and so the initial and final values for the total air resistance.

S2.31 What can you say about these figures?

We can now calculate the power developed at take-off and at normal cruise. We use the formula *power = thrust × velocity*. We already have the data for take-off. We are told that at cruise, the thrust is 2.9×10^5 N (less than half the take-off value) and cruise speed is 0.8 Mach at 35 000 feet. (This is the one occasion when it is all right to use feet. By convention, metres are reserved for horizontal distances, feet for vertical.)

S2.32 First derive the formula for power.

S2.33 Now calculate the cruise speed, assuming that the speed of sound is 320 m s^{-1} at 35 000 ft. This is lower than the value at room temperature; at 35 000 ft, the temperature is about 0 °C.

S2.34 Calculate the power output at take-off and at cruise.

S2.35 What is going on here?

S2.36 When the plane lands, its mass is down to 180 000 kg, its maximum speed is 76 m s^{-1} and it needs 1.8 km of runway. Find the deceleration of the plane and the total force of air resistance, braking and reversed engine thrust.

S2.37 Comment on these results.

S2.38 In marked contrast to the DC10, we consider a typical ultralight aeroplane. Kate Eipper formed the Eipper Formance company (sorry!) originally to make hang-gliders and then added engines. Her Quicksilver has a loaded mass of 400 lb (180 kg) and a cruising speed of 32 m.p.h. (15 m s^{-1}). We wish to find the power developed and compare it with the quoted value of 8 h.p. (6 kW) at cruise. Unfortunately we are not given the air resistance or drag. We are told that at 22 m.p.h. (2000 ft min^{-1}) It has a sink rate of 260 ft min^{-1}. Thus we can get the glide angle, and from this get the air resistance at the speed of 22 m.p.h.

S2.39 Now find the air resistance at the cruising speed of 32 m.p.h., assuming that this is proportional to the square of the speed.

S2.40 Finally, work out the power developed at cruise and compare it with the quoted value of 6 kW.

S2.41 We have data for the Airbus 320:

> take-off mass = 72 000 kg;
> total thrust of the two engines = 220 kN;
> range = 4500 km;
> fuel capacity = 23 000 l;
> energy content of the fuel = 10^8 J l^{-1};
> lift:drag ratio of the wings = 8:1.

Calculate the total drag force of the wings and compare it with the total thrust of the engines. Account for the discrepancy.

S2.42 Assuming the lower value for the thrust, calculate the total work done by the engines and so get their efficiency.

S2.43 The Tomahawk air-launched cruise missile has a total mass at launch of 1443 kg and its rocket motor develops a constant thrust of 2.7 kN. Calculate the lift:drag ratio of its wings. How can it fly with such tiny wings?

S2.44 If the Tomahawk's cruising speed is 885 km h^{-1} (250 m s^{-1}), what is the power output of its motor?

S2.45 A car built by my neighbour for stock car racing has a large metal sail (2 m × 2.2 m) on one side. It is intended to make it more stable when cornering fast. I calculated the sideways force on this sail as 5 N, when the car was going at 3 m s^{-1}. (Note that this is not the forward speed of the car, but the sideways speed as it corners.) Compare the restoring torque of the wind with the restoring torque due to the weight of the sail. Mass of sail = 20 kg; distance between wheels (track) = 1.2 m; height of centre of sail = 2.0 m.

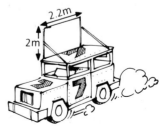

S2.46 Do you think sails are worthwhile for stock cars?

S2.47 The advertising brochure for the Honda Civic says that it can cover the standing quarter-mile (say 400 m) in 17.5 s. Calculate the average acceleration. The mass is given as 820 kg, so find the accelerating force. The maximum power is given as 76 h.p. (1 h.p. = 750 W), so find the speed at the end of the quarter-mile. Compare this with the value found from the acceleration.

S2.48 The braking system on my car has hydraulic disc brakes worked by a master cylinder, 2 cm in diameter. There are eight slave cylinders (two for each wheel), each 1 cm in diameter. How does the force at each brake pad compare with the force exerted by my foot? (In fact my car, like most modern ones, has a form of power-assisted braking called a 'booster'. As I cannot find out how it works, neglect it for this question.)

S2.49 When the brakes of a car are applied, the car often assumes a nose-down position (as if bowing), much exaggerated in cartoons. Why?

S2.50 Does it make any difference if only the back brakes are used?

S2.51 The opposite effect is obvious when a fast motor boat starts – it tips back. In this case there is a different, more likely cause; what is it?

S2.52 What are the energy changes involved in a car braking system? Hence, why are disc brakes now preferred to the older drum brake system (still used on some motor bikes)?

S2.53 A car of mass 800 kg is travelling at 20 m s^{-1}. Calculate its k.e. If all this energy were converted to heat energy, how hot would the discs get if there were no cooling draught? Assume there are four discs, each mass 2 kg, made of steel of specific heat capacity 500 J kg^{-1} K^{-1}. Is it fair to assume that all the heat goes into the discs?

S2.54 Some male ballet dancers have the reputation of being able to make very long jumps during the step known as the *grand jeté*. (Nijinsky was especially famed for this.) The illusion is created by the dancer raising his centre of mass while he is at the highest point of the jump. How does he do this? How does it create the illusion?

3 Rotational mechanics

S3.1 The formula for the rotational inertia of a sphere is $I = \tfrac{2}{5} Mr^2$. What can you deduce from the fact that the measured value for the Earth conforms to the formula $I = 0.344 Mr^2$?

S3.2 A modern method of making mirrors for reflecting telescopes is to melt the glass in a furnace and then rotate it at high speed while the glass solidifies. Show that this will, in fact, give a parabolic surface.

S3.3 One such mirror has an aperture (diameter) of 2 m and a focal length of 2 m also ($f = 1$). At what rate should the glass furnace be rotated?

S3.4 Pulsars are stars that emit light in short pulses of constant frequency. They are thought to be emitting light in one direction relative to the surface of the star, but to be rotating at great speed. One pulsar emits light in bursts of 30 Hz. How do you know that it must be small?

S3.5 The Stanford Torus is a design for a permanent space station that would have a staff of 1000 people. It would have a diameter of 1.5 km. At what speed should it rotate if its inhabitants are to experience Earth gravity?

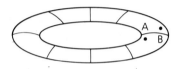

S3.6 Should the space travellers stand on the inside of the inner or outer ring? At A or B?

S3.7 Why would such a scheme not work well for a one-man ship, a torus of 10 m diameter?

S3.8 A 'dust devil' is a twisting column of rising air often seen in dry hot deserts. Very little is known about them – why they rotate, why they are seen at some places and not others, why they go faster higher up. But we do know why they spiral upwards. One dust devil had dust particles moving with a linear speed of 2.5 m s^{-1} high up, where the radius of the column was about 2 m. What was the speed of the particles at ground level, where the radius of the column was about 10 m? (There is obviously great uncertainty in all the values quoted here.)

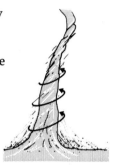

S3.9 Is the Sun a typical star?
To answer, consider the centripetal force acting on the Sun. The Sun is moving with a speed of 250 km s^{-1} relative to the centre of the galaxy, 30 000 light-years (3×10^{20} m) away. The Milky Way galaxy is said to consist of 10^{11} stars and most of these will be in a spherical shape. If the Sun is a typical star (mass 2×10^{30} kg) we can find the mass of the galaxy.

S3.10 Why, for the purpose of doing the previous question, is it fortunate that most of the stars in the galaxy are within a sphere with the Sun outside (in one of the spiral arms)?

S3.11 Many small motorcycles have 'centrifugal' clutches. How do they work?

S3.12 When Indian cooks make chapattis, they do not use a rolling pin to get a thin circular disc of dough. Rather they thin it out by hand and then spin it out by a circular flick of the wrist. How does this work?

S3.13 When a jet plane is taking off, the pilot pulls back on the control column and the plane 'rotates'. The plane then tends to veer sideways slightly. What law is in action here? Pilots are so used to this that they compensate for it without thinking.

S3.14 The engines on jet aircraft are only fixed by two or three bolts of carefully determined strength. The bolts are designed to break and allow the engine to fall off if it stops rotating, that is, if it ingests some foreign matter like a seagull. We call this a mechanical or structural fuse. What principle is involved here?

S3.15 The DC10 has three engines, one under each wing and one in the tail. One of the three stops. Does it make any difference to the total angular momentum which one stops?

S3.16 What would happen to a Boeing 727 if one engine stopped and did not fall off? This aeroplane is not yet obsolete and is the only one for which I can find data. It has three jet engines, each with low-pressure rotor with $I = 11.5$ kg m^2, $\omega = 881$ rad s^{-1}. For the high-pressure rotor, $I = 7.2$ kg m^2, $\omega = 1290$ rad s^{-1}. Calculate the angular momentum of one engine.

Now find the rotational inertia of the two wings. You may neglect the rotational inertia of the rest of the plane, as we only want a rough result. Treat the wings as rods of mass 10^4 kg and length 20 m, with $I = \frac{1}{3}Mr^2$. All three engines are in the tail and do not contribute to the rotational inertia.

Finally, find the rate at which the body of the plane would rotate.

S3.17 For a hand centrifuge in my lab, the radius of the circle in which the bottom of the tubes move is 14 cm. I can, with great effort, turn the handle once in four seconds. The rotation speed of the tubes is geared up in the ratio 22:1. What is the linear speed of the bottom of the tubes? What is the inward acceleration, and what is this in terms of Earth gravity?

S3.18 The friction in the centrifuge bearings is terrible and it stops rotating in 2 s. What is the average angular deceleration?

S3.19 For a centrifuge in the biology lab, the equivalent data are radius = 14 cm and maximum speed of rotation = 5000 r.p.m. Work out the same quantities as in question **S3.17**.

S3.20 For a centrifuge in the pathology lab of our local hospital, the radius is again 14 cm (this seems to be standard) and the maximum speed 12 000 r.p.m. They tell me that the acceleration is enough to separate viruses. The friction is so low (due to air bearings and the fact that the tubes rotate in a vacuum) that when the motor is switched off it continues to turn for over ten minutes, so that no measure of the angular deceleration is useful. Again calculate the same quantities.

S3.21 At the Wright Patterson Air Force Base, the U.S. Air Force maintains a vast centrifuge in which its fighter pilots are given a taste of the 'g' forces they will experience when making tight turns at high speed. They are also taught how to counteract these forces. Several pilots have been killed because loss of consciousness can last for over half a minute after the plane has pulled out of the tight turn. The simplified graph for human behaviour under high 'g' forces is shown here.

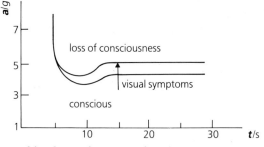

One can stand high accelerations for about 5 s, because there is a reserve of oxygen in the brain. One can stand low accelerations (about $5g$) indefinitely, because one's cardiovascular reflexes can cope. Planes now carry accelerometers so that if the pilot is subject to excessive 'g' forces, the automatic pilot takes over.

In the U.S. Air Force centrifuge, pilots are subject to a force of $9g$ for a short time. The radius of the machine is 5 m; how fast is the pilot travelling if he undergoes a $9g$ acceleration?

S3.22 What is the linear acceleration on the pilot if this acceleration is applied at the rate of $1.5g \text{ s}^{-1}$?

S3.23 When you are being taught to drive, you are told to go slowly into a curve and to accelerate out of it. Why?

S3.24 If you take your hands off the wheel while the car is turning a corner, the car straightens automatically. Why? (I am told that this is a very dangerous practice; when straightening, you should pass the steering wheel through your hands.)

S3.25 You are driving your car, harming no one, when you see hanging in the rear window of the car in front a hideous model pussycat. What happens to this monstrosity when that car makes a right turn?

S3.26 A young man goes on a fast circular ride at a fun fair. He begins to feel sick and wants to lie down. He can only do this lying along a radius in the car. Should he lie with his feet or his head towards the centre of the circle?

S3.27 Racing cyclists attach great importance to having their machines as light as possible, especially wanting lightweight 'sewn up' tyres. Why?

S3.28 The brochure for an automatic washing machine says, 'During the spin cycle, the clothes are dried by centrifugal force'. What do you say?

S3.29 Why do horses and other fast-running animals have very large buttock muscles and very small calf muscles?

S3.30 While watching a display of trampolining recently, I saw that the athlete was able to turn round in mid-air. To prove that she was not getting a push off the canvas, she was only told whether to turn left or right when she was near the top of her bounce, some 5 m high. Does this not contravene the Law of conservation of angular momentum?

S3.31 Like all right-thinking people you loathe having to mow the lawn, so you think up this brilliant scheme. You attach the mower (a powered-drive model) to a thick pole by a long rope. As the mower moves, more rope is wrapped round the pole. If the width of the cut swath equals the circumference of the pole, all the lawn will get cut while you sit in a deck-chair. The mower has constant mass and moves at constant speed but the radius gets less. Thus angular momentum ($L = mvr$) is not conserved. What do you say?

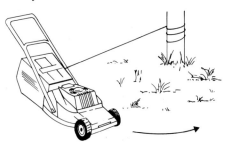

S3.32 Why do tight-rope walkers hold their arms fully outstretched? When Houdini crossed the Niagara Falls on a tight rope, he went further (sorry) and he carried a heavy pole, 6 m long. Why?

S3.33 Some tight-rope walkers carry an open umbrella in each outstretched hand. What is the point of this?

S3.34 Male ballet dancers can make themselves spin faster during the step called *tour jeté*. How do they do this?

S3.35 The wind turbine MOD 5B on the Hawaiian island of Oahu is used for electricity generation (its basic load is 3.2 MW). It has a double propeller blade of diameter 100 m and rotates about a horizontal axis at 17.5 r.p.m. What is the angular velocity of the blade, the linear speed of the blade tip and its centripetal acceleration?

4 Properties of matter

S4.1 During each heart beat, approximately 70 ml of blood is pumped at a pressure of 90 mm of mercury (1.2×10^4 pascal). If the pulse is 72 beats per minute, calculate the power developed by the heart. Comment on your answer.

S4.2 When a giraffe is lying down its blood pressure is 120 mm of mercury, but when it is standing up its blood pressure is 260 mm of mercury. Make an estimate of the height of a standing giraffe, assuming its heart is 1.8 m above the ground; take the relative density of mercury as 13.6.

S4.3 Someone says, 'the answer to question **S4.2** is nonsense. Most of the giraffe's height is in its neck, which is very thin. You should spread that pressure over its whole body.' What do you say?

S4.4 A pool in a dolphinarium (horrible word) has an underwater viewing window. This is a rectangular pane of reinforced glass, 3 m × 0.5 m. If the centre of the glass is 1.2 m below the surface, calculate the force of the water on the glass.

S4.5 The greatest depth to which anyone has ever dived without special clothing is 282 feet (90 m). What would have been the maximum force on the diver's ear drums (area 0.6 cm^2) if he had not worn ear plugs? (He also had to wear goggles.)

S4.6 In the shower, it is possible to pinch two or three jets of water together to make a single jet. What is going on? Would the single big jet of water be more stable in cold or hot water?

S4.7 Many cars now have pistons with domed heads instead of the older flat type. What is the purpose of this? Increasing the area of the piston would decrease the pressure exerted by the gas, wouldn't it?

S4.8 You are given a cup of coffee with the handle facing away from you. You turn the cup round. Does the coffee stay still or does it move with the cup?

S4.9 A typical needle has a mass of 0.1 g and length of 3.5 cm. Can it be made to float on water? Show that the two upward surface forces on the needle are greater than the weight of the needle. Take the surface tension of water as 0.07 N m^{-1}.

S4.10 If, in question **S4.9**, the upward force is greater than the downward force, why does the needle not jump out of the water?

S4.11 Three beakers are filled to the brim with water and also contain respectively a solid lump of ice, a lump of ice containing a large air bubble and a lump of ice with a large bubble of water. What happens to the water in the beakers when the ice melts?

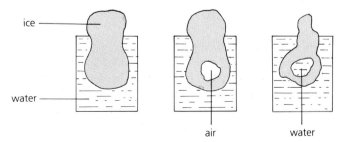

S4.12 When a weather balloon is on the ground it is very tall and thin, but when it gets to altitude it becomes spherical in shape. Why does the volume of gas change? Does the force of buoyancy change? As the balloon rises the temperature falls; does that affect your answers?

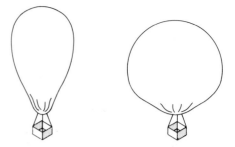

S4.13 A book on climbing says that ropes should have a 'breaking strain' of 2000 kg. What do you say?

S4.14 The hot tap in the kitchen has not been used for some time so that when you open the tap, cold water comes out. The tap is not fully opened so that the width of the jet is about 9 mm. After a minute, the water and tap have become hot and the width of the jet, at the same place, is now about 8 mm. What is going on?

S4.15 A scuba diver at a depth of 10 m had used up all her compressed air and so had to come to the surface. Unfortunately, she forgot the instruction to empty her lungs on the way up and held her breath. What happened?

S4.16 A visitor to the Orient will be offered noodles which vary in diameter from about 2 mm to 1 cm. Which size should a westerner choose?

S4.17 The diameter of the tubes in the xylem of plants is about 5×10^{-5} m. How high could water rise in such a tube due to its surface tension? (The surface tension of water = 73×10^{-3} N m^{-1}.)

S4.18 Why is a submerged submarine in an unstable situation?

S4.19 Why would it be impossible to make plastic submarines?

S4.20 Does it require more force to break a long rope or a short one? Does it require more energy?

S4.21 The first third of a ten-pin bowling track is oiled, so that the ball skids along this length. Explain why it begins to roll when it reaches the unoiled part.

S4.22 Many ten-pin bowlers deliver the ball with backspin. Would this spin operate over the whole track or just the oiled part?

5 Simple harmonic motion

S5.1 The Lucas BL9 is a warning lantern. It consists of a stationary 55 W quartz–halogen lamp, with a concave mirror behind that rotates to send a beam of reflected light sweeping out periodically. The lamp is at the focus of the mirror. For simplicity, assume that the mirror occupies half its circular path and that it rotates with a period of 1 s. Draw a sketch graph of the intensity of light received by a distant observer in the plane of the lamp.

S5.2   In fact, the mirror only occupies one-third of its circular path. Assuming the same period, draw a sketch graph of the intensity, as before.

S5.3   In the sport of bungee jumping, a participant ties one end of a stout elastic rope round his middle (or, if very brave, round an ankle) and the other end to a fixed member of some bridge or high building. The jumper then throws himself off and performs a set of damped vertical oscillations. Success is achieved if the jumper just does not hit the water or earth below on his first descent.

   In a recent exercise, a 80 kg man used a rope of unstretched length of 30 m. He jumped from a girder some 50 m up on the Auckland Harbour Bridge, and achieved success, coming within a few cm of the water on his first fall. What was the period of his oscillations?

S5.4   A 60 kg woman was then preparing to repeat the feat but was stopped by the police. If she had been allowed to proceed, what length of rope should she have used? (The data in these two questions have been slightly rounded to make calculation easy, but are essentially accurate.)

S5.5   In answering these questions you may have been tempted to say that at the bottom of the fall the jumper is stationary, so $mg = kx$. Why is that not permissible?

S5.6   A 'baby bouncer' is a device for quietening fractious infants. It consists of a small seat suspended by four elastic ropes from the lintel of a doorway. One such device had ropes with unstretched length of 1.2 m. When baby, mass 8.5 kg, was gently put in the ropes stretched by 20 cm (near enough). Mother then pulled baby down about 10 cm and released her. What was the period of the motion, and what was the maximum speed of the baby?

S5.7   The baby's sister then pulled the seat down 30 cm before releasing the tot. In this case, what was the period of the motion, what was the maximum speed and what happened at the top of the first rise?

S5.8   Why can the formula $\frac{1}{2}kx^2 = mgh$ not be used in this question?

S5.9   The needle of a sewing machine moves with a motion that may be taken for s.h.m. If the total vertical movement in one machine is 8 mm and it makes 20 stitches in 9 s, what is the maximum speed of the needle?

S5.10 The maximum permitted rate of rotation of a certain motor cycle engine is 4800 r.p.m. (revolutions per minute). If the stroke of the engine (total vertical movement of the piston) is 12 cm, what are the maximum vertical speed and maximum acceleration of the piston? (Assume s.h.m.)

S5.11 The cone of a moving-coil loudspeaker moves with s.h.m. It is desirable that the natural period of vibrations of the cone be below the level of audible detection, say 30 Hz. What should be the characteristics of the mass of the cone and its suspension?

S5.12 In the Orient, coolies carry two heavy loads on the ends of a long pole which is carried on a shoulder. What can you say about the flexibility of the pole?

S5.13 The Black and Decker GS400 is a hedge-trimmer with a blade 400 mm long. The blade moves back and forth with an oscillatory motion of frequency 1600 min^{-1} and a total movement of 2 cm in each stroke. The oscillatory motion is derived from the rotation of the electric motor by the device sketched here. There is a slot in the end of the blade and this engages a stud in a wheel attached to the motor shaft. Show that the blade moves with an accurate s.h.m.

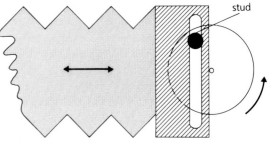

S5.14 Calculate the maximum speed and maximum acceleration of the cutting blade.

S5.15 At the Institute of Aviation Medicine there is a rig that gives pilots vertical oscillations (s.h.m.). The purpose of this is to test how well they can continue to recognise objects while being vibrated. In this machine, the frequency can be varied from 0.01 to 40 Hz and the amplitude can be up to 2 m for low frequencies. What are the maximum velocity and acceleration for a pilot being tested at 40 Hz, amplitude 0.5 mm?

S5.16 A bungee jumper recently performed a fall (under police supervision) from the top of the Auckland Stock Exchange (height 23 m). I timed his oscillations as having a period of 4 s. If the mass of the jumper was 80 kg, what was the force constant of the rope?

S5.17 What was the unstretched length of the rope?

S5.18 During a test match at Eden Park, Auckland, recently, the crowd performed a 'Mexican wave'. I estimate that the perimeter of the ground is about 400 m long and that the 'wave' took about 40 s to complete one circuit. What is a better name for this manoeuvre, rather than 'wave'?

S5.19 If the motion had been continuous, what would have been the amplitude, wavelength, frequency and speed of the wave?

6 Heat

S6.1 A solar-powered pump has been developed by VSO workers for use in Africa. It consists of a metal tank inside an insulated glass house. It is designed to be built from scrap materials at negligible cost. How does it work?

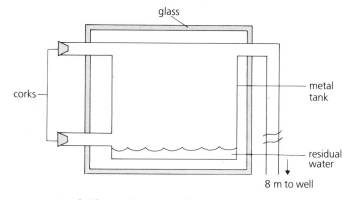

S6.2 In many parts of Africa, there is a desperate shortage of wood for cooking and the women have to walk for many hours to get a few twigs. Relief agencies have introduced solar cookers, although the poorest communities cannot pay for them. One such cooker consisted of a concave spherical mirror of aperture (diameter) 1.4 m. If the solar insolation is 260 W m^{-2}, calculate the power developed by the mirror.

S6.3 In Mali (one of the poorest parts of Africa), a cheaper solution has been found in the Fresnel concentrator. This consists of a flat circle of wood that is covered in aluminium cooking foil. The wood is then cut into one continuous spiral. If the outside of the spiral is given the correct sharp twist, the rest of the spiral conforms to a parabolic section. The reflector (1.2 m diameter) produces abut 500 W. How long would it take to heat half a litre of water from 30°C to 70°C? Assume that all the heat energy is absorbed by the water container.

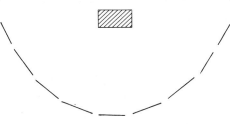

S6.4 In Tondo, equatorial Zaïre, VSO workers have devised a solar hot-water system for incubating eggs. Two panels, each 4 m^2 in area, heat 2580 litres of water per day (8 hours) from the ambient temperature (25 °C) to 65 °C. If the solar insolation is 250 W m^{-2}, what is the efficiency of the system?

S6.5 Does it matter that the efficiency is so low?

S6.6 In Madras, India, VSO workers have devised a cooking system that makes no demands on the critically short supply of wood, used traditionally. They dug a pond about 1 m deep and 8 m in diameter and lined it with impermeable plastic. The pond was filled with water and enough salt poured in to give a saline concentration of 20 per cent at the bottom. The concentration of salt gradually decreased from the bottom to the top of the pond. At the bottom of the pond, the temperature reached over 80 °C. Food is placed in sealed pots and left in the pond for a whole day. (This kind of cooking is equivalent to an electric 'crock pot' which takes 75 W for 8 hours.) How does the Indian system work?

S6.7 Given that the resonance curve for the molecules in a sheet of glass is as shown and that AB represents the range of visible wavelengths, explain how the glasshouse effect works. (There are other maxima at other wavelengths, but they do not affect the issue here.)

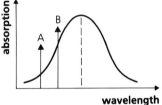

S6.8 Why is there a greenhouse effect for the Earth as a whole?

S6.9 Why is the concentration of carbon dioxide in the atmosphere increasing?

S6.10 Why would an increase in temperature cause a rise in sea levels worldwide?

S6.11 A person enjoying the rigours of the 'negative calorie diet' imbibes ice water only. How much water at 273 K would a person have to drink each day to have the opposite effect of the normal intake of 2000 calories (8400 J)?

S6.12 Even more severe is the 'ice only' diet. How much ice per day would someone have to eat to have the same negative effect?

S6.13 In the desert regions of Rajasthan, India, where there are frequent strong winds and it is usually very hot (often over 40 °C), schools and hospitals are cooled by a 'tatti'. This consists of a large panel (2 m × 1 m) of thick compressed vegetable matter. It is kept completely damp by a continual drip of water from above. How does it work, and what is the disadvantage of this method of cooling?

S6.14 Many swimming pools are in the hot sun all day but never get really warm. Why? What is the simplest way of overcoming this failing?

S6.15 How much thermal pollution is caused by a 1000 MW power plant that works at 33 per cent efficiency, if all the waste heat is discharged into a river flowing at the rate of 6×10^5 kg s^{-1}?

S6.16 Power stations that are not near a river get rid of their waste heat by evaporating water to steam. How much water would a large power station (6000 MW of heat to dissipate) have to evaporate per second? The latent heat of vaporisation of water is 2.26 MJ kg^{-1}.

S6.17 During the day, the temperature in the centre of Australia often reaches 40 °C, yet at night the temperature may well fall to 5 °C. Why?

S6.18 How much heat energy do you supply when you eat a 50 g ice block?

S6.19 In printing, it is essential to dry the ink quickly. In the old days, the paper was passed through a gas-fired oven for this purpose. Now a bank of u.v. lamps is used. Why is this much better and cheaper?

S6.20 Some modern kitchen cookers no longer have radiant heat elements but use 500 W quartz–halogen lamps over a metal reflector. What is the advantage?

S6.21 The same cookers often have a continuous glass top, over the heating lamps. Why is this an advantage?

S6.22 What simple experiment tells you that microwave ovens are more efficient than those relying on radiant heat from resistive elements?

S6.23 At geothermal power stations, the water is drawn up from a depth of about 6 km, where it is at a temperature of about 300 °C. Why is it liquid at that temperature? What happens to it as it is brought to the surface?

S6.24 A man working flat out can evaporate 1.5 kg of sweat per hour. If the latent heat of vaporisation of water is 2427 kJ kg^{-1}, at what rate is he working? Can he maintain that rate for long?

S6.25 Why is making toast an unstable process?

S6.26 Polar bears have black skin but appear white because their fur reflects all colours equally. Each hair is a tube and acts as a natural optical fibre, with the result that they absorb solar u.v. radiation with an efficiency of about 95 per cent, compared with the best man-made solar energy converters which are about 40 per cent efficient. What would be the result of photographing a polar bear in a snowfield with film sensitive to (a) visible light, (b) i.r. radiation, (c) u.v. radiation?

7   Fields

S7.1   A Penning ion trap is a device for holding single ions (usually protons) in place long enough to study them. It is suspected that in certain circumstances a single proton behaves differently from protons in bulk. The trap consists of a negatively charged ring and two positively charged studs, above and below. There is also a vertical magnetic field.

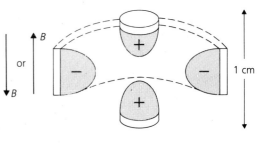

   Without the magnetic field, how would a single proton in the middle of the trap move?

S7.2   Sketch the shape of the electric field in any plane of the trap.

S7.3   How does the magnetic field keep the proton in the centre? Is the direction of the field up or down?

S7.4   Why not arrange the magnetic field to send the proton back to the centre?

S7.5   The sketch shows an electrostatic paint gun at a potential of −90 000 V and the earthed object to be painted in front of it. What must be the charge on the paint particles? Sketch in the electrostatic field lines.

S7.6   If you have drawn the field lines correctly, the main advantage of this method of painting will be immediately apparent. What is that advantage, and can you think of any others?

S7.7   In a typical electrostatic dust precipitator, the plates are 0.3 m apart and the wire electrode is at a potential of −45 000 V. Sketch the general shape of the electric field lines in the top half of the system, and of the equipotentials in the bottom half. Calculate the intensity of the field at the collecting plate.

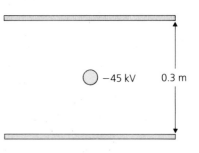

S7.8 Electricity is sent round town by a three-phase a.c. system, each current at all times being out of phase by 120° with the other two. At a certain instant, the currents in one system were as shown in the sketch. Sketch in the general shape of the magnetic field around the wires at that instant. Which wires will attract each other, and which will repel?

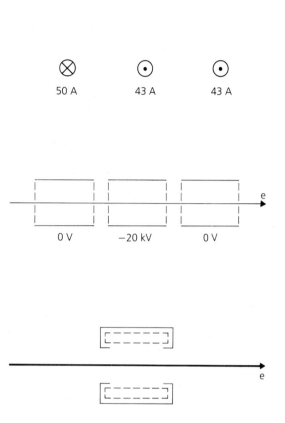

S7.9 The Einzel lens system is used to focus electron beams in electron microscopes and elsewhere. It consists of three short tubes, with potentials as shown in the diagram. Draw in the general shape of the field lines. Will this system give a convergent or a divergent beam?

S7.10 An alternative method of focusing is to use magnetic fields. In this case, a solenoid is encased in a soft-iron can in which there is a gap, as shown.

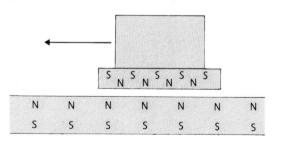

Draw in the magnetic field lines for this application. Is this a convergent or divergent system?

S7.11 The electromagnetic system does something to the electron beam that the electrostatic system does not do; what is it?

S7.12 Some trains are suspended by a magnetic levitation system. This has the enormous advantage of reducing frictional resistance. It would be possible to have either an attractive system in which the train hangs from a magnet or a repulsive system in which the train rides above a magnet. Why is the repulsive system always chosen?

S7.13 The gap between the electrodes in the plugs in my car should be between 0.7 and 0.8 mm. If the coil provides a potential of 20 000 V, what is the maximum electric field during a spark? Is it permissible to treat this as a parallel-plate capacitor?

S7.14 When Halley's comet is at its closest to the Sun (88×10^9 m) its linear velocity is 55 km s^{-1}. What is its linear speed when, 38 years later, it is at its greatest distance from the Sun (5.4×10^{12} m)?

S7.15 What assumption do you have to make to do the sum in the previous question? Is it a very daring assumption?

S7.16 The path of the planet Pluto is the most elliptic of all the planet paths. (At the time I am writing – 1987 – Pluto is inside the orbit of the planet Neptune; they will never collide as they move in different planes.) When closest to the Sun, at a distance of 4.4×10^{12} km, its speed is 7.5 km s^{-1}. At its furthest from the Sun, its speed is 2.9 km s^{-1}. What is its greatest distance from the Sun?

S7.17 The condition that a star be a black hole has to be worked out by relativity theory. Happily, it turns out that you get the same condition if it be stated that the escape velocity must be greater than the velocity of light. How small would the Sun have to be if it were to become a black hole? (Mass of Sun = 2×10^{30} kg.)

S7.18 The astronaut Alan L. Bean measured his mass while in stable orbit round the Earth during the second Skylab mission. How did he do it?

S7.19 The field ion microscope is a device for examining the arrangement of atoms in a small metal sphere. The image of the atoms appears on the fluorescent screen.

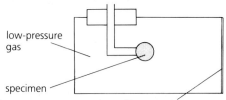

low-pressure gas

specimen

fluorescent screen

In one such device, the voltage on the sphere of metal was 10 kV. The electric field round the sphere was then 3×10^{10} V m^{-1}. What was the radius of the metal specimen?

S7.20 Some of the flares on the Sun are due to great rope-like filaments of ionised hydrogen and calcium spurting up and returning to the Sun's surface, as shown. What magnetic fields are associated with these solar flares?

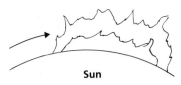

Sun

8 Waves

S8.1 The breast feathers of a peacock, seen head on, are brilliant light blue in colour. But if the bird turns away from you, the same feathers seem much darker in colour. Why?

S8.2   I am told that in expensive dress shops in Beverly Hills and elsewhere, the mirrors are not exactly plane but slightly curved so as to make the customers appear slimmer than they really are. What kind of mirror would do this?

S8.3   How could you detect the imposture optically, without actually examining the mirror closely?

S8.4   For the acceptance of nuclear test bans, it is very important to be able to distinguish earthquakes from underground nuclear explosions. How would you expect the seismic waves from earthquakes and nuclear explosions to be different in these ways: (a) depth of explosion, (b) type of seismic wave (compression or shear), (c) frequency of the wave?

S8.5   A person being treated for the bends is made to inhale a helium–oxygen mixture. What difference does this make to his or her speaking voice?

S8.6   Dolphins emit sounds at a frequency of about 250 kHz. In sea water, the speed of sound is about 1.56 km s^{-1}. What is the wavelength of these waves?

S8.7   If we hear these sounds, we say that they sound like 'clicks'. Why is this, bearing in mind that the dolphin uses this sound as a prey-detection system and its prey could be only a few metres away?

S8.8   Parallel waves are approaching the sea shore when they flow over the submerged remains of a child's sand castle. What happens to the waves thereafter?

S8.9   The minimum length of tubing in a trombone is about 210 cm. The tubing can be extended by pushing a loop out to arm's length, 45 cm. If the speed of sound is 340 m s^{-1}, what is the range of frequency of the trombone? (This will be approximate only because the effective length of the tubing is changed by the horn.)

S8.10   Certain of the fibres in the human cochlea support waves with a velocity of 17 m s^{-1}. How long should such fibres be if they are to detect sound of frequency 200 Hz?

S8.11   The human ear is especially sensitive to notes in the range 3–4 kHz. Relate this to the fact that the distance from a point outside the outer ear to the ear drum is about 2.5 cm.

S8.12   The Omega navigation system is used by ships to help them determine their position to within a few hundred metres. It consists of two transmitters 13 km apart, emitting radio waves at a frequency of 10.2 kHz. What is their wavelength? What is the distance between two nodes, on a line parallel to and 500 km from the line joining the sources?

S8.13 Most of the colours in nature are due to selective absorption of light of different wavelengths, but a few are due to interference effects. How can you, in general, tell which is the cause by a casual glance?

S8.14 The 'yellow eye' on the wing of a certain butterfly is due to constructive interference in a thin film. What is the minimum thickness of such a film if its refractive index is 1.4 and the wavelength of yellow light is 580 nm? Assume that this film rests on a matrix of higher refractive index.

S8.15 It is often necessary to protect old paintings by a glass pane, but this usually introduces reflections. How thick should a layer of magnesium fluoride (refractive index 1.38) be if it is to act as a destructive interference film in the most sensitive part of human perception, 500 nm?

S8.16 The beetle *Serica serica* has a set of parallel grooves on its back, 1000 nm deep and 1200 nm apart. If white light is normal on this surface what colour would you see, looking at an angle of 36° to the normal?

S8.17 A pulse Doppler speedometer measures the speed of an aeroplane by noting the change in frequency of radio waves reflected back off the ground. The formula is $\Delta f/f = 2v \cos \theta/c$. In one device $\theta = 60°$ and $f = 13.3$ GHz. What would be the change in frequency for a plane travelling at 200 m s^{-1}?

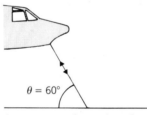

$\theta = 60°$

S8.18 What happens to the tuning of wind and string instruments as the temperature of the concert hall increases? Consider a 5 °C rise, remembering that the speed of sound is proportional to the square root of the temperature. The coefficient of linear expansion is about 10^{-5} K^{-1}.

S8.19 In Balzac's novel *Cousin Bette* we read that Steinbock worked by the 'light of a little lamp whose rays were concentrated by passing through a globe filled with water'. Steinbock does very fine work, so what is going on?

S8.20 If you are holding a rope that is fixed at the other end and send a pulse down the rope, the pulse is reflected. It also comes back upside down. Why is it reflected, and why is it inverted?

S8.21 A bat flying at 10 m s^{-1} emits a bleep of sound of frequency 60 kHz. What is the frequency of the sound reflected off a stationary morsel of food? The speed of sound in air is 340 m s^{-1}.

S8.22 For ultrasonic examination of unborn babies, a frequency of 2 MHz is used. If the speed of sound in blood is 1.5 km s^{-1}, what is the wavelength of these waves? Hence, what is the size of the smallest detail visible? How do you know that the velocity of ultrasound in flesh must be different from that in blood?

S8.23 The weather radar on an aeroplane usually has a frequency of about 3 GHz (3×10^9 Hz). It emits a pulse for 1 μs and then rests for 1 ms awaiting the return signal. What is the wavelength of the emission, how many waves are sent out in each pulse and what is the maximum possible distance over which it can detect a severe storm? The power rating of the emitter is 200 kW, so what is the energy in each pulse? As a matter of interest, the power in the reflected signal can be as low as 10^{-12} W, so it must be amplified greatly before it can show on an oscilloscope tube.

S8.24 A lightning flash may take a fraction of a second to travel from the cloud to earth, yet the roll of thunder it produces may last for several seconds. Why?

9 Current electricity

S9.1 If two electrodes are placed on your skin a few centimetres apart, the resistance between them is of the order of 100 kΩ. If a mains voltage of 250 V was switched on momentarily, would you be killed?

S9.2 If the same voltage was applied for some time and you could not snatch the electrodes away, you probably would be killed. Why? (Hint: what would be your reaction to the shock?)

S9.3 Fibrillation is the state wherein the different electric pulses to the heart muscles get out of sequence and the heart does not pump properly. For most people, fibrillation is caused by a short pulse of d.c. giving 200 mA or by 40 mA a.c. Why is the a.c. more dangerous than d.c.? (For these currents, the heart will usually start to beat properly once the voltage source is removed.)

S9.4 Some years ago in Irving, Texas, a parachutist landed astride two parallel cables, both at a potential of 138 kV. (Presumably it was a three-phase system.) His parachute got caught in a pair of wires, some 4 m above, at a different potential. Why was he not killed instantaneously? Why did he get severe burns to his hands and legs?

S9.5 If your car won't start, the A.A. man uses jump leads to connect his battery to your car. Does he connect the batteries in series or in parallel? Does he connect + to + or + to −? What would happen if he got the wires the wrong way round?

S9.6 How much should you pay the A.A. man for the electrical energy he supplies from his car? Assume that in 5 s your car starter motor takes about 50 A and that 1 unit costs 5p.

S9.7 You have a 3 V, 0.25 A lamp which has to be tested urgently. But you have only a 240 V supply and a set of 240 V lamps. How could you do it?

S9.8 Loudspeakers are usually made with impedances of 4 Ω, 8 Ω and 16 Ω. The output stage of most amplifiers has an internal impedance of 8 Ω, so if you are connecting one loudspeaker there is no problem. For hi-fi you need two loudspeakers, however. How can they be connected?

S9.9 The recent discovery of high-temperature superconductors was almost entirely a matter of trial and error. There are many surprising things about them.

(a) Firstly, they are ceramic.
(b) They are metallic oxides (Y–Ba–Cu–O).
(c) Because they are ceramic they will be difficult to use.
(d) The most important use for them is expected to be in high-speed 'chips'.

Comment on these four points.

S9.10 In the refining of zinc a large sheet of the refined metal, area 2.4 m^2, carries a current density of 480 A m^{-2}. If the voltage across this cell is 3.5 V, what power is used in this one cell?

S9.11 The 'electric fish' or 'torpedo' (a kind of ray) can give a shock of about 16 A at 60 V for 5 ms. The electric potential across almost all animal cells is about 90 mV; assume this is true for the torpedo. Calculate the power developed and energy delivered in one shock. The torpedo usually gives a series of shocks with a frequency of up to 150 Hz, varying for different species. Assuming an average frequency of 75 Hz, how much energy is delivered in one second? How many cells must be connected in series to give the voltage of this fish?

S9.12 In south London, the electric trains pick up their power (d.c., at 750 V) from a third rail, the bottom of which is about 5 cm above the ground in insulated supports. In winter, it often happens that snow piles up to the top of these live rails, with no apparent ill effects. What does that tell you about the properties of snow?

S9.13 The resistance of the live rail is about 0.017 Ω per km. The resistance of the running rails is about twice that, 0.034 Ω per km (because they are made from much harder steel). What is the total resistance for 1 km of track? During normal running the train draws about 3000 A. What is the voltage drop when the train is 1 km from the supply point? and what is the power loss then?

S9.14 Why is it preferable to put the supply points near stations?

S9.15 The tandem Van de Graaff generator at the Florida State University delivers a current of 15 μA at a potential of 90 MV. At what power rate is it working?

S9.16 What is the resistance of a typical nerve axon? Assume it is in the form of a cylinder 1 cm long and radius 5 μm and contains a liquid, axoplasm, with resistivity $\rho = 2\ \Omega\,\mathrm{m}^{-1}$.

S9.17 At my bank, the main safe can only be opened by turning two switches, each worked by a separate key. (The same system is used in underground missile silos – two keys are needed to fire the missiles.) Are these switches in series or in parallel? (In fact there is a relay between the switches and the lock mechanism.)

S9.18 What happens if you connect a 230 V, 15 W lamp in series with a 230 V, 150 W lamp to a 230 V supply? (Make a guess first.)

    (a) The 15 W lamp will burn out.
    (b) The 15 W lamp will be dim and the 150 W lamp bright.
    (c) Both lamps will glow dimly.
    (d) The 15 W lamp will be slightly dimmer than if used alone and the 150 W lamp will not glow at all.

S9.19 It is a bitterly cold night and you have only two blankets, a thick fluffy one and a thin worn one. Which blanket do you put on top and which underneath?

S9.20 A set of lights for a Christmas tree works off the 240 V supply. If each lamp is marked 12 V, 6 W, how are the lamps connected, what current do they draw, what is the total wattage, and don't they look terrible?

S9.21 My electric blanket has two resistive elements and yet has three heat settings. How is that possible?

S9.22 If each element in an electric blanket has a resistance of 480 Ω, what are the three power ratings? (The supply is 240 V.)

S9.23 My method of committing the perfect murder will only work if the victim is a junkie who lives in the back blocks, in country too rough for wheeled transport. You only need a battery, wires and two needles. Can you work it out?

S9.24 The electric room heater in my house has its element inside a silicon rod which allows the element to run hotter than it otherwise could. The brochure for the heater says that it is thus more efficient than all other heaters. A physics teacher has criticised this statement, saying that all heaters convert electrical energy into heat energy only and so must be 100 per cent efficient. What do you say?

S9.25 A battery charger gives an e.m.f. of 14 V, with internal resistance ¼ Ω. If it is used to charge a battery of p.d. 12 V and negligible internal resistance, what is the charging current?

S9.26 What happens if you connect a 240 V, 60 W lamp in series with a 3 V, 0.25 A lamp in series to a 240 V supply?

S9.27 I have a friend who recently built on an extension to her house. I noticed that she was not putting any fibreglass insulation in the walls. She said that as there was no insulation in the original part, there was no point in putting any in the new part. What do you say?

S9.28 Are the heater and fan motor of an electric hair-drier connected in series or parallel?

S9.29 In most cars, an interior light (with a warning light) comes on when any one of the four doors is opened. How are the switches connected? What kind of logic circuit is represented here?

S9.30 How can these switches work when there is only one wire to them?

S9.31 In my car, the rear window heater consists of eight elements (each of resistance 6 Ω) connected as shown. What is the total equivalent resistance?

S9.32 How much power is developed in the heater (12 V, of course)?

S9.33 Why did the designer choose such an unusual arrangement? Why not, for example, have all the elements in series?

S9.34 I have run out of 10 A fuse wire but have plenty of 5 A fuses. Should I connect them in series or parallel?

S9.35 Will the two 5 A fuses blow at 10 A?

S9.36 Several books on logic give this as a realisation of a NOT statement and recommend that students put it together. Why is it not a good idea?

S9.37 The separation of the power lines outside my house is such that they cannot be spanned by any local bird in flight. They are about 30 cm apart. We know, however, that birds can safely sit on power lines; is not the local electricity supply department being over-cautious?

S9.38 So does the wing span of birds determine the separation of the high-tension wires (say 100 000 V) carried by pylons?

S9.39 The surface of the Earth is generally a good conductor and so is the upper part of the ionosphere. The air between in the troposphere and stratosphere is a poor conductor of electric current. As the top of the ionosphere is at a potential of 300 000 V and the resistance between Earth and ionosphere is about 200 Ω, there is a constant current flowing through the atmosphere. Calculate the size of this current and the average power generated. If each thunderstorm discharges a current of 2 A, on average, how many thunderstorms are happening at any given time on our planet? Why would you expect the ionosphere to be a good conductor?

10 Capacitors

S10.1 You have bought a job lot of 1 μF capacitors, going cheap, but the circuit you are wiring calls for a 1.5 μF value. What do you do?

S10.2 An Airbus 310 flies through a thunder cloud and picks up a charge of 10^{-6} coulomb. When the plane lands, its wings form a parallel-plate capacitor with the ground. If the wings are 220 m^2 in area and 3 m above the ground, what is the capacitance of the plane? What is its potential? What is the significance of all this?

S10.3 An electrostatic loudspeaker consists of a rectangular sheet of plastic film (as used for wrapping food) coated on both sides with graphite. This sheet is placed between two sheets of metallic mesh, 1.5 cm apart. If the area of the plates is 80 cm $\times$ 60 cm, calculate the total capacitance of this arrangement.

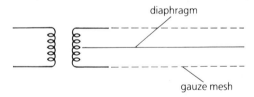

diaphragm

gauze mesh

This capacitor is fed from a centre-tapped transformer with a potential of 1000 V across each half. Calculate the charge on each mesh and the energy stored. Why are open meshes used and not solid sheets of metal?

S10.4 Some electricians can work with 10 kV wires while the power is on. How is this possible?

S10.5 An electret is the analogue of a permanent magnet. It is a piece of insulator that carries a permanent electric charge. Electrets are used in microphones and one such had an area of 2 cm $\times$ 2 cm and carried a permanent charge of 20 nC per square cm. The air gap between the charged surface and the fixed plate was 20 μm. Calculate the value of the capacitance and the voltage produced by the charge.
($\varepsilon_0 = 9 \times 10^{-12}$ F m^{-1}.)

S10.6 In small spot-welding machines, it is sometimes the practice to store the energy for each weld in a bank of capacitors. In one such machine, the energy for one weld is 2500 J. How many 0.01 F capacitors would be needed, in parallel, if the d.c. voltage was 336 V? Why is the d.c. voltage 336 V, if the mains is 240 V a.c.? Does it matter that the machine cannot be used while the capacitors are recharging?

S10.7 The ions inside and outside a cell are separated by a membrane 10^{-8} m thick and of relative permittivity = 8. Find the capacitance of 1 cm^2 of such a membrane. The permittivity of free space is 9×10^{-12} F m^{-1}.

S10.8 A 50 μF capacitor in an electronic flash gun supplies an average power of 10 kW for 2 ms. To what voltage must the capacitor be charged, and what charge must it carry?

S10.9 What simplifying assumption have we made in the previous question?

11 Electromagnetism

S11.1 In Colombia, some VSO workers have been able to install a very small hydroelectric system. A stream with a fall of 50 m and a flow rate of only 58 litres per second is used to drive a power saw. Formerly the villagers only sold logs of timber; now they can sell prepared timber at much greater profit. In the evening the power is used for cooking, but as there is only a maximum of 20 kW, villagers have to take it in turns. What is the efficiency of this system?

S11.2 A moving-coil loudspeaker has a radial magnetic field of strength 0.6 T. What is the force on the coil if it has 200 turns, each of diameter 6 cm, and if it carries a current of 2 mA?

S11.3 Would such a loudspeaker act as a microphone?

S11.4 An electromagnetic pump is used in nuclear power stations and elsewhere to move molten metals about, in particular molten sodium. One such pump consists of a rectangular section of pipe as shown. A current of 1000 A is passed horizontally in a vertical magnetic field of 0.02 T. What is the force on the element of molten metal shown?

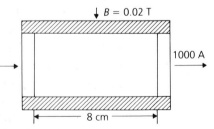

S11.5 It is believed that the magnetic field of the Earth is due to convection currents in the molten part of the core. Moving charges will constitute an electric current and this will have a small magnetic field. What is the next stage in the argument?

S11.6   Induction heating is an important industrial technique. The crucible is placed inside a large solenoid, a few turns of thick wire. A.C. is then passed through the coil at a high current (several hundred amperes). Normally the current is at a high frequency; why? One way of getting a big current at high frequency is to use a special alternator; how would it be special?

S11.7   One of the problems facing suppliers of electric power is that there is little call for their product at night and thus their machinery is standing idle. One proposal is to store electrical energy in the form of magnetic energy in a large coil of superconducting wire. In one such design, a coil of radius 100 m carries 150 000 A and produces a magnetic field of strength 5 T. The problem is that this produces enormous electromagnetic forces that would tend to tear the coil apart. What would be the force on 1 m of the wire in this field?

S11.8   What would be the force between any two turns of the wire carrying this current, supposing them to be 1 mm apart?

S11.9   Many television tubes work with the anode at a potential of 20 000 V. What would be the speed of an electron leaving the electron gun? (Disregard relativistic effects.)

S11.10   Would this be the speed of the electrons as they hit the screen?

S11.11   What would be the force on this electron if it moves horizontally in a vertical magnetic field of strength 6×10^{-5} T, supposing the tube to be unshielded?

S11.12   Hence find the sideways acceleration on the electron. Then get the sideways deflection on the electron.

S11.13   Someone says, 'This deflection would not matter as it would apply to all the electrons.' What do you say?

S11.14   In a mass spectrometer, a velocity selector passes those ions with speed of 1.6×10^5 m s^{-1}. The ions are then passed into a perpendicular magnetic field of strength 0.8 T and bent into a circular path. What would be the separation of singly ionised neon isotopes, ^{20}Ne and ^{22}Ne, after their tracks had been bent through half a circle? The masses are 20 u and 22 u, where $u = 1.66 \times 10^{-27}$ kg.

S11.15   In industry, induction heating is widely used; that is, a metal object is placed inside a larger copper coil (usually water-cooled) carrying alternating current. An e.m.f. is then induced in the object causing an induced current, and it gets hot by Joule heating. From your known formulae, explain why the applied a.c. is usually at high frequency.

S11.16   Following on from this, explain why the iron in many electrical machines is not solid but made of many thin laminations, each with an insulated coating.

S11.17 The most powerful source of ultra-violet and X-rays is synchrotron radiation. When an electric charge is accelerated, electromagnetic radiation is emitted. Thus protons or electrons orbiting in synchrotrons are plentiful sources of radiation and some synchrotrons have been specially built for this purpose. For one electron synchrotron, the focusing device is of the quadrupole design, sketched here. Sketch the shape of the magnetic field in the space between the poles and show that the field does focus errant electrons.

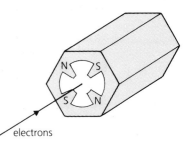

S11.18 To increase the intensity of the beam of radiation, the electron beam is passed through a 'wriggler'. This consists of a set of magnets with alternate polarities. If the electron beam is bent as shown, mark in the polarity of the magnets (one pair will be enough).

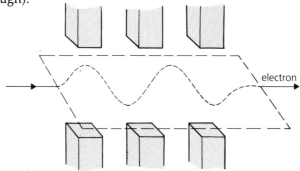

S11.19 What causes 'sferics' (the loud crackling noises picked up by a radio receiver during a thunderstorm)?

12 Alternating current

S12.1 In arc welding, a series inductor is used to even out the power demands during welding. In one such device, the power supply was 300 A at 80 V (50 Hz). If the p.d. across the load was 40 V, what was the p.d. across the inductor? What was the value of the load resistance, and what was the value of the inductance? In some welding machines, a series capacitor is used to make the power factor unity; what value of capacitance would have been needed in this case?

S12.2 In resistance (spot) welding, two metals are held together under pressure and a very large current passed. This causes a weld by melting the metals locally and allowing them to flow together while still held in position. For high temperatures it is essential that there be a high resistance; how is that achieved if the metals have low specific resistivity?

S12.3   For resistance welding, the voltage can range from 1 to 25 V, the current from 1000 to 100 000 A and the time from half a cycle of 50 Hz a.c. to several seconds. Taking typical figures, 10 V, 10 000 A and 0.5 s, calculate the rate of power supply, and the energy supplied. If the specific heat capacity of steel is 420 J kg^{-1} K^{-1}, how hot would a piece of steel of mass 0.1 kg get?

S12.4   In a radio receiver, the tuning coil has an inductance of 10 μH. What series capacitor will tune in a station, $f = 1.5$ MHz?

S12.5   A ballast inductor is included in the wiring to all fluorescent lights. Its purpose is to limit current through the lamp. What equation is in action here?

S12.6   In one fluorescent light system, the inductor was 5 H in value. What series capacitor was also included? Its purpose was to make the power factor unity (50 Hz mains supply).

13   Modern physics

S13.1   President Reagan gave approval for the construction of the 'Super Collider' particle accelerator. This will speed beams of protons and anti-protons to energies of 20 TeV (1 TeV $= 10^{12}$ eV). It will have a radius of 14 km and use superconducting magnets to keep the protons in a circular path. If the protons travel at, essentially, the speed of light, what must be the strength of the magnetic field?

S13.2   A stream of protons is fired into a magnetic field ($B = 0.02$ T) and bent into a circular path of radius 5 cm. If the direction of the protons' path was perpendicular to the magnetic field, what was the speed of the protons?

S13.3   A ruby laser emits light of wavelength 694.3 nm. How big was the energy change for this emission?

S13.4   A nuclear battery consists of a positive terminal (a rod carrying a β-source) inside an evacuated negative can. Such a battery can provide a steady current of 2 μA at 10 000 V. How many β-particles are emitted per second? What determines the e.m.f. of this battery? What could this battery be used for?

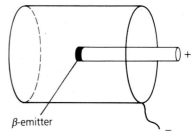

β-emitter

S13.5   Calculate the k.e. given off in the following reaction, and estimate how much is carried by the α-particle and how much by the radon nucleus.

$$^{226}\text{Ra} \rightarrow {}^{222}\text{Rn} + {}^{4}\text{He}$$

Data: ^{4}He $= 4.002\ 60$ u, ^{222}Rn $= 222.017\ 53$ u;
^{226}Ra $= 226.025\ 36$ u; 1 u $= 931$ MeV.

S13.6   Why does a mountain of uranium ore not explode as a bomb?

S13.7   The supernova 1987a was remarkable in that we know what the star it came from was like. It was very young (only 20 million years old), very hot (surface temperature 20 000 K) and a giant (50 times more massive than the Sun). How are these three factors self-consistent?

S13.8   A domestic microwave oven gives out 500 W of radiant energy at a frequency of 2450 MHz. What is the wavelength of this radiation? A book put out by my local electricity supply department says that standing waves are set up in the oven; is that possible? What is the energy carried by one photon? How many photons are emitted each second by the magnetron?

S13.9   All naturally occurring isotopes that are not being continually produced have very long half-lives (of the order of billions of years). The 40 radionuclides with half-lives between 1000 and 1 000 000 years are never found naturally and have to be made in nuclear reactors. What does that tell you about the age of the Earth?

S13.10   A wooden bowl has one-eighth of the radioactivity of ^{14}C observed in a contemporary bowl of the same wood. Estimate its age. (Half-life of ^{14}C = 5670 years.)

S13.11   A fission bomb contains about 10 kg of uranium-235. Calculate the energy released if 3.2×10^{-11} J is given off per nucleus.

S13.12   In a breeder reactor, three reactions are needed to make the fissile plutonium isotope ^{239}Pu. They are:

$$^{238}U + n \rightarrow {}^{239}U + \gamma$$

$$^{239}U \rightarrow {}^{239}Np + \beta$$

neptunium

$$^{239}Np \rightarrow {}^{239}Pu + \beta$$

Calculate the minimum energy carried by the γ-rays and the two β-particles from the following data: n = 1.0087 u; ^{238}U = 238.0507 u; ^{239}U = 239.0543 u; ^{239}Np = 239.0529 u; ^{239}Pu = 239.0521 u.

S13.13   For nuclear fusion, it is better to use tritium rather than deuterium only (T + D, rather than D + D). Unfortunately tritium is radioactive, with a half-life of 12 years. Thus it is usual to make the tritium using this reaction:

$$^{6}Li + n \rightarrow {}^{4}He + {}^{3}H + Q$$

Calculate the energy Q given off in this reaction, first in mass units and then in joules, using the following data: ^{6}Li = 6.015 12 u; n = 1.008 67 u; ^{4}He = 4.002 604 u; ^{3}H = 3.016 049 u; 1 u = 1.66×10^{-27} kg.

S13.14 I read recently in an astronomy book the following: 'Every second, the Sun converts 600 million tonnes of hydrogen into 596 million tonnes of helium . . .'. The mass of the Sun is given as 2×10^{21} million tonnes. Surely it is not possible to measure the mass of the Sun to one part in 10^{21}?

Answers

Acceleration due to gravity

1.1 The answer is (b), the separation stays the same. If the people had been looking out of the same window, the bricks would have fallen side by side, accelerating all the while. The separation of the bricks is the distance between the windows.

1.2 The answer is (c) and we may see this by doing quick calculations, using the formula $d = \frac{1}{2}at^2$.

> After 1 s, first stone has fallen $d = \frac{1}{2} \times 10 \times 1^2 = 5$ m; separation $= 5 - 0 = 5$ m.
> After 2 s, first stone has fallen $d = \frac{1}{2} \times 10 \times 2^2 = 20$ m; separation $= 20 - 5 = 15$ m.
> After 3 s, first stone has fallen $d = \frac{1}{2} \times 10 \times 3^2 = 45$ m; separation $= 45 - 20 = 25$ m.

As you see, the separation goes up in a nice arithmetical progression.

1.3 The distance fallen is always the area under the v–t graph and we get the results of the previous answer, but very much more elegantly.

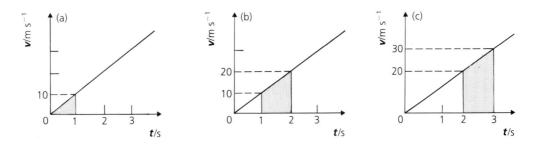

1.4 The answer is (d), as long as friction is negligible. The angle of the slope is decreasing and so must be the component of the acceleration due to gravity. While the acceleration is positive, the speed must increase.

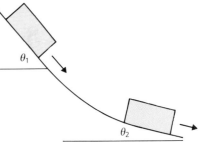

1.5 Certainly the acceleration will continue to decrease. Towards the end of the journey, however, the acceleration is so small and the friction so big that the speed may well begin to decrease. The speed will decrease as soon as the force of friction F is greater than the component of the force of gravity down the slope, that is, when $F > mg \sin \theta$. If μ is the coefficient of friction, then $F = \mu mg$ and the condition becomes $\mu > \sin \theta$. We may take the coefficient of friction as about 0.4, and so the speed will begin to decrease once the angle of the slide is less than about 20°.

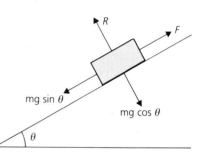

1.6 We know that friction is considerable for at least two reasons. The flat portion at the end of the slide is not very long and yet the child does not hurtle off the end. The seat of one's pants gets quite hot too (remember?).

1.7 The ball will lose its speed of 20 m s^{-1} in 2 s, and in that time will rise 20 m. It must also fall 20 m, so the total distance travelled is 40 m.

1.8 The total displacement is zero. The ball is back where it started.

1.9 The increase in speed is negligible, because the acceleration due to gravity is so small. Using the formula $v^2 = u^2 + 2ad$ gives us that $v^2 = 225 + 2 \times 1.6 \times 4 = 225 + 13 = 238$, so $v = 15.4$ m s^{-1}. On Earth the speed would have gone up only to about 17 m s^{-1}.

1.10 I think the film was a fake and I think they should have said so. Supposing that the man times his jump perfectly, that he just clears the car as it approaches him. The time to jump 1.8 m is given by $d = \frac{1}{2}at^2$ and this is 0.6 s. The time to jump 1.5 m is 0.55 s. Thus he has $0.05 \times 2 = 0.1$ s to clear the car (0.05 s going up and 0.05 s coming down). Travelling at 20 m s^{-1}, he can only clear the car if it is less than 2 m long. He would have to be pretty good to get higher than 1.8 m without using some exotic high jump technique. I don't think anyone could do it with the normal knees-together take-off.

1.11 During the reaction time, the car travels $30 \times 0.7 = 21$ m. It takes 4 s to stop from the given initial speed and at an average speed of 15 m s^{-1} will go a further 60 m.

1.12 A day is the time it takes to go from light to dark and back to light again. For both Prevolvans and Subvolvans, the number of days in a year is the number of times the Moon goes round the Earth in a year. Actually it is one less than this because the Earth goes round the Sun once in a year. The disadvantage of living on the Moon from this cause is having to experience the great extremes of heat and cold in the long lunar day.

1.13 The time taken for the cable to fall 6 m (taking your height to be 2 m, to the nearest metre) is given by $d = \frac{1}{2}at^2$. This turns out to be 1.1 s and this is more than the 1 s given for the power to be shut off. In fact, the cable would be fairly stiff and would take more than 1 s to fall.

1.14 The distance from the power station does not come into it. Although electrons travel fairly slowly in wires, the current is switched off and on almost instantaneously.

1.15 The water is accelerating as it falls. The volume of water at any level is constant, so as the speed goes up, the cross-sectional area must go down.

1.16

$$\text{Area of jet at top} = A_0 = \pi(0.7)^2 = 1.5 \text{ cm}^2$$
$$\text{Speed at top} = v = 75/1.5 = 50 \text{ cm s}^{-1}$$
$$= 0.5 \text{ m s}^{-1}$$

$$\text{Area of jet at bottom} = A = \pi(0.35)^2 = 0.35 \text{ cm}^2$$
$$\text{Speed at bottom} = v_0 = 75/0.35 = 200 \text{ cm s}^{-1}$$
$$= 2 \text{ m s}^{-1}$$

Hence
$$v_0{}^2 = 4 \text{ m}^2 \text{ s}^{-2}$$

$$v^2 + 2ad = 0.25 + 2 \times 15 \times 10$$
$$= 3.25 \text{ m}^2 \text{ s}^{-2}$$

Thus we see that the two agree pretty well, especially considering that the essential measurement, the rate of water flow, was made so sketchily.

1.17 If the flea takes off at 1 m s^{-1}, it takes 0.1 s to reach its apogee (lovely word, it means highest point). In 0.1 s it will fall ($d = \frac{1}{2}at^2$) 5 cm.

1.18 It takes about 0.75 s for the 'roo' to fall 2.8 m and so its take-off speed was about 7.5 m s^{-1}, about as fast as you can run.

1.19 You must hold the string with the small separations at the bottom and the bottom weight must touch the floor. I must say that whenever I have done this experiment, I have found it rather unconvincing.

Weightlessness

2.1 Light the candle and close the jar, but do not drop it; the candle will stay alight for at least half a minute.

2.2 Drop the weight, but not the can.

2.3 The motors of the space craft are not working.

2.4 The Earth has been circling the Sun for about 4.5 billion years. If any frictional force acted, the Earth would have fallen into the Sun long ago. In both this question and the last one, the force is at right angles to the displacement. *Work = force × distance*, but only when they are in the same direction. The same applies in our model of atoms with electrons circling a nucleus: no work is done.

2.5 They were weightless for all the journey – ever since leaving the cannon's mouth (if the effect of air resistance was small).

2.6 If the Moon were stationary and your space craft also. You would have to be quick because the Moon would not stay motionless for very long.

2.7 Using the formula $a = v^2/R$ and inserting the data, we get a value of about 12 m s^{-2} for the acceleration – good enough agreement, considering the roughness of the data.

2.8 Electric shielding arises because we have two kinds of electric charge, positive and negative. In an electric field, any substance becomes polarised (that is, the charges become separated) and there is no field inside a hollow conductor. In the case of gravity, we have only one kind of gravitating mass (unless there is some anti-matter somewhere in the cosmos – if there is, do not hang about; there would be nasty effects if you came in contact with any anti-matter).

2.9 Negative mass would still go down. It is true that the force of gravity between the Earth and the lump of negative mass would be directed upwards. But then as $F = ma$, an upwards force on a negative mass would give a downwards acceleration.

2.10 Two empty spaces would still attract. We know that two masses attract. Now think about the two voids. Fill one of the voids with matter. A point in between, like Q, experiences a gravitational field to the right, as if a void repels matter. Hence, a void attracts a void.

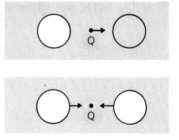

2.11 When the helicopter is rising at constant speed, its actual speed is irrelevant as far as the tension is concerned. The tension has the same value as if the chopper were stationary, namely 600 × 10 = 6000 N.

2.12 There is now an extra tension due to the helicopter's upward acceleration. The tension is 6000 + 1200 = 7200 N.

2.13 The work done by your thigh muscles would be the same on Earth as on Jupiter. If your mass is 60 kg and you can jump a height of h m on Jupiter, then $60 \times 10 \times 1.6 = 60 \times 25 \times h$, leading to $h = 0.6$ m. Remember your mass is the same everywhere. This question is unrealistic, though: on Jupiter, you would not be able to get much of a run up to the bar.

2.14 Suppose your mass is 60 kg. Then on Jupiter, the force of gravity on you would be 1500 N, which is 900 N greater than on Earth. So you would get around on Jupiter just as you would on Earth if you were permanently carrying a weight of 90 kg, like Obelix with his menhir. You could stand up with this and could even run, but not very far or fast. So your high jumping would be restricted.

2.15 For a mass of 3 g and force of 0.45 N, there is an acceleration of 150 m s^{-2}. If this acts for a distance of 4 cm, the take-off speed is 3.5 m s^{-1}. The vertical component of this is $3.5 \cos 60 = 3$ m s^{-1}. The locust thus will take 0.3 s to reach the top of its jump and so will attain a height of 0.45 m. This is correct; the locusts in my lab, when disturbed, can hit the top of the cage and this is 40 cm high. The horizontal distance travelled is $2 \times 0.3 \times 3 \cos 60 = 0.9$ m. I have not been able to test this as my locusts seem to jump much more nearly vertically – I have never seen them jump more than 20 cm horizontally. Notice that the difference between a vertical jump and one at 60° will hardly affect the height reached.

Plastic bullets

3.1 Using $v^2 = 2ad$, $v = 70$ m s^{-1} and $d = 100$ m yields a deceleration of about 25 m s^{-2}.

3.2 Inserting the value of 70 m s^{-1} for the muzzle velocity u in the formula $v^2 = u^2 + 2ad$ yields a value for the final speed v of about 60 m s^{-1}.

3.3 The k.e. comes out to about 330 J for the plastic bullet.

3.4 For the cricket ball the k.e. comes to about 70 J.

3.5 The area of the bullet is $\pi \times 2 \times 2$ cm$^2 = 1.2 \times 10^{-3}$ m^2. This leads to a force of about 4 N.

3.6 Using $a = F/m$ we find that the acceleration $= -4/0.134 = 30$ m s^{-2}, and this agrees very well with our first value – it is slightly bigger because this is the maximum value. This happens when the speed is at its maximum. The previous value was an average one.

3.7 A cricket ball is round, the plastic bullet could hit you with a sharp edge.

3.8   The time for the water to get to its highest point is given by

$$v \sin 45 = at$$

Hence
$$t = \frac{v \sin 45}{a}$$

Then time to travel distance $d = (2\,v \cos 45)t$

Thus
$$d = \frac{v^2 \sin 45 \cos 45}{a}$$

and this leads to
$$v = 14 \text{ m s}^{-1}$$

$V = 14$ m s^{-1}

$45°$

20 m

3.9   The rate at which water is emerging is $1400 \times 2 \times 2$ ml s^{-1} and this equals about 5.6 kg s^{-1}. Multiplying this value by our previous calculation for v we finish up with a force of about 80 N, certainly enough to knock you over.

3.10   The deceleration is 10 000 m s^{-2} and this gives us a force of about 1000 N.

3.11   The momentum of the rhino $= 500 \times 5 = 2500$ kg m s^{-1}.
The momentum of the bullet $= 0.1 \times 400 = 40$ kg m s^{-1}.

So even if it died instantly, the rhino would continue to slither some way in the dust.

3.12   We are going to say that the momentum of the bullet equals the momentum of the gun. Hence the recoil speed of the gun is 10 m s^{-1}. Using the same well-trodden path, if the gun stops in 1 cm we find that its deceleration equals 5000 m s^{-2} and so the force exerted on the shoulder of the hunter is $5000 \times 4 = 20\,000$ N – an enormous figure. This is the force that would be felt if the hunter allowed the gun to spring back on to his shoulder. He takes good care to hold it firmly.

3.13   The rubber bullet would be more likely to knock you over and this is why it is used. If it were perfectly elastic it would rebound with the same speed as it hit you. Thus its change in momentum would be $2mv$, and this would be equal and opposite to your change in momentum. The brass bullet would hardly bounce off your body and its change of momentum would be $1mv$. In practice, of course, the rubber bullet would not be perfectly elastic so your change in momentum would be between $1mv$ and $2mv$.

$+mv$

rubber bullet

$-mv$

$+mv$

brass bullet

3.14   In this case, the brass bullet would do more damage to you. When it stopped, it would lose almost all its k.e. and your body would have to absorb this energy; there would be work (= Force × Distance) provided by your muscles. The rubber bullet, as we have seen, would lose less k.e. and so would do less damage to you. The answers to both this question and the last hinge on the fact that momentum is a vector quantity and involves v^1, while energy is a scalar quantity and is proportional to v^2. Thus when something rebounds its change in momentum is added (two minuses make a plus).

3.15 The horizontal component of the muzzle velocity is 950 cos 17 = 900 m s^{-1}. Similarly, the vertical component is 950 sin 17 = 220 m s^{-1}. The time for the shell to reach its highest point is 22 s, so the total time of flight is 44 s and so its range would be 40 km.

3.16 For resistive force of 400 N, the deceleration is − 20 m s^{-2} and so the shell would stop completely in 45 s. Of course this is unreasonable, but then the resistive force gets less as the shell slows down. This problem is not amenable to a simple solution.

3.17 In this case the vertical component is 900 sin 40 = 580 m s^{-1}. The shell takes 58 s to reach its apogee. The whole journey takes 116 s. As the horizontal component of the speed, 900 cos 40 = 690 m s^{-1}, the range turns out to be about 80 km. This again is far out, but is not so bad as the previous case. This is to be expected as the muzzle velocity, and hence the air resistance, is lower.

3.18 The idea is rubbish. The tanker would continue to go at constant speed. The petrol in the tank has the same forward momentum when it leaves the tank, and it goes forward with the tanker until it hits the ground which it then causes to speed up by a minute amount.

3.19 There is a hole in the back of the barrel so that the hot gases (or cartridge) may move backward with momentum equal and opposite to that of the missile. They can be very dangerous to those firing them. But surely, if there is nothing for the gas to press on, the shell cannot go forward. What do you say?

3.20 The data are as follows:

v/m s^{-1}	823	650	508	391	325
x/m	0	225	450	675	900

The graph is plotted here.

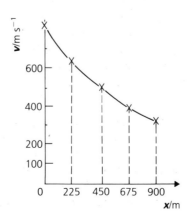

Reading off the slopes and average values for v, in each interval of distance, we get:

v/m s^{-1}	736	579	450	358
$-dv$/m s^{-1}	173	142	117	66
dx/m	225	225	225	225
$-a$/m s^{-2}	566	365	234	105
v^2/× 10^4 m^2 s^{-2}	54	34	20	13

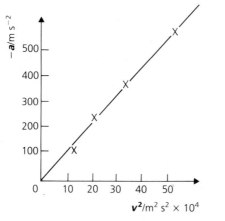

When we plot the graph of $-a$ against v^2, we get a pretty good straight line. This confirms the assumption (made in question **3.5**) that air resistance is proportional to the square of the velocity.

ICBMs

4.1   The centripetal force needed to keep the missile in circular orbit is given by

$$F = \frac{mv^2}{r}.$$

The force is provided by the gravitational attraction between the missile (mass m) and the Earth (mass M),

$$F = \frac{GMm}{r^2}$$

Putting these two together, we get

$$v^2 = \frac{GM}{r}$$

Here r is the Earth's radius plus the height risen, so

$$r = (6.4 + 0.6) \times 10^6 \text{ m}$$

This yields a speed of about 8×10^3 m s^{-1}.

4.2 Over a distance of 8000 km, a height of about 1000 km means that the path is very nearly circular.

4.3 As the distance is about 8000 km, then the time is 1000 s or about 16 minutes.

4.4 To travel 600 km at a speed of about 8 km s^{-1} takes about 70 s.

4.5 The increase in speed due to the acceleration due to gravity is $70 \times 9.8 = 700$ m s^{-1} or 0.7 km s^{-1}, which is negligible compared with the speed of the missile.

4.6 The increase in speed is 8000 m s^{-1} and this happens in 120 s. So the average acceleration is $8000/120 = 70$ m s^{-2}.

4.7 The initial acceleration will be much less than the average, and the final acceleration much more, because during the flight fuel is burnt (and liquid oxygen is used) and also the first two stages are discarded. The maximum occurs just as the last of the fuel is burnt.

4.8 The useful work done (if you can call it useful) is given by

$$W = mgh$$
$$= 1000 \times 10 \times 1.2 \times 10^6$$
$$= 1.2 \times 10^{10} \text{ J}$$

The chemical energy supplied in burning 5000 kg of hydrogen (5×10^6 g $= 2.5 \times 10^6$ mol) is 7.5×10^{11} J.

The business is very inefficient, but that is hardly surprising since a great deal of work has to be expended in lifting the fuel, the oxygen and the first two stages.

4.9 No work is done as there is no resistance force (no air friction) in the horizontal direction. The force and distance are perpendicular to each other.

4.10 When the ball is pulled into its new, smaller orbit, it increases speed. This is because the Law of conservation of angular momentum is in action. This says that the quantity $L = mvr$ is conserved. As r is decreased, so v is increased.

4.11 The Law of conservation of angular momentum is a generalised statement of Kepler's second law.

Consider the two rubber balls circling a common centre. Then in order that the two balls sweep out equal areas in equal periods of time, it is necessary that the inner ball goes faster than the outer one. If the two areas shown are equal, then the arc of the smaller circle must be longer than the arc of the larger. The Law of conservation of angular momentum is more general because it allows for the planet (which interested Kepler) or the rubber ball (which our question was about) to change mass.

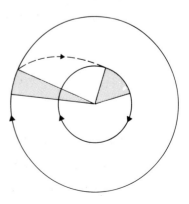

4.12 A component of the force which is pulling the ball inwards acts to accelerate the ball. When the ball is changing from orbit A to orbit B it is acted on by a force towards the common centre of rotation. This force can be resolved into two components: one of these (the centripetal force) will be perpendicular to the motion and will serve to keep the ball in a circular path, while the other component will accelerate the ball, increasing its speed until it is appropriate to the orbit with smaller radius. Note that if the ball had been going fast enough not to need to be tethered by a string but held in place by gravitational attraction, then the increase in speed (and hence increase in k.e.) would have come from the decrease in gravitational p.e.

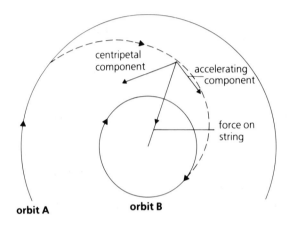

4.13 Protons, missiles and planets all follow a circular path (near enough). For missiles and planets, the centripetal force is provided by the gravitational attraction. For protons in a synchrotron, the magnetic force provides the needed inward pull.

4.14 The momentum is $p = (1.6/3) \times 10^{17}$ kg m s^{-1}. Equating the centripetal and magnetic forces, $Bev = mv^2/r$, or $B = p/er = 0.25$ tesla.

4.15 At least we can see that the units are right. In $p = E/c$, both sides have the units (dimensions) of mass $\times$ velocity.

Some sporting controversies

5.1 Surprisingly, the balls will tend to stay in the air stream. This is an example of the action of Bernoulli's equation which itself is an extension of Newton's laws. If a ball strays out of the air flow, the air will flow faster where its streamlines are straight. An increase in speed means a decrease in pressure, and so the ball tends to move back into the air flow.

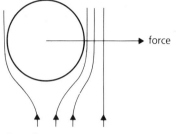

5.2 The inverse-square law does not apply here. It is true that the intensity of illumination decreases the further you are from the source but no light photons are lost. Reflectors ensure that all the light energy from the lamps reaches the playing field and so contributes to the illumination.

5.3 It would be better to call these 'conditioned reflexes'. A reflex action is one that does not depend on training. If a football is coming straight at your head your reflex action is to duck, whereas a soccer player is trained to head the ball without thinking.

5.4 The vertical component of the speed is 5 m s^{-1}, so it takes 0.5 s for the jumper to reach his highest point and 1.0 s is the total time of flight. The vertical component of the velocity is 8.7 m s^{-1} and so the distance moved by the centre of mass is 8.7 m. This compares with the record of 8.4 m. The two agree pretty well.

5.5 The calculation in the previous question disregards air resistance and also the thrust of the leg on take-off. To eliminate this last effect, you would have to jump vertically at the end of the runway. Alternatively, you could see how far you could jump from a standing-still position. I suspect that you can jump further than the sum of the two effects taken singly.

5.6 When a jumper takes off, his body is bent forward. He wants to land with his body bent backwards, with his feet reaching forwards, since it is the centre of mass that follows the (approximate) parabolic path. The kick conserves angular momentum during the flight.

5.7 The k.e. of the high-jumper is $\frac{1}{2}m \times 7^2 = 24.5\,m$ J. If this energy is converted to p.e., the height reached is 2.45 m. The agreement with the record of 2.4 m is fortuitous; again the effect of the leg thrust has been neglected.

5.8 Considering the torques about the toes, the height of the centre of mass d, is given by $80 \times d = 53 \times 156$, so d is 103 cm. That is about 60 per cent of my height. This is higher than usual for males but I had my arms raised.

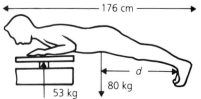

5.9 To find the position of the centre of mass we consider the whole body, add the effect of the raised arms and subtract the effect of the missing lowered arms.

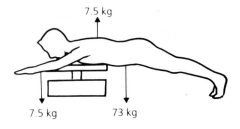

If d is the height of the centre of mass and considering torques about the toes, we have:

$$73 \times d = 73 \times 1.03 + 7.5 \times 1.53$$
$$- 7.5 \times 0.87$$
$$= 73 \times 1.03 + 7.5 \times 0.66$$

This yields the result that the centre of mass is raised by about 6.8 cm. The books give a figure of 6 cm as the result of actual measurements.

5.10 The angular velocity of the hammer is $\omega = 4\pi$ rad s^{-1}, the linear velocity is $v = \omega r = 20$ m s^{-1} and the acceleration 240 m s^{-2}. This leads to a force of 1680 N. Whether you could stand such a force in your shoulders depends on whether you can hang from a bar by one arm with two people hanging on to you.

5.11 We plot x against t and y against t^2.

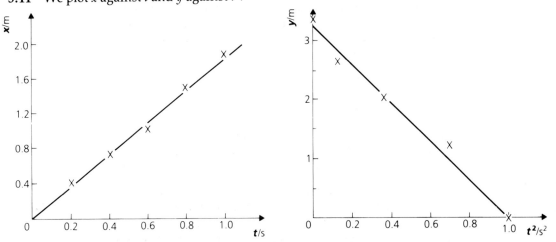

We see that both give a reasonable, though not perfect, straight line. The value for g, twice the slope of the second graph, turns out to be under 8 m s^{-2}.

In my experience of taking measurements from photographs, we always seem to get very low values for g and I put this down to poor values for the rate of flashing (or opening of the slits) of the stroboscope.

5.12 The centre of mass of the diver continues to move in a parabola, whatever circular motion be imposed on it.

5.13 The karate stance is very stable. If the non-striking hand is moved backwards as the striking hand goes forward, linear momentum is conserved and this again preserves stability.

5.14 The energy diverted by the fist is ½mv^2 and all karate training aims to increase fist speed. Whether the outlandish cries that accompany the blows have any effect, I leave to you.

5.15 The loss in energy in breaking a thin plank of wood is very small; there is little change in hand speed. Thus very little more energy is needed to break a stack of thin planks than to break one. When you break a thin plank, the underside is stretched and there is nothing to counter that extension. In a thick plank there are other layers of wood to resist the extension. If you had a stack of a hundred sheets of paper-thin wood, very little energy would be needed to break them all.

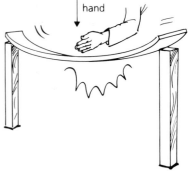

The effects of nuclear war

6.1 The smoke from the fires adds to the fog, which becomes smog and stays around for days, under the inversion layer.

6.2 The intense sunlight reacts with the fumes from the million or so car engines to produce 'photochemical smog'. This is reddish-brown, due to the oxides of nitrogen present. Smog is one reason why California has led the way in pressing for 'catalytic converters' to clean up car emissions.

6.3 The heat ray travelled at the speed of light (3×10^8 m s^{-1}), whereas the blast wave travelled at approximately the speed of sound (about 330 m s^{-1}).

6.4 A black surface is a better absorber of heat than a white one. We may assume that the cloth was the same throughout, and the only difference was in the dye.

6.5 The blackened soil might absorb enough heat to melt the permafrost, in comparison with the snow-covered soil which tends to reflect the Sun's rays. (If once the Antarctic ice began to melt it would all go very quickly; this is one of the fears if the atmosphere began to reflect heat because of the 'greenhouse effect'.) In fact these fears have proved groundless. The pipeline has broken many times; on one occasion, the oil poured out for nearly a day before the leak was noticed. The damage has been no more than the pollution caused by the oil.

6.6 It is quite possible to get blisters on the bottom of your feet if you stand for long on black sand, which absorbs the heat rays. Nearby golden sand is comfortable. The black sand is the very valuable iron oxide.

6.7 Electromagnetic waves travel at 3×10^8 m s^{-1}. Hence the time to travel 1.2×10^6 m is 0.4×10^{-2} s or 4 ms.

6.8 They would have to be shielded by being placed in a continuous metal can; there is no electric field inside a hollow cylinder.

6.9 Signals can be sent down optical fibres as pulses of light, a method coming increasingly into use. Many messages can be sent down one fibre by varying the wavelength of the light.

6.10 The principle here is that if a current is perpendicular to a magnetic field, then there is a force on the conductor in a direction perpendicular to the other two.

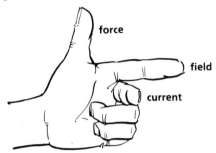

It is for this reason that we only normally get the aurora at the poles. At the Equator, the cosmic rays tend to get turned away. At present, all testing of nuclear bombs in the atmosphere is forbidden by the test ban treaty of 1962. One reason why this treaty has been upheld scrupulously since its signing is because any infringements would be so easy to detect. Everyone thought that the aurora would never be seen in the tropics.

However, a very important part of the American 'Star Wars' programme for defence against nuclear missiles is the X-ray laser. This involves detonating a hydrogen bomb in space, directing the resulting X-rays down laser tubes and pointing them at the missiles. All this happens in the fraction of the second before the bomb explodes and blows the whole apparatus to bits. The only way it would be possible to test such a weapon would be to detonate a hydrogen bomb in space and end the treaty.

6.11 Whenever a free electron is accelerated, it emits electromagnetic radiation. (Bohr had to assume that accelerated electrons in the atom do not radiate, as otherwise they would quickly lose all their energy.) The charged particles spiralling round a magnetic field line are accelerated and emit electromagnetic radiation, which happens to be in the visible region.

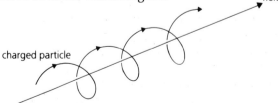

In the same way, electrons and protons being accelerated in synchrotrons and other devices emit electromagnetic rays as they follow their circular paths.

6.12 We calculate the product pt (density × thickness) and see how constant it is:

Substance	Lead	Steel	Concrete	Soil	Wood
Product pt/g cm^{-2}	20	22	24	11	15

6.13 Similarly, we calculate the product for β-rays.

Substance	Lead	Steel	Concrete	Soil	Wood	Air
Product pt/g cm^{-2}	9	12	12	6	10	13×10^{-1}

Thus we see that the law is better upheld for β-rays than for γ-rays. We also see how any threat from β-rays is much easier to eliminate than the danger from γ-rays. There is no likely harm from α-particles, as they are absorbed by a few cm of air.

An American Under-Secretary for Defense recently published a book called *With enough shovels*. His argument was that there was no need to fear an all-out nuclear war as Americans are able to protect themselves by their own efforts. All they need to do is to dig a trench, cover it with boards and then pile dirt on top. Leaving aside the fact that most Americans live in cities, with no access to soil, and also the Japanese experience that in a nuclear war it is not the radiation that kills most people but the blast and firestorm, the figures show that even 14 cm of soil only cuts down the intensity of γ-radiation by half. Several metres of soil would be needed to make the danger from γ-rays negligible. Nor does the book mention that it would be necessary to live in this trench for several months while the radiation level decayed to a safe level. It was only after several months that the Russians allowed citizens back to their homes 10 km from the site of the nuclear reactor explosion at Chernobyl.

6.14 A subcritical mass is one that is too small to sustain a chain reaction; in a subcritical mass, on average, more neutrons are lost from the mass than are produced in it. If the mass of uranium is compressed, then any neutron is more likely to cause further splitting than to escape from the mass.

6.15 I make the density come to 30 000 kg m^{-3}, so the uranium is compressed to two-thirds of its normal volume by the explosion. Note that uranium is one of the densest materials, almost twice as dense as lead.

6.16 Einstein expressed regret that physics, to which he had devoted his life's work, should be used for wholesale destruction. He, along with others who worked on the bomb, believed that they had assurances that it would never be used against people. He thought that the bombs would be dropped on uninhabited islands in the Pacific to demonstrate their power. Even now, forty years later, there is still controversy on this matter. In 1987, another book was published arguing that the bombs had to be dropped, that millions would have been killed if the Japanese islands had had to be invaded and that the Japanese would have defended their homeland with the utmost ferocity. Against that, some argue that the Japanese had previously made peace overtures to the Russians, that they were in no state to defend themselves and that a demonstration of the fearful power of the bombs would have been enough. My own view is that some American soldiers and physicists were determined to see the bombs tested in a real situation. They had worked so hard and for so long on what they called 'sweet problems' that they longed to know what their weapons could do.

6.17 When a uranium bomb is exploded, the required heat is produced but there is also a strong blast wave. The problem is to hold the bomb together long enough for the heat to ignite the hydrogen before the blast blows it apart. This is more likely to happen if the explosion of the TNT pushes the uranium inward towards the central hydrogen.

Galileo at Arcetri

7.1 The graph of d against t^2 is plotted below. It is a straight line through the origin. The slope is of no significance, as the time was measured in ml of water.

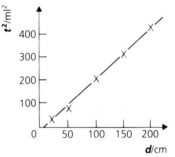

7.2 This time we plot height h against $1/t^2$ and again we have a straight line through the origin, demonstrating the conservation of energy.

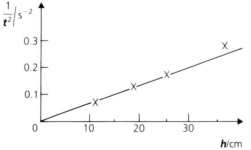

7.3 Babies have a large surface area for their mass and so dissipate a lot of heat energy. They have to be wrapped closely in sleeping suits and shawls.

7.4 Baby dinosaurs, newly hatched from eggs, were particularly vulnerable as they were unable to control their body temperature. They depended on sunlight to keep warm. If that was not forthcoming, they would be too cold to move and would become easy prey for any prowling carnivores.

7.5 Other things being equal, there is less skin per unit mass of fruit for big oranges.

7.6 Often other things are not equal and small oranges have thinner skins. There is always less waste in peeling large oranges rather than small ones, however.

7.7 In scaling down from a full-size aircraft, the structural members can be thinner and can even be made of balsa wood. Many early pioneers of flying went wrong over this. Their small models did well but failed at full size. One full-sized machine with eight wings collapsed under its own weight before it got the chance to fly.

7.8 The formula *work = force × distance* only applies if the force is constant. If, as in a spring, the force goes up with the distance (extension), then the area under the force–distance curve is the work done.

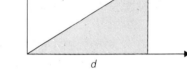

7.9 The work done in moving a charge q against a constant potential V is qV. But the work done in charging a capacitor, where the charge and potential go up together, is $\frac{1}{2}qV$.

7.10 The energy stored in the bow is $\frac{1}{2} \times 350 \times 0.6 = 105$ J.

7.11 The strain energy of the bow is almost all converted to k.e., giving a speed of about 45 m s^{-1}.

7.12 If the bow is pre-stretched by having it initially bent backwards, then work has to be done in getting it to the unstretched position and the 60 cm can begin later. In the diagram,
    AD is the initial tension,
    AB is the 60 cm extension produced by the straightening of the archer's arm.
    Then ABCD is the work done by the archer, approximately 170 J.

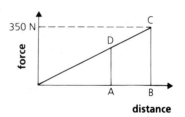
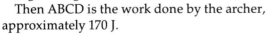

7.13 All the surface and shallow mines had been worked out and it was necessary to go ever deeper. The pumps were needed to remove the water that drained into them.

7.14 Plasticine behaves plastically, that is, it does not recover if its shape is changed (although it must have limited elasticity).

The end of the world

8.1 No energy is lost; the first law of thermodynamics tells us that energy is conserved.

8.2 At present, the forces on the Sun are nicely balanced; the force of gravity is just equal to the force exerted by the radiation of heat and all the electromagnetic radiation (and all the particles emitted). If the radiation stopped, gravity would win and the Sun would collapse.

8.3 All our energy on Earth comes ultimately from the Sun. Locally, we have been enabled to lose entropy as the Sun has gained entropy. It has gained more entropy than we have lost because of our inefficient energy conversion.

8.4 There are the black dwarf stars that have burnt out, leaving only charred remains. (There are other sources of 'hidden mass' as well.)

8.5 If you talk about how 'heavy' something is you mean how big is the force of gravity on it, but you cannot speak about weighing a galaxy – what scales would you put one in?

8.6 If gravity had been a little stronger, then the galaxies would all have been pulled together in a comparatively short time. There would not have been the 4.5 billion years needed for human beings to have evolved from the primeval soup.

8.7 If gravity had been a little weaker, the primitive matter of the Big Bang would not have formed into galaxies. Stars like the Sun are made from clouds of hydrogen gas at the centre of galaxies. So, no galaxy, no Sun. Obviously, the first generation of stars were not made in the centre of a galaxy as no galaxy then existed. However, our Sun is one of a later generation of stars, it is only 4.5 billion years old: the Big Bang occurred about 15 billion years ago.

8.8 The Earth would lose its oxygen because the molecules would move faster. They would not all 'boil off' at once because their average speed would still be less than the escape velocity for the Earth, but we should lose them more quickly.

8.9 The forms of life that have evolved on this planet are suited to the conditions that have existed on Earth.

8.10 If the mass did not change significantly, the rotational inertia would be much less and so the angular velocity would be much more, in accordance with the Law of conservation of angular momentum.

8.11 It certainly could tear itself apart and the calculation is not too difficult. It would go like this. First calculate the new rotational speed of the star, then the linear speed of a particle on the rim.

Hence find the centripetal force on this particle. If this force is less than the gravitational force on the particle from the rest of the star, then the star blows itself apart.

8.12 We know that the galaxies are rotating and so we know the speed of the stars on the edge of the galaxy. We can then equate the centripetal force (mv^2/R) on such a star with the force of gravitational attraction (GMm/R^2).

8.13 We can also estimate the mass of a galaxy by adding up the masses of all the stars. When we do this, the answer turns out to be less than the result got by the method in the previous question. It is therefore assumed that there is a lot of invisible matter in each galaxy. A great deal of work is now proceeding to try to discover what this dark matter could be.

8.14 $\log P = \log C + n \log d$.

		$\log P$	1.92	1.54	1.14	0.84
Air:		$\log d$	0.60	0.85	1.08	1.28
Ground:		$\log d$	0.52	0.70	0.91	1.11

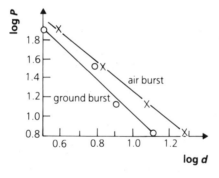

8.15 We see that both graphs are pretty well linear and both have approximately the same slope of -1.4. We expect the slope to be less than that for an inverse-square law, which would be -2, since we should get that slope if the ground had no influence, that is, if the detonation point was very high. The effect of the ground must be to make the pressure fall off at a lesser rate. With the air burst higher up, we might have expected its graph to have a steeper slope; if anything, it is flatter.

8.16 We see that for a given distance, the air burst causes a higher over-pressure than a ground burst. We should expect that, since in the ground burst, energy is used in gouging out a hole and flinging dirt into the air.

Newton's mistakes and Einstein's blunder

9.1 $F = ma$ will not work if the mass is changing. For example, if you have a rocket on its launch pad its mass is decreasing rapidly due to the hot gases being shot out of its rear end, so you cannot use $F = ma$. Again, if you want the force exerted by a stream of water or the force of the wind on the side of a building, you cannot use $F = ma$, since the speed can be constant and $a = 0$, but there is certainly a force.

9.2 Newton said that the force was proportional to the rate of change in momentum, or

$$F = \frac{d\,(mv)}{dt}$$

If we use the product rule we get

$$F = m\frac{dv}{dt} + v\frac{dm}{dt}$$

and the second term takes care of both the cases mentioned in the previous question.

9.3 Any object moving round in a circle must have a centripetal force to keep pulling it to the centre of the circle. It is the force of gravity that keeps the Moon circling the Earth.

9.4 The theory of relativity tells us that it is impossible to detect absolute motion at constant speed. Thus if you were out in deep space and the only thing you could see was another space ship, there would be no way you could tell how fast each was moving. But as soon as one space ship began to accelerate you could tell, since acceleration implies a force and we can measure forces absolutely.

9.5 If the two galaxies became a little further apart, the attractive force would get a little less ($1/d^2$) and the repulsive force would get a little more ($F \propto d$) and so the system would be unstable. The galaxies would move even further apart.

9.6 Conversely, if the galaxies became a little closer the attractive force would get more, the repulsive force would get less and the two galaxies would move even closer together – a highly unstable situation.

9.7 The galaxies are getting further apart, the system is not stable. We do not live in a stationary universe.

9.8 We think the galaxies are getting further apart for many reasons, the most important of which is the 'red shift'. The spectral lines of the galaxies are shifted towards the red end of the spectrum indicating, according to the theory of the Doppler effect, that they are going away from us.

9.9 On the contrary. Their mistakes were made at the very edge of human thinking. 'The foolishness of God is wiser than the wisdom of men.'

9.10 There is far too much visual pollution on Earth. Telescopes are now placed on mountain tops as far from the glare of cities as possible, but can still be used only occasionally. The telescopes placed on mountains in Hawaii have suffered from the obscuring effects of volcanic debris. There is also a very real threat that may prevent the use of all optical telescopes on Earth. The Celestis Corporation of Florida is actively promoting a scheme whereby the cremated remains of 15 000 people are to be compressed into 3 cm cubes, packed into a satellite of mass 150 kg and put into orbit round the Earth. The satellite would be provided with a large mirror so that it could easily be seen from Earth. It is expected that many hundreds of these would be sent up and they would collectively be so bright that visual astronomy would be at an end.

The French also had a scheme to send up a set of 100 large spheres joined into a ring. This was planned for 1989, to commemorate the anniversary of the building of the Eiffel Tower. Each sphere would appear twice as bright as the Pole Star. The whole ring would be at a height of 800 km and would circle the Earth every 90 minutes. We were assured, however, that these would have only a limited life and would not prevent visual astronomy for long. I do not know if it took place.

9.11 No, it is not a geostationary orbit (one in which the period of the satellite is 24 hours). It is much lower and the reason is so that it can be taken up and serviced by the space shuttle. All the proposed experiments that are waiting for the shuttle to return to service are planned for heights of 500–600 km. I make the period to be about 6000 s or about 100 minutes.

9.12 The age of the universe is thought to be about 15 billion years. The telescope will thus glean some information about the very early universe, and this may help cosmologists to decide between rival theories concerning the history of the universe.

9.13 The faint-object spectrometer (f.o.s.) will be used to study the light from very distant quasars; an f.o.s. attached to the telescope at Palma has already analysed light from quasars that are nearly as old as the universe. The f.o.s. has fewer optical parts than conventional spectrometers have, and so suffers less loss in light intensity.

9.14 It is possible to determine absolutely the motion of rotating objects since they experience centripetal forces. Einstein's theory of special relativity only applies to inertial observers (those moving in straight lines at constant speeds relative to each other).

The space shuttle

10.1 Total thrust = 28.6 MN.

Total initial mass = 2.2×10^6 kg.

Net thrust = $28.6 - 22 = 6.6$ MN (taking $g = 10$ m s^{-2}, near enough).

Acceleration = $6.6/2.2 = 3$ m s^{-2}.

10.2 Starting from rest, $v = at = 3 \times 120 = 360$ m s^{-1}, and the height $d = \frac{1}{2}at^2 = \frac{1}{2} \times 3 \times (120)^2 = 21.6$ km.

10.3 Our answer is far too low. Obviously the acceleration goes up as the mass decreases. Note, the craft does not go up exactly vertically, in fact the orbiter seems to turn on its back; but that will hardly affect things.

10.4 After two minutes, the total mass is 0.83×10^6 kg and the force of gravity on this mass is 8.3 MN. The net thrust is 22.7 MN and so the new acceleration is $22.7/0.83 = 27.5$ m s^{-2}.

10.5 Taking the average of this acceleration, 27.5 m s^{-2}, and the initial acceleration, 3 m s^{-2}, we have the average of 15 m s^{-2} (near enough). Then we find the speed after 120 s is $15 \times 120 = 1800$ m s^{-1} and the height reached is $d = \frac{1}{2} \times 15 \times (120)^2 = 108$ km.

10.6 Now our answer is too big, no nearer than before. Taking the average assumes the acceleration goes up linearly – obviously, we were wrong.

10.7 After 1 minute, the total thrust is 30 MN and the total mass is 1.5 million kg. The force of gravity on the mass is 15 MN and so the net thrust is $30-15 = 15$ MN. Hence the acceleration is $15/1.5 = 10$ m s^{-2}. We plot the three points for the acceleration, and join up in a smooth curve.

Then we find the area under the graph for the four 30 s intervals and find this:

(a) 30 × 4.2   126 m s^{-1}
(b) 30 × 8   240
(c) 30 × 13   390
(d) 30 × 21.5   645
Total   1400 m s^{-1}

and by a piece of good luck (thoroughly deserved) this has come out very near the given value of 1390 m s^{-1}.

10.8 We really ought to have taken smaller intervals than 30 s.

10.9 We now plot the speed–time graph, using the values we got in an earlier part.

Again we find the areas under the graph for each of the 30 s intervals. Then we get the distance travelled as:

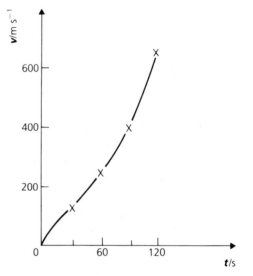

(a) 30 × 120   3.6 km
(b) 30 × 240   7.2 km
(c) 30 × 390   11.7 km
(d) 30 × 645   19.2 km
Total   41.7 km

and this compares with the figure given by NASA of 45.6 km.

10.10 Again we have taken too large steps, 30 s, for our integration. Note, too, in plotting this last graph we assumed that for each interval, the speed was the average of the first and last. In fact, the speed would go up more as the mass got less.

10.11 The wings and control surfaces of the orbiter tend to set up forces leading to instability and extra rudder surface is needed to counteract these. It cannot be an effect of the extra weight of the orbiter vehicle, as the 747 is designed to carry that weight in its cargo holds.

10.12 The orbiter vehicles are essentially gliders and so the pilots have only one chance when landing. There is no option of going round and trying again. The pilots must become very skilled at handling the craft.

10.13 The acceleration is given by $a = F/m = 0.54$ m s^{-2} and so the speed is given by $v = u + at = 0.54 \times 160 = 86$ m s^{-1}. This is near enough to the given value of 90 m s^{-1}.

10.14 Unless I have made a mistake, the agreement is hopeless (and the data came from NASA). From the distance and time, I get $v = 9 \times 10^3$ m s^{-1} and so $v^2 = 8 \times 10^7$ m^2 s^{-2}. From the gravitational force, I get GM/R to be 6×10^7. At least we agree on the number of zeros and if I have made a mistake it is probably in converting the Imperial units to civilised ones and the error is pardonable.

10.15 This is a real puzzle. We would expect the ratio of the masses to be 8:1, since the relative atomic mass of oxygen is 16. I can only assume that because it is lighter, the hydrogen issues from its tank at greater speed than the oxygen and thus a proportion of it does not take part in the reaction. But if this is so, why is the ratio so close to 6:1?

Earth satellites

11.1 The mathematical answer is that the mass m cancels in the equation. In fact, you probably know already that the mass does not come into it. When the space shuttle is circling the Earth in stable orbit, it can open its cargo doors and a communications satellite can be taken out and placed in orbit. The speed of the shuttle and satellite stays the same. When an astronaut gets out of a space ship to take a 'space walk' the speed of the ship does not change, even if its mass does.

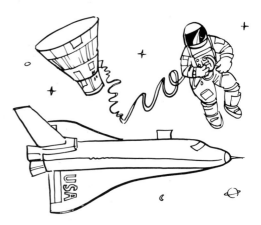

11.2 It depends on the speed and the way it happens. If the satellite is given an enormous speed, it can shoot off into space. At lower speeds, it may go into an elliptical orbit or it may go into a higher stable circular orbit (trading k.e. for p.e.). Strictly speaking, it will be an elliptical orbit but it may be so nearly circular as makes no difference.

11.3 The child will swing out, so that the chain follows a conical path. The horizontal component of the tension in the chain provides the centripetal force to keep the child going round in a circle.

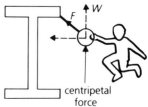

11.4 When the top of the roundabout jams, the child will continue to rotate round the pole, but as the radius gets less (as the chain wraps round the pole) the speed will increase.

11.5 When you are doing the standard experiment of whirling a rubber bung round on the end of a string, put your fist in the way; the string will wrap round your fist and the bung will go faster (incidentally showing the conservation of angular momentum).

11.6 The formula includes v^2, so it must always be positive.

11.7 We know that the further from the Sun, the longer is the periodic time. Thus Mercury orbits the Sun in 88 days, Mars in 687 days and Pluto in 248 years.

11.8 Unless the satellites (or the electrons) collide, there can be no other forms of energy to concern us. (We are assuming that there is no dust – normally – to provide friction.)

11.9 If we assume that the electron is a massive object circling a stationary nucleus and put the numbers in the formula (as was first done by Nils Bohr), we get the right answer for the wavelengths of the emitted light and you can't ask for more than that. To say that an electron is a probability cloud is not more 'realistic' than to say that it is a lump of matter. Use whichever picture turns you on.

11.10 The missile is slightly behind the target because, being lower, it has to travel faster and so will catch up with its target. Conversely, if it is put into a higher orbit it would have to be in front of its target to allow the target to catch up. Clearly, it is better to put the missile into the lower orbit.

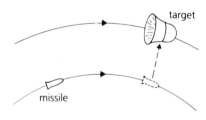

11.11 The Russian system is very slow because each requires the launch of a liquid-fuelled rocket, which takes time. They can only reach 2400 km. They may have to wait an average of 6 hours for the satellite to come into view. The American system is far more advanced. A small homing vehicle, mass 15 kg and diameter 30 cm, is fitted with infra-red sensors and carried aloft by an F15 fighter. It can be launched in minutes. It is so accurate that it destroys its target by hitting it directly, without explosives.

11.12 Putting the centripetal force mv^2/r equal to the gravitational force GMm/r^2, we get $v^2 = 5.6 \times 10^7$ m^2 s^{-2} and this gives a speed of 7.5 km s^{-1}.

11.13 The k.e. is then 2.8×10^{10} J.

11.14 The work done in lifting the satellite to this height is $mgh = 7.4 \times 10^{10}$ J.

11.15 The precise formula for the work done is $GMm(1/R_1 - 1/R_2)$ and this equals $GMmh/R(R+h)$, where R is the radius of the Earth and h is the height above the surface of the Earth. The approximate formula is $mgh = GMmh/R^2$. Thus the two formulae are the same except that $(R + h)$ is replaced by R. In this case, $(R + h) = 7140$ km and R is 6400 km; they differ by a little more than 10 per cent.

11.16 The k.e. is equal to half the p.e. of the satellite measured from the centre of the Earth, not the work done in raising the satellite from the surface of the Earth to its working height. The p.e. measured from the centre of the Earth is $GMm/(R + h) = 5.6 \times 10^{10}$ J.

11.17 There is a repulsive force between your head and the football, but an attractive force between Jupiter and *Voyager*.

11.18 There was never any contact between Jupiter and *Voyager*, so there could be no form of energy for any loss to be converted into.

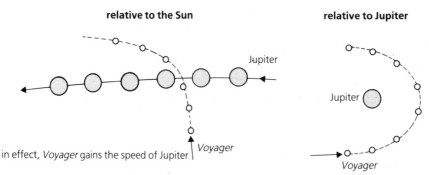

relative to the Sun

relative to Jupiter

Jupiter

in effect, *Voyager* gains the speed of Jupiter | *Voyager*

Jupiter

Voyager

11.19 As there is no conceivable way in which the change in speed of Jupiter (of the order of 10^{-20} m s^{-1}) could be measured, we may assume it never happened. I suppose that astrologers must be very worried about this sort of thing though.

11.20 Equating the centripetal force with the force of gravitation, we get

$$m\omega^2 R = \frac{GMm}{R^2}$$

or

$$M = \frac{\omega^2 R^3}{G}$$

Here $\omega = 2\pi/1.77 \times 24 \times 60 \times 60$ rad s^{-1}, and $R = 3.5 \times 10^8$ m. Inserting the figures, I find that the mass of Jupiter is, near enough, 2×10^{27} kg, or about 300 times the mass of the Earth.

Moon rocket

12.1 Total mass = 2.7 million kg.
Total thrust = 33.8 MN.
Net thrust = 33.8 − 27 = 6.8 MN.
$a = F/m = 6.8/2.7 = 2.5$ m s^{-2}.

12.2 Total mass = 0.6 million kg.
Total thrust = 33.8 MN
Net thrust = 33.8 − 6 = 27.8 MN.
$a = F/m = 27.8/0.6 = 46$ m s^{-2}.

12.3 The average acceleration = 24 m s^{-2}.
Speed after 2.5 minutes = 24 × 150 = 3600 m s^{-1}.

12.4 Obviously our figure is too high. When we plot a graph of the acceleration against time, we get the dotted line, as shown, and not the straight line we assumed. We should really have calculated the acceleration for several time intervals.

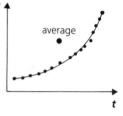

12.5 Total thrust = 5.2 MN, and this is less than the force of gravity on the total mass remaining. Clearly there is something fishy about our figures.
Acceleration $a = F/m = 5.2 \times 10^6 / 6 \times 10^5 \approx 9$ m s^{-2}.

12.6

Average distance /km	Change in speed /m s^{-1}	Acceleration /m s^{-2}	aR^2 /m^3 s^{-2}
27 668	−272	−272/600 = −4.5	3.6 × 10^{14}
55 362	−73	−73/600 = −1.2	3.6 × 10^{14}
6 400	−	= −9.8	3.9 × 10^{14}

The last figure is for the surface of the Earth, and this shows a bigger disagreement than I would have expected.

12.7 There are free electrons in a conductor and they can absorb the energy of incident photons. The Earth is a conductor and will not transmit radio waves; they have to be beamed up to Earth satellites for long-distance transmission.

12.8 In a bridge there are conductors (usually the steel reinforcing rods in concrete) which absorb the radio signal.

12.9 I have not noticed this myself. It could be because the radio wave is polarised and absorption will happen more noticeably when the electric vector of the radio wave is aligned with the metal rods.

12.10 The whole car is metal and acts as a Faraday cage, so radio waves must be picked up outside the car. The same would happen if you lived in a house clad with corrugated iron.

12.11 The craft passes through this critical part very much more quickly – it goes almost straight up. On the return journey the craft hits this layer almost tangentially, so as to get the greatest slowing effect. It is possible for a returning space ship to 'bounce' off the atmosphere and go out into space if the angle is too shallow.

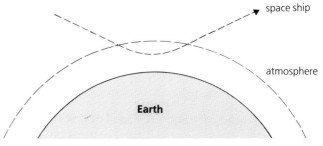

Gullibility

13.1 We assume that above a flat earth the value of g is constant at the value $g = GM/R^2$. Above a spherical earth at a height h above the surface it is $g' = GM/(R+h)^2 = GM/R^2(1+h/R)^2 \approx GM(1-2h/R)/R^2$ if $h \ll R$. Therefore $g - g'/g = 2h/R$. For this fractional difference to be less than 5% we must go up less than 2.5% of the radius of the Earth, namely 160 km. For a difference of 1% a height of 32 km is needed. Clearly as far as ordinary living is concerned we can consider that g is constant, and that we live on a flat Earth. But when the motion of ICBMs and Earth satellites is considered we have to use the inverse-square law.

Tychonian system

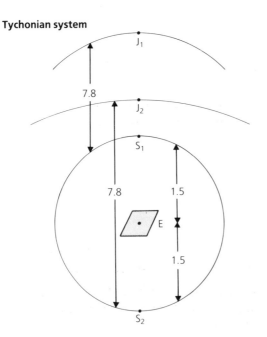

13.2 When, in six months, the Sun goes from S_1 to S_2, Jupiter goes from J_1 to J_2. The Earth–Jupiter distance changes from 6.3×10^{11} m to 9.3×10^{11} m.

Copernican system

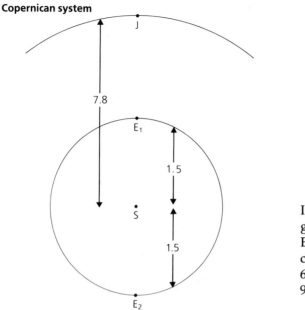

In six months, the Earth goes from E_1 to E_2. The Earth–Jupiter distance changes from 6.3×10^{11} m to 9.3×10^{11} m.

And the same will be found for all positions of the planets.

13.3 For Venus, one of the inferior planets, the position is quite different. In the Tychonian system, it circles a stationary Earth and so its distance from the Earth is constant. In the Copernican system, its distance varies from 0.5×10^{11} m to 2.5×10^{11} m.

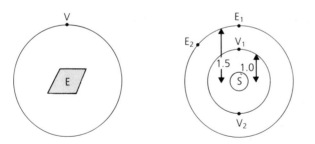

13.4 If the Sun goes round a fixed Earth, the force of gravitational attraction provides the necessary centripetal force, so

$$\frac{GM_SM_E}{d^2} = M_S\omega^2 d$$

or

$$\omega^2 = \frac{GM_E}{d^3}$$

Substituting the figures, we get $\omega = 2.5 \times 10^{-10}$ rad s^{-1}, and $T = 3 \times 10^{10}$ s or about 1000 years (our present years, that is).

13.5 The Tychonians' reply would be, 'Newton's law of gravitation was framed for a heliocentric system. As that system does not exist, neither does Newton's law.'

13.6 We need Newton's Law of gravitation, $F = GMm/d^2$.

The force on the baby due to the midwife
$= 6.7 \times 10^{-11} \times 80 \times 4/(0.5)^2 = 8 \times 10^{-8}$ N

The force on the baby due to Mars
$= 6.7 \times 10^{-11} \times 6.4 \times 10^{23} \times 4/(2.2 \times 10^{11})^2 = 3.5 \times 10^{-9}$ N

Thus the midwife exerts about twenty times the gravitational force on the child as Mars. A similar result holds for all the other planets. Jupiter is more massive than Mars, but is further away.

13.7 'The astrological influence is neither gravitational, magnetic nor anything else known to man. It is a completely distinct effect which cannot be detected by any physical means.'

13.8 We equate the centripetal force acting on the Sun, $F = m\omega^2 r$, with the force of gravitation, $F = GMm/r^2$. This leads to $\omega^2 = GM/r^3$. When I insert the figures, I get $\omega = 3.4 \times 10^{-10}$ rad s^{-1} and I find that this leads to the period of one revolution of about 580 years. But the problem is ridiculous since it is not possible for 'the Earth to rotate about the Sun' or 'the Sun to rotate about the Earth'. In fact they rotate about each other, the centre of rotation being their common centre of mass. Because the Sun is very much more massive than the Earth, this is very close to the centre of the Sun. So to say 'the Earth rotates about the Sun' is very nearly correct.

13.9 If we now substitute the value of 9×10^5 m in the formula of the previous question, we get $\omega = 0.02$ rad s^{-1} and this gives a period of 300 s or 5 minutes.

13.10 When you plot the graph, you get a figure for the population of the world in 2500 B.C. of about 800. We may then assume that 80 people (men, women and children) were available for the job. As it is known that the pyramid took only about 20 years to build, they must have been busy. It is generally thought that, in fact, about 100 000 men were used when they could be released from their jobs on the farm. The Pharaoh of the time could not have borrowed labourers from other places in the world as vast building projects in China, India, Indo-China and the Middle East were also going on at the same time.

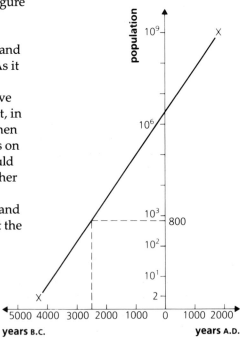

Credulity

14.1 The acceleration is found from $a = v^2/r$, and so we have $a = 4000$ m s^{-2}.

14.2 We know that the human body can only stand an acceleration of about 50 m s^{-2} for any length of time, without special clothing to restrict the flow of blood.

14.3 Presumably there are alien beings on some other planet, circling some other star in our galaxy (though it is certain none of them have visited us). We can only guess what they must look like, but they will have been subject to the same evolutionary forces as us. They will also be based on the same kind of replicating molecule as DNA and on the same basic chemistry. Precursor molecules to DNA have been found elsewhere in the solar system and probably exist in other parts of the galaxy. Although they may use different proteins they will not be all that different in shape. They will not have blue heads or have eyes sticking out on stalks, and they are unlikely to be super-resistant to acceleration. They could be totally different from us, like the creatures in *The hitch-hikers' guide to the galaxy* – just a blue flash of light – but then they would not zoom about in space ships.

14.4 At a temperature inversion, the temperature changes from cold to hotter and the speed of light increases. This is analogous to waves on a string encountering a lighter string. The wave is reflected (actually without being turned upside down – i.e. without phase change) at the join.

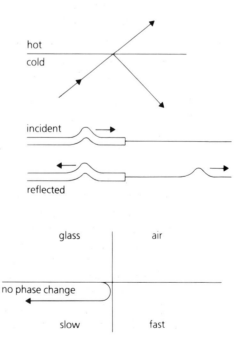

14.5 The analogy here is with light waves reflected at a glass–air boundary, as in the Newton's rings experiment.

14.6 We expect that radar waves will not be able to go through clouds because they will be scattered as light waves are. We know that radar waves are easily absorbed by water in bulk as submarines are not able to use radar to detect enemy ships; sonar waves have to be employed.

14.7 Radar systems basically measure the time between the sending of a radio wave and the receipt of its reflection. Knowing the speed of electromagnetic waves, its range can be calculated. If the plane's height can be given, then its direction is also known.

14.8 (a) The Earth's magnetic field is maintained by electric currents in the core of molten iron. It is difficult to see how these currents could flow in a hollow Earth.

(b) Hollowing out the centre of the Earth would remove about one-eighth of the volume of the Earth, but the most dense part. We may guess that the mass would be reduced by about a quarter. If we know the value of the gravitational constant G and the acceleration due to gravity at the surface g, we can calculate the mass of the Earth from

$$\frac{GMm}{r^2} = mg$$

(c) In a similar way, the rotational inertia of the Earth would be changed, although not by so much. This can be estimated from the small effects on the Earth's rotation due to the Moon.

14.9 Any food that we digest liberates some of its stored energy as heat energy which we need to live.

14.10 At these dilutions, the chances are that not a single molecule of the medicine remains. At the recommended dilutions it is virtually certain that the medicine is as pure water as we can get. Homoeopaths counter this by saying that the water retains the 'memory' of the medicinal molecules and try to baffle you with science by talking about nuclear magnetic resonance which they have read about in one of their texts and which they do not understand. They also say that the shaking and banging are important and help to intensify the healing properties.

14.11 I found the volume of a drop of water by counting one hundred drops into a measuring cylinder. With one dropper I found this to be 3 ml and with another to be 7 ml (to the nearest ml). It is interesting that droppers can vary so much. Presumably when their use is prescribed in medicine, no great precision is needed. We will take 5 ml as the result. Then the volume of 10^{60} drops I find as 5×10^{55} litre. The length of a cube of this volume I make to be 4×10^{17} m, and this is about the distance from Earth to the star Vega.

14.12 The kinetic theory says that the molecules of a liquid are in ceaseless motion; they are also under the influence of attractive, cohesive forces (the cause of the viscosity of a liquid). Any void in a liquid, the space formerly occupied by a medicine molecule, would be quickly occupied.

14.13 Cooling a liquid increases its viscosity and so should, on a homoeopath's view, increase the 'remembering' of absent molecules. Hence cooling should increase the curative powers of the medicine.

14.14 Banging the medicine bottle should, if anything, shake up the molecules even more.

14.15 There would be an inverse law of magnetism, light, electricity and gravitation: $B \propto 1/d$. We now have an inverse law for the magnetic field due to the current in a long straight wire. A magnetic field is due to electrons moving in a circle; in a two-dimensional world, all the electrons would circle in the same plane. Thus all iron would be permanently magnetised.

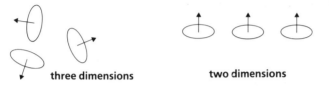

three dimensions   two dimensions

14.16 The power of garlic to kill bacteria is open to objective testing. But the advertiser is such a naive, guileless fellow that I have not the heart to threaten him with the Trades Description Act.

The risks from radiation

15.1 Total cost of motoring £2000 per year. If you are paid at £5 per hour, that is 400 hours work and that means approximately 50 km per hour. If you include the actual time spent driving that distance at 80 km per hour (250 hours) and all the hours the average car-owner spends washing the wretched thing, changing the spark plugs and whatnot, we easily get a total of 800 hours, that is 25 km per hour – a bit more than Illich calculated, but still slower than cycling. R. North, in a fascinating book called *The true cost*, says that the average American devotes 1600 hours per year to his car (driving it, washing it, sitting in traffic jams and working to pay for it). On average, he drives about 12 000 km a year and this works out at about 8 km h^{-1}.

15.2 That all those who died from smoking in New Zealand were heavy smokers; we could perhaps infer that if you smoke less than 20 per day, you won't die from it. In fact, we know that even one cigarette a day adds something to the risk.

15.3 We assumed that people start smoking at the age of 20; 15 would be nearer the mark. We assumed that all smokers consume only 20 per day; unfortunately some smoke as many as 100, that is one every ten waking minutes.

15.4 Both these errors will decrease the calculated risk; smokers do so for up to 55 years on average, and the risk is spread over more cigarettes.

15.5 We compare 0.17 and 0.000 34, approximately 600:1.

15.6 About half of all accidental deaths are due to cars (250 per million compared to 476 per million). That is about 1 in 60 of all deaths.

15.7 Your life expectancy goes up as all the weaklings die off. Imagine you are blindfold and try to cross a busy street; your chances of making it improve the further you go.

15.8 Presumably the level of damage needed to hurt your sex cells is more than that needed to kill you. A massive dose of X-rays will damage the DNA in almost every cell in your body, making repair and production of new cells impossible.

15.9 Of all the human eggs that are fertilised, most fail to implant successfully into the wall of the uterus. When implantation is taking place, the first tissues go to make the support systems that surround the embryo (such as the yolk sac). Among the cells left over are those that will make the embryo (called the primitive streak). In over half the cases, the primitive streak fails to form and the implantation fails. Foetuses damaged by radiation are usually among those that are spontaneously aborted at a very early stage, usually without the mother being aware of her pregnancy. This is one of the dangers of radiation that is not detected.

15.10 I guess that the hydroxyl ion, being much more massive than the proton, would cause much more damage.

15.11 The break in a single strand of DNA is the easiest to repair. There is a very efficient repair system at work all the time. It must also be easy to make up for a loss of a cross-linking base, if there are enough of them about, as this happens naturally when DNA splits.

Isolation transformers

16.1 Those that combine water and electricity, like concrete mixers. Also those like hedge-clippers and power saws where it is only too easy to cut the power line.

16.2 If you grab both wires you can kill yourself, but it takes a determined effort. However, there will be the resistance of both your hands, which may be more than the resistance of your feet and shoes. In that case, the shock might not be lethal.

16.3 Certainly; neither side of the secondary is earthed (we say the supply is floating). So you cannot complete the circuit. In any case, the voltage of most lab transformers is so low that the current through you will not be harmful.

16.4 For trains and trams, the return can be through the earth. Trolley buses run on rubber tyres and so the circuit cannot be completed in this way. You would think that trolley buses could trail a wire behind them as an earth, but it does not seem to work.

16.5 Gumboots have a very high resistance, but not an infinite one. Thus if you grab a live wire while wearing this item of the national costume, a small current will flow through you. The current may be too small for you to notice, but it will not be zero. In the same way, if you grab both terminals of a 1½ V cell, there will be a minute current through you.

16.6 The inside of the television tube is coated with a conducting layer that looks like carbon. This is earthed to provide a Faraday cage to shield the electrons from any stray electric fields which might cause the picture to be distorted. The electrons are accelerated by a voltage that is positive with respect to this electrode.

16.7 A 6 V transformer connected to a 12 V supply will give twice the voltage on the secondary as a 12 V transformer.

16.8 The snag is that the 6 V transformer will draw twice the current from the battery, and might burn out. The current is limited by the ballast resistor.

16.9 In the transformer, the power is almost the same for primary and secondary (*power = voltage × current*). In the brake system, the work done (the integrated power) is the same (*work = force × distance*).

16.10 You can't, unless you know whether it is a step-up transformer or a step-down one. If it is a step-up transformer, then the primary will have the smaller voltage, the bigger current and so the thicker wire. If you can open up the transformer you can count the number of turns in a winding and work out the voltage since, as a rule, there are ten turns per volt.

16.11 In an isolation transformer there is no difference between the primary and secondary, since both handle the same voltage and so carry the same current.

16.12 Since it is 99 per cent efficient, 1 per cent of the power is transformed into heat energy. (I suspect there is something wrong here. You cannot transform power into energy, they are different quantities; never mind.) 1 per cent of 90 kW is 900 W or, roughly, one kW, the heat given out by a single-bar electric heater. In practice, most transformers are better than 99.5 per cent efficient.

16.13 There is still quite a lot of heat energy to be dissipated to the atmosphere. That is why there are the cooling fins which you can see: they look like tubes, about 3 cm in diameter. They carry cooling oil from the iron core which tends to get hot (not so much the copper windings). The oil moves by convection. A tiny amount of energy is lost as sound; you can hear the transformer humming merrily away.

The Mitsubishi Lancer

17.1

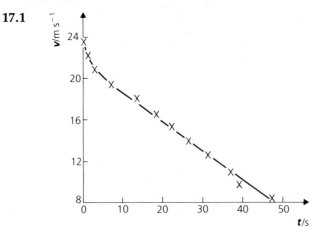

17.2 For the last part, the graph is a straight line of negative slope. This shows that there was a constant deceleration. Before this, the gradient is steeper, showing a greater force of air resistance.

17.3

v/m s^{-1}	23.6	22.2	20.8	19.4	18.0	16.6	15.3	13.9	12.5	11.1	9.70	8.30
v^2/m^2 s^{-2}		494	434	378	326	278	233	193	156	123	95	69
t/s		1.3	3.19	7.51	13.3	18.4	22.2	26.7	31.5	37.2	39.2	47.1
Δt/s		1.3	1.89	4.32	5.78	5.11	3.85	3.54	4.88	5.7	1.2	7.93
a/m s^{-2}		1.1	0.74	0.32	0.24	0.26	0.36	0.4	0.29	0.24	–	–

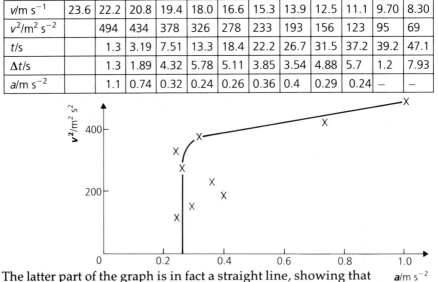

17.4 The latter part of the graph is in fact a straight line, showing that there the force is proportional to the (speed)^2. What is surprising is that the graph goes off the linear relationship at such a high speed (about 20 m s^{-1}). This is the speed below which air friction is negligible. The books say that air resistance begins to be important at speeds as low as 50 km h^{-1} (14 m s^{-1}). This can only mean that my car has so much rolling friction that it swamps the air resistance.

17.5   It is best for her to let the car stop by itself and only apply the brakes when she has to. In theory the faster the car is going, the greater the slowing due to air resistance. If the car is travelling slowly, air friction will not slow it further. If the data for my car means anything, however, air resistance has virtually no effect at speeds that are legal within built-up areas. Moreover, if she keeps her speed up, she will be able to zoom away if the light should change in her favour unexpectedly quickly.

17.6   Horizontally the car goes at 80 km h^{-1}, so in one second it goes about 22 m. Vertically, the engine turns at 6000 r.p.m. and this is 100 r.p.s. The piston will rise and fall by equal amounts in each cycle. Hence, in one second, it will move vertically 200×10 cm = 20 m. Thus we see that the horizontal and vertical distances are nearly the same.

17.7   For an s.h.m., the frequency f is 200 Hz and so the angular velocity ω is $2\pi f = 2\pi \times 200 = 400\pi$ rad s^{-1}. The amplitude A is half the stroke = 5 cm. The maximum speed is given by $v = \omega A = 20\pi$ m s^{-1}. Thus the maximum vertical speed is about three times the average horizontal speed.

17.8   The car travels about 10 km on one litre of gas, so we want the cross-sectional area of a tube 10 km long of capacity 1 litre. As $V = A \times 1$, $A = V/l$: thus the area of the tube is 10^{-3} m^3/10^4 m. This gives us a (radius)^2 given by $r^2 = 10^{-7}/\pi = 3 \times 10^{-8}$ m^2. So r is 1.7×10^{-4} m = 0.17 mm. The trough would be about the size of a fine fuse wire. It wasn't such a brilliant idea after all.

17.9   If all the mass is on the rim, we have $I = Mr^2 = 1$ kg m^2.

17.10   The k.e. $= \frac{1}{2}I\omega^2 = 1.28$ MJ.

17.11   For the bus, k.e. $= \frac{1}{2}mv^2 = 1.35$ MJ. These two values are nearly equal and so the flywheel stores enough energy to get the bus to full speed from rest.

17.12   The angular acceleration of the flywheel is

$$\alpha = \frac{d\omega}{dt}$$
$$= \frac{1600}{50 \times 60}$$
$$\alpha = \frac{8}{15} \text{ rad s}^{-2}$$

The frictional torque is

$$I\alpha = \frac{8}{15} \text{ N m}$$

In stopping from 1600 rad s^{-1} the wheel turns through

$$\theta = \tfrac{1}{2} \times 1600 \times 50 \times 60$$
$$= 2.4 \times 10^6 \text{ rad}$$

The work done is then

$$\text{torque} \times \theta = \frac{8}{15} \times 2.4 \times 10^6$$
$$= 1.28 \text{ MJ}$$

This is the answer we got for question **17.10**.

17.13 The caravan swings behind a car like a compound pendulum. Putting more mass at the back will increase the period and make it swing slower. If it swung with bigger amplitude, there must have been a resonance between the new period and the period of the instabilities in the car.

17.14 Inserting the figures in the formula gives $F = 1$ kN.

17.15 Power is given by $P = F \times v$, which gives 37 kW. This is less than the quoted value of 43.4 kW. The discrepancy lies in the fact that there is no way that I could find the constant rolling friction from the brochure and I have neglected it.

17.16 The acceleration is F/m and I make this about 1.4 m s^{-2}.
   When I measured the acceleration of my car, using the home-made accelerometer in the drawing, I got a value of about 1.0 m s^{-2}. I have little confidence in this measurement, however, as the calibration of the accelerometer is tricky. As the car starts up the engine is running more slowly than when it is moving fast so the initial force is certainly less than that found in **17.14**.

air bubble

water–alcohol mixture

17.17 Power P is also given by $P = torque \times angular\ velocity$. In this case, torque $= 105$ N m and the angular velocity $\omega = 3500 \times 2\pi/60$, giving a value of 38 kW – comfortingly close to the previous value.

Firewalking

18.1 The whole quiche has just come out of the oven and it has been cooking long enough for the whole to have reached the temperature of the oven.

18.2 The hot-water bottle is cuddly because water has such a high specific heat capacity. A hot-copper bottle would be pretty useless since copper has a specific heat capacity about one-tenth that of water; it would be cold within a few minutes. Best of all, of course, is to share one's bed with one's spouse, who is continually converting chemical energy into heat energy and who therefore has an almost infinite store of heat energy.

18.3 The air in the oven is at a high temperature but there is very little of it. The whole ovenful has a mass of less than 100 g, and the air in contact with your hand has mass of only a few grams (air is a bad conductor of heat).

18.4 The steel of the oven tray has a mass of at least a kilogram and so the tray contains much more heat energy than the air, even though the specific heat capacity of air is about twice that of steel. The main point, however, is that steel is a much better conductor of heat, so that as your blood takes heat energy away from your fingers, the steel supplies copious quantities, enough to burn your skin. The coefficient of thermal conductivity of steel is about 10^4 times that of air.

18.5 Pumice is full of air holes and so has a very small specific heat capacity; it is also very light, so a lump of it will have very little heat energy. There is no need to go into a trance to walk on it but the Fijians are canny. They will not let tourists try it (they want the tourist dollars).

18.6 The teacher's feet will scorch (and no sympathy for him); once again it is not the temperature that matters here, it is the heat energy.

18.7 The heat energy converted from electrical energy is $1000 \times 2 = 2000$ J $= 2$ kJ. The heat energy stored in the hot-plate is $0.5 \times 0.1 \times 300 = 15$ kJ. The total energy $= 17$ kJ.

18.8 The hot-plate will continue to lose heat energy until its temperature is the same as that of the guru, until both are at a common temperature. This is analogous to what happens when you earth a charged object. In fact, you share the charge between the object and the Earth until their electrical potential becomes the same. However, because the Earth has such an enormous capacity for charge compared to any object anyone is likely to have, we can say that all the charge goes into the Earth and none remains on the object. In the same way, if we put a hot object touching a cold one, heat energy will flow from the hot one to the cold one until they are at the same temperature.

18.9 It is not the boiling point that matters, but the temperature difference between the boiling point and the skin temperature. Thus water is cooled from 373 K to 293 K on touching a human, and the heat energy needed to cool 1 kg of water is $4190 \times 80 = 335$ kJ. The oil would be cooled from 570 K to 293 K and so the equivalent heat energy value is $290 \times 1970 = 571$ kJ, about 1.5 times the value for water. Strictly, the calculation should take into account the lower density of oil because a cauldron full of oil would weigh less than a similar volume of water, but that would be comparatively unimportant.

18.10 I estimate that the area of shoe supporting my foot is 18×8 cm. The normal pressure on the ground is then $60 \times 10/1.44 \times 10^{-2}$ Pa and I make this to be about 40 kPa. For the soldiers in the minefield, the area is 0.1 m^2 and the pressure is 6 kPa. When you are running across white-hot embers, I guess the area to be 2 cm $\times$ 1 cm and this leads to a pressure of 30 000 kPa. Thus great pressure is exerted by firewalkers and this must increase the damage to the feet.

18.11 If you add the milk first, the volume of the drink increases, the surface of cup that is heated is increased and so more heat energy is lost from the sides. Moreover, china (or polystyrene) is a poor conductor of heat, so the part of the cup above the level of the drink does not get hot and therefore does not radiate heat energy.

18.12 The hotter the liquid is, the more quickly it loses heat (Newton's law of cooling). So if you delay adding milk, the coffee will cool quickly; then you can add the milk for more cooling.

18.13 Newton wanted to find out how old the Earth was, and so needed to calculate how long it would have taken to cool down from a molten mass. Some of the first studies of the effects of scaling were undertaken in this field. People heated iron spheres of different sizes and compared the rate at which they lost heat. They then scaled up to calculate the rate at which the Earth would have lost heat since it was a molten lump. In the last century, Lord Kelvin repeated the calculation and got an answer of only a few million years. He thought this was too short a time for humans to have evolved from primitive creatures and so decided not to accept the theory of evolution. We now know that the rocks at the centre of the Earth are kept in a molten state by the heat evolved in the decay of radioactive atoms in the core. When this is taken into account, we can see that the Earth may be billions of years old. Lord Kelvin did not know about radioactivity.

18.14 The work done is $14 \times 10 \times 2 \times 2 \times 20 = 10\,000 = 10^4$ J.

18.15 The energy needed to heat 7 kg of water by 1 K is $4200 \times 7 = 30\,000$ J. Hence the maximum temperature rise that Joule could measure would be about $\frac{1}{3}$ K. Joule's experiments, apart from being so important for theoretical reasons, were especially noteworthy for their great attention to detail. Joule allowed for the heat energy that went into heating the water container (although he made sure that this was very small). He even allowed for the sound energy lost when the weights hit the floor.

18.16 If 1 kg falls 100 m, the p.e. lost is 1000 J and so the maximum temperature rise would be about $\frac{1}{4}$ K. For these experiments Joule made several mercury-in-glass thermometers that were very sensitive. They were very long, with very thin mercury columns and very thin glass bowls at the bottom for mercury reservoirs. He had to calibrate them individually.

18.17 The gravitational field due to a flat Earth has parallel flux lines. As far as our daily lives are concerned, we live on a flat Earth. In the eighteenth century, one ingenious scientist measured the curvature of the Earth by observing the curvature of the water on a very long canal. Unfortunately some members of the Flat Earth Society then came along and their measurements proved that the Earth is flat.

18.18 Light from a point source is made parallel after passing through a convex lens (or reflected from a concave mirror) if the source is at the focus.

18.19 We now account for Marco Polo's observation by saying that the boiling point of water would be about 360 K at 4000 m altitude, a drop of over 10 K. Polo's explanation was in line with the beliefs of his contemporaries and no one can do better. The fact that decreasing atmospheric pressure causes a fall in the boiling point was not known for 400 years after Polo's day. Some of the answers given in this book will no doubt be considered laughable by anyone reading them in a hundred years' time.

The Fokker Friendship

19.1 For a mass of 17 700 kg and an acceleration of 2.13 m s^{-2} we have a thrust of 37 700 N. The rolling friction of the plane is not known but we will estimate it from the fact that for a cyclist, it is about 5 N for a mass of 80 kg. This gives about 10 000 N for the aircraft. The total thrust then is 47 700 N. The area under the graph gives a speed at the end of 4 s as 5.65 m s^{-1} and so the power is $F \times v = 47.7$ kN $\times 5.65 = 280$ kW. The total power of both engines is 3670 h.p. $= 3670 \times 750 = 2750$ kW. The discrepancy between the two values is embarrassing. Presumably, the full power of the engines is not being delivered to the craft.

19.2 The acceleration is now 1.76 m s^{-2} and so the thrust for this is 31 000 N. Adding on the rolling friction, assumed constant, we get 41 000 N for the total thrust. The total area under the graph now becomes 13.4 m s^{-1} and so the power = 550 kW. Better, but still not equal to the power at take-off.

19.3 At V_2, we can no longer ignore the air resistance generated by the wings, the drag which is the penalty for the lift they produce. We may estimate this ('guess' is a better word) as one-fifth of the lift. The mass is 17 700 kg, so the weight is 177 000 N. The guess for the drag force is then 35 000 N. The inertial force ($F = ma$) is 17 700 $\times$ 0.88 = 16 000 N. The rolling friction is still 10 000 N and with the drag force gives us a total force of

60 000 N. Multiplying this by the V_2 of 48 m s^{-1}, we get the total power of 2880 kW, gratifyingly close to the value given above. Thus we see that the engines only develop their full power at take-off.

19.4 The accelerometer no longer works – the plane tilts too much as it climbs.

19.5 The centripetal force is mv^2/r. The weight of the plane is mg. If L is the lift provided by the wings, we have the force triangle shown. Then

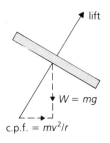

$$\tan \theta = \frac{\text{centripetal force}}{\text{weight}}$$

$$= \frac{v^2}{rg}$$

19.6 The data are given by this table:

$r/\times$ 1000 ft	35	20	13	10	7.5
$\theta/°$	6	10	15	20	25
$\tan \theta$	0.0945	0.176	0.268	0.364	0.464
$1/r/\text{ft}^{-1} \times 10^{-3}$	0.0286	0.050	0.077	0.1	0.133

We plot the graph of $\tan \theta$ against $1/r$ because $\tan \theta \times r = \text{constant } (mv^2)$.

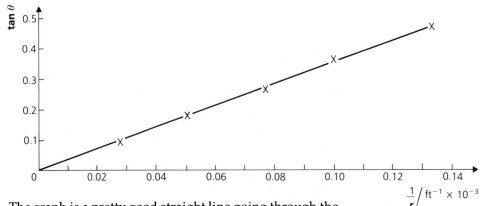

The graph is a pretty good straight line going through the origin.

19.7 The Pitot tube device with only one tube would work but it would not be compensated for changes in atmospheric pressure and these can be almost as big as the changes due to the motion of the aeroplane. The second tube is protected from the effects of movement but is open to the atmosphere.

19.8 When the plane is stationary it does not take in as much air as when it is moving. Thus although the pilot pushes the engine control levers as far forward as possible at the start of take-off they do not deliver maximum power until later. Once the plane begins to move, air resistance increases and so the acceleration begins to go down. The first effect will be roughly proportional to the speed and the second will depend on the square of the speed.

19.9 The higher up you go, the less the atmospheric pressure. This was first shown by Blaise Pascal, who persuaded his brother-in-law Perrier to carry a barometer up the Puy de Dôme. Pascal was too much of an invalid to do this himself. As the mountain is well under 2000 m high, great precision was needed to detect the change in barometer level. It is for this experiment that we name the unit of pressure after Pascal.

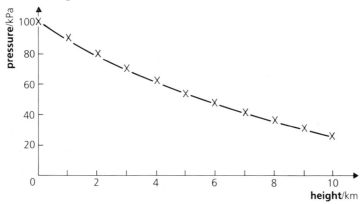

19.10 The defect of this scale is that it is by no means linear with height – in fact the relationship is exponential. Also the barometric pressure at ground level is variable by several kPa. A change of height of about 1000 feet, the difference in height of the different air lanes, corresponds to a difference of 4 kPa per 1000 m at 10 000 m, or about 1 kPa per 1000 feet. Thus the daily differences in barometric pressure at sea level are greater than those due to differences in height of 1000 feet. It is interesting that for flights across the Atlantic and the United States, heights of 30 000, 32 000, 34 000 feet and so on are reserved for travel in one direction and heights such as 31 000, 33 000 and 35 000 feet for the reverse direction. As fuel is consumed, the planes fly at greater heights. Special precautions have to be taken when they change from one height to another.

Presumably, the Chinese have been saved from a great number of mid-air collisions by having so few air liners. In the west, altitudes are no longer measured by barometric means but by radar altimeters, which detect the time for a radar pulse to be reflected back off the Earth. It is difficult to think of an advantage for the Chinese method, except that it relates what is measured to the means of measuring.

19.11 The line of thrust being above the line of drag, the plane is liable to pitch forward when the thrust is increased.

Helicopters

20.1 The torque reaction of the small propeller would tend to make the machine tip forwards or backwards; this could be countered by adjusting the angle of the main propeller, as is normally done to control the forward speed.

20.2 We have the angular speed of the main rotor as $\omega = 33$ rad s^{-1}, and its radius is 7.61 m. The linear velocity of the tip of the rotor is given by $v = \omega r$, and so $v = 33 \times 7.61 = 250$ m s^{-1}. Combining this with the forward speed of the machine, we get the advancing tip's speed as $250 + 61 = 310$ m s^{-1} and the retreating tip's speed as $250 - 61 = 190$ m s^{-1}.

20.3 The speed of the advancing tip is less than the speed of sound, 330 m s^{-1}. If the speed of the main propeller exceeded that of sound, there would be all sorts of trouble with vibrations. It is true that as the temperature gets less, so does the speed of sound, but helicopters do not normally fly at any great height. They do not go high enough for the speed of the rotor to exceed the local speed of sound.

20.4 The tension in the rope due to gravity is $600 \times 10 = 6000$ N and that due to the upward acceleration $= 600 \times 3 = 1800$ N, giving a total tension of 7800 N. We have to add the tensions: the helicopter has to support the insensate animal and at the same time give it an upward acceleration.

20.5 The helicopter is going 7 m s^{-1} faster than its prey. So if the dart is fired directly at the deer, it will pass in front because the dart will have the forward momentum of the aircraft. The catcher must aim at the animal's rump.

20.6 The speed of the advancing tip is $320 - 110 = 210$ m s^{-1} through the air relative to the aircraft, and the corresponding speed of the retreating tip through the air is $210 - 110 = 100$ m s^{-1}.

20.7 There is a twofold difference in the speed of the tips relative to the helicopter, that is, while it is hovering. Hence there has to be a twofold difference in lift provided by the blade. That is why such an enormous angle of attack – 22° – is used. (In aeroplanes 3° is usual.) Notice too, that the speed of the advancing blade tip is kept less than the speed of sound.

20.8 As the star contracts, its rotational inertia decreases and so its speed of rotation increases markedly. We know that white dwarfs and neutron stars rotate at enormous speeds.

20.9 As the child goes towards the centre, the rotational inertia is smaller and so the speed of rotation is bigger.

20.10 Surprisingly, if friction can be neglected it would make a difference. The rotational inertia of the roundabout is $\frac{1}{2}Mr^2$ or 640 kg m². The angular momentum of the child $L = mvr = mv^2/\omega$ (since $v = \omega r$) and this comes to $25 \times 16/\omega = 400/\omega$. Thus when the child is at the edge, the total rotational inertia is $640 + 400 = 1040$ kg m², and when it is at the centre, the total $I = 640$ kg m². So the child really makes a difference. I suppose that the result surprised me because in the days when I pushed children round roundabouts they (the roundabouts) all had so much friction that they stopped long before my children could have reached the centre.

20.11 The ball will go to the right of Q as we see it. The ball has linear momentum to the right before P throws it and will continue to have such after the ball is thrown. Also, if the ball is thrown directly to Q, by the time it arrives Q will have moved to Q'. These two effects would add, for suppose that by some magical means we could dispense with the law of conservation of linear momentum, the second reason would still hold.

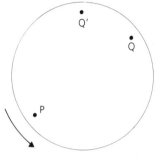

20.12 The mass of the plane is 22 000 kg, so its weight is 220 kN. This equals the thrust in hover, and so the thrust in level flight is 73 kN. The power developed is then $73\,000 \times 130$ (the speed in m s⁻¹) = 9.5 MW. The power of both engines is given as 12 000 h.p. = 9 MW, good enough agreement.

Lightning strikes

21.1 When standing radially, the cow cuts across several equipotential lines, as in A. The cow that is sideways on, as in B, is almost entirely on one equipotential line. These lines are, of course, always perpendicular to the electric field. Thus cow A is in a strong electric field. Cow B is in no electric field.

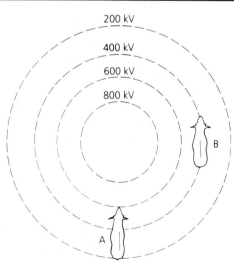

21.2 Electric field is given by $E = dV/dx$. For cow A, $dV = 600\,000 - 200\,000 = 400\,000$ V and $dx = 2$ m; hence the field strength = 200 000 V m⁻¹, quite enough to cause bovine distress.

21.3 The energy stored in a parallel-plate capacitor is given by $E = \frac{1}{2}QV$. So the energy in the discharge = $\frac{1}{2} \times 20 \times 10^8 = 10^9$ J.

21.4 A typical power bill of mine shows a consumption of 700 units in two months (of winter). Now 1 unit is a kilowatt hour $= 1000 \times 60 \times 60$ J. So my monthly consumption comes to $700 \times 1000 \times 3600 = \frac{1}{2} \times 10^9$ J. Hence the average lightning stroke generates enough electrical energy to supply a typical home for a month.

21.5 It is quite all right to treat a thunder cloud as a parallel-plate capacitor. The base of the cloud is parallel to the Earth and its distance from the ground is small compared with its length. There will be some barrelling of the electric field lines at the edge of the cloud, but the effect will be small.

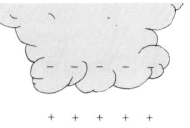

21.6 Using the formula $C = A\varepsilon/d$, I make the capacitance to be about 14×10^{-8} F.

21.7 With the formula $C = Q/V$ we got a value of about 20×10^{-8} F. This agrees very well with the value from the previous question. It shows that the estimates for the dimensions of a thunder cloud were reasonable.

21.8 Current is given by $I = Q/t$ or, if you prefer, $I = -dQ/dt$. So if $dQ = 20$ coulombs and $dt = 1$ ms, then the average current is 2×10^4 A. Incidentally, I prefer to write out the word coulomb in full so as not to confuse it with the symbol C in the formula for a capacitor, $Q = VC$.

21.9 If the flash travels 1 km in 1 ms then its speed is 1000 km s^{-1} or 10^6 m s^{-1}. This is not as fast as one-sixth of the speed of light, which is 5×10^7 m s^{-1}. I think that the time I have given for a lightning flash, about 1 ms, is correct – this has been measured by the rotating camera technique. I think the $c/6$ for the speed of lightning is wrong.

21.10 If the base of the cloud is at 10^8 V and the electric field needed to ionise the air and initiate a discharge is 330 000 V m^{-1}, then the maximum height of the bottom of the cloud is 300 m, a typical figure (it can range from 100 m to 3 km).

21.11 A moving electric charge constitutes an electric current. As it flows it will heat the air surrounding it. As we have seen, the charge moves very quickly and so the sudden heating causes a sudden expansion of the air. This causes the peal of thunder – like the sudden contraction of air when you clap your hands.

21.12 This is a real old wives' tale. There are certain places which are especially prone to thunder and lightning. Parts of West Africa have thunder storms of frightening intensity every day of the rainy season, and sometimes they go on for hours. By contrast, where I live in New Plymouth, New Zealand, electrical storms are very rare; we have maybe one a year at the most. It is necessary for there to be rain clouds with a strong updraught to separate the positive and negative electric charges. High humidity seems to help as well.

21.13 The two clouds must be the same distance above the Earth and so are presumably at the same potential. (There is no spark when they join.) We may also assume that the charge density σ is the same for each as presumably, since they are at the same temperature, the same charge-forming mechanisms are at work. The total charge will then be the sum of the separate charges and the energy will add up in the same way.

21.14 The charge passed is given by
$Q = VC = 6 \times 10^3 \times 16 \times 10^{-6} = 96$ mC. The energy in the discharge is given by $E = \frac{1}{2}QV =$ about 300 J and the current is about 50 A, an enormous figure, certainly enough to stop all heart action.

21.15 The charge is given by $Q = VC = 5$ coulomb. The energy $W = \frac{1}{2}QV = 12.5$ J, about as much as the work done in lifting a 1 kg mass from the floor to the bench top.

21.16 Since $I = Q/t, t = Q/I = 12.5/0.006 = 2000$ s $= 30$ minutes. I would not think that you always get the power on in that time, better put two capacitors in (in series or parallel?).

21.17 The current is 120 μA and that is supposed to be quite safe, causing no more than a tingle, but I would not like to receive it. The power is 960 W, an enormous amount for an electrostatic machine. The high voltage is now usually achieved by a very clever device, the tandem machine. Suppose that the Van de Graaff gives a large positive voltage; then the atoms to be accelerated are first given an extra electron and are attracted to the high-voltage terminal. These negative ions then pass through an 'ion stripper', where two electrons are removed, leaving the ion with a net positive charge. These positive ions are then repelled from the positive terminal and so the effective voltage is doubled.

Washing up

22.1 White light is a mixture of light of many wavelengths, so if the thickness is just right for one wavelength, it will not be right for another. Remembering that a thick film will be many wavelengths thick, there cannot be constructive interference for any range of wavelengths. Even using light from a sodium lamp, which consists almost entirely of light of two wavelengths, we cannot get interference if the film is more than a few wavelengths thick.

There is another point. If the film is thick, then the wave reflected from the bottom surface cannot lie exactly on top of the wave reflected from the upper surface, since it is impossible that the two surfaces could be exactly parallel. The two waves will be out of phase by a variable factor and cannot interfere. It is possible to get interference in thick films if special care is taken to get the two reflecting surfaces exactly parallel (as, in effect, in the Michelson interferometer). It is also possible to get interference in thick films if laser light is used. This deals with both the points raised: the light is essentially monochromatic (of one wavelength) and also coherent (in phase across the wave front).

22.2 You can see very good polarisation effects in a pane of glass. If you look into a pane of glass at an angle of about 50° and rotate a Polaroid sunglass in front of your eye, you will see a variation in the intensity of the light reflected from the glass. The glasses are supposed to reduce the glare from light reflected off water and so must have their planes of polarisation set vertically.

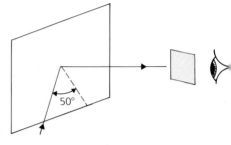

22.3 Yes, a laser gives almost monochromatic light (that is light of a very narrow range in wavelength). There will be no fringes unless both surfaces of the block of glass are optically flat, however.

22.4 Put the surface to be tested on to a surface that is known to be flat and look for interference at the interface between the two. This is how telescope mirrors are tested for accuracy.

22.5 You will see a set of parallel fringes. The distance between each fringe and the next corresponds to an extra distance of one wavelength travelled by the light.

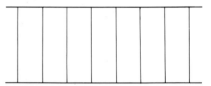

22.6 Newton's rings in transmission have a bright spot in the centre. This is because light is reflected at two surfaces and there is a phase change of $\lambda/2$ at both, bringing both rays back into phase.

22.7 The wavelength quoted ($\lambda = 600$ nm) is for light in air. To get the wavelength in the film we use the definition of refractive index:

$$refractive\ index = \frac{speed\ of\ light\ in\ air}{speed\ in\ the\ medium} = \frac{wavelength\ of\ light\ in\ air}{wavelength\ in\ the\ medium}$$

Hence λ(medium) = 600/1.4 = 444 nm. As $2t = \lambda/2$, $t = 111$ nm.

22.8 The wavelength of the light is 550 nm in air and so is 550/1.4 = 390 nm in the destructive material. The light traverses this thickness twice and so, for destruction, $2t = \lambda/2$, giving the thickness $t = 98$ nm.

22.9 We need to know whether the refractive index of the glass is greater or less than that of the calcium fluoride so as to determine if there is a phase change at that interface or not. In this case, glass has the greater refractive index and so there will be a phase change of π radians. There will also be the same phase change at the surface of the coating because its refractive index is greater than that of air, hence $2t = \lambda/2$. Note that in this case, you could still have got by even if you had forgotten the rule. At both surfaces (the coating and the glass) there is an increase in refractive index so whether there is a phase change or not, the behaviour is the same at both interfaces and so there is no net phase change.

22.10 The thickness of the coating will give total destructive interference in the middle of the visible spectrum, but not so good at the edges. Thus some blue and red light will be reflected, together giving a purple hue. If this is not acceptable, it is necessary to use several films of different materials and thicknesses to produce interference right across the visible spectrum.

22.11 The wavelength in air is 650 nm, so the wavelength in the material is $650/1.5 = 433$ nm. In this case $2t = \lambda/2$, so $t = 108$ nm.

22.12 We always use the thinnest film so as to reduce the amount of light absorbed in it. Also the use of thick films would mean that constructive interference would occur at other, unwanted, wavelengths in the visible region.

22.13 The formula here is the same as for the more common transmission grating, $d \sin \theta = n\lambda$, and $n = 1$ here. Hence $d = 400/0.17 = 2350$ nm $= 2.35\ \mu$m.

22.14 Here $\theta = 30°$, $\sin \theta = 0.5$ and so $\lambda = 1175$ nm. This is beyond the visible range. But if we take the second order of diffraction, $n = 2$, we get $\lambda = 587.5$ nm, and this is yellow.

22.15 Colours that are due to selective absorption do not change as the angle of incidence is changed.

22.16 The formula we want here is $\lambda = xd/D$ or $x = \lambda D/d$, where x is the distance from the centre to the first antinode. I make this to be 10 m and so the first node is 5 m from the centre. Hence, if there was destructive interference for one ear there would also be for the other. The student could, for once, be telling the truth. For the high-frequency sound, the distance from a node to an antinode is 10 cm, the separation of her ears, and so the sound could not be destroyed by interference at both ears. These sounds are just the ones which the loudspeakers are unable to handle, however. Give her the benefit of the doubt.

22.17 The speed of light is 3×10^8 m s^{-1} and so the wavelength of the radiation is 1 cm. As the separation of the sources is 7 cm and as, for first-order diffraction, $d \sin \theta = \lambda$, $\sin \theta = 1/7$ and $\theta = 8°$.

22.18 The reflected pulse is the same way up, it is not inverted. This is analogous to the reflection of light at a glass–air interface. In neither cases is there a phase change.

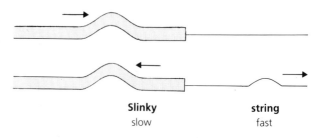

Slinky
slow

string
fast

Waves at the seaside

23.1 The amplitude of the wave gets less and this is due to friction, within the wave and with the sand below.

23.2 As $v = f\lambda$, $\lambda = 10$ m and $f = \frac{1}{8}$ Hz, $v = 1.25$ m s^{-1}.

23.3 As the speed of the waves is constant, at any particular depth of water, then a long wavelength implies a small frequency or a long period. Thus if there is a big distance between waves, then there is also a long wait for the next one. Which seems obvious, doesn't it?

23.4 A big wave is one with a large amplitude, corresponding to a loud sound or a bright light. There is no truth in the belief that every seventh wave is of large amplitude. You can easily check this next time you are at the beach. It is all part of the general belief in the mystical powers of the number seven – seven days of the week, seven colours of the rainbow and Snow White and the seven dwarfs.

23.5 The idea of walking over rocks to get into deep water quickly generally does not work because as a rule the water gets shallow at the edges of the bay. When that happens, the waves will tend to bend and come in parallel to the shoreline. The wave in deep water travels faster than a wave in shallow water. The wave is refracted. Alternatively, we could regard this as a case of diffraction at the edge of a large object.

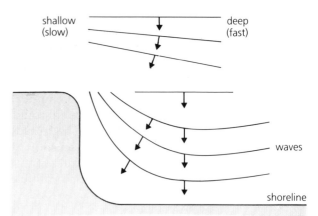

shallow
(slow)

deep
(fast)

waves

shoreline

23.6 The Lion Rock at Piha juts out into fairly deep water; in that case there will be no refraction, and the waves come straight into the shore. Unfortunately, there are often dangerous currents there.

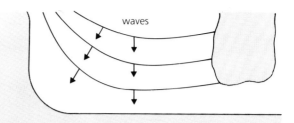

23.7 The waves go straight past the paddling surfie because the surfboard is much shorter than the wavelength of the sea waves. When this happens we have diffraction; the water waves do not 'see' the surfboard, just as a microscope cannot 'see' a particle smaller than the wavelength of light.

23.8 You take path (c). You can run faster than you can swim and so want to minimise the time in the water. It is true that if you take path (d) you will go a slightly shorter distance in the sea, but the distance on land will be very much greater.

23.9 A ray of light going from air into glass (that is, from a fast medium to a slow one) is refracted in the same way. The path chosen is that which makes the time taken as short as possible. This is the principle of least time. There is more. If I throw a rock into the sea it will take a path similar to that shown in the sketch.

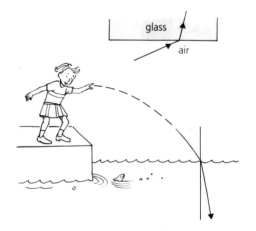

In this case the law of least action applies. 'Action' is defined as *energy* × *time* (the unit of Planck's constant, a fact of enormous significance). The path chosen is just the one that will make the action a minimum. It can also be shown that the laws of quantum mechanics can be written in very similar terms. This is the source of the real satisfaction we get from studying physics. We do one piece of work and then find that it applies, almost exactly, in a completely different part of physics. For example, when you have studied electric fields you find that a great deal of the work can be taken over, without change, to apply to magnetism and to gravity. The work also has links with light beams and heat flow. Physics is a 'seamless robe'.

23.10 The waves go round the rock and give an excellent example of an interference pattern. The sand joining the rock to the shore is a little higher than elsewhere and the waves bend round to cross.

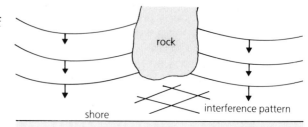

23.11 The X-rays, having higher frequencies than those of visible light, will be the other side of the resonance curve and so we expect little absorption by glass.

23.12 Chlorophyll appears green because it reflects green light to our eyes, the red and blue light being absorbed by the chlorophyll molecules. You can guess that a number of resonances are involved because there is a wide band of absorbed colours.

23.13 At the first sharp frost the chlorophyll molecule is destroyed – it is no longer needed. The carotene molecule survives and gives the brilliant colours of autumn, perhaps best seen in up-state New York.

23.14 Melanin absorbs most light at the short wavelengths, that is, at high frequencies. Since $E = hf$, this means that the most energetic photons are absorbed. Without melanin, the blood vessels and the skin cells in our dermis would be destroyed.

Nuclear winter

24.1 The graph suggests that the temperature would stay 5 °C below the ambient for over 200 days. There could be no agriculture during this period.

24.2 The marked rise in temperature after about a year in the northern hemisphere is a surprise. It could be due to the loss of the ozone layer, permitting the passage of electromagnetic radiation of wavelengths that are normally absorbed high up.

24.3 The graphs are as shown. In the northern hemisphere, the graph is a straight line, approximately. In the southern hemisphere, the temperatures are higher and return to something like normal more quickly.

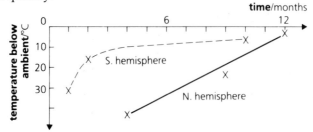

24.4 The monsoons are predicted to cease because there would be so much less evaporation from the colder seas. There would thus be virtually no agricultural produce in the whole of Asia.

24.5 Erosion would be very much more severe because of the loss of trees. This would be more significant if missile silos were the targets of the bombers rather than cities. About one-third of the land surface of the northern temperate zone is covered by forests.

24.6 Normal weather patterns would go, and there would be much greater variations in temperature (something we seem to be noticing anyway; if this continues, it could be due to the 'greenhouse effect' caused by increased levels of carbon dioxide in the atmosphere transmitting shorter visible wavelengths from sunlight and reflecting longer wavelengths). The clouds would be heated by the Sun's rays prevented from reaching the ground. There would probably be temperature inversions, with the temperature in the stratosphere higher than lower down.

24.7 The islanders would be unable to survive because they have lost the skills that enabled them to thrive in past times. In the same way, many aborigines can no longer live in the bush.

24.8 Without an atmosphere the temperature of the Earth would fall immediately to that of the Moon (which is, on average, the same distance from the Sun). The heat energy from the Sun would be re-radiated out into space immediately. Many people do not appreciate that the Earth radiates as much heat energy out into space as it receives from the Sun; otherwise, its temperature would rise without limit.

24.9 We deduce that light rays can pass through the atmosphere (along with radio waves) but that infra-red rays (heat rays) are absorbed. This is why i.r. telescopes are mounted on Earth satellites at a height of over 500 km.

24.10 Soil particles reflect the heat energy, so it remains in circulation. Soot absorbs it and so removes it from circulation.

24.11 In the troposphere, the rain could wash the soot particles to Earth and clean the air. In the stratosphere, there is no rain to do this. It is for this kind of reason that the TTAPS and other reports carry so much conviction. Although they are merely computer simulations (and pray God they are never realised in practice), they are said to be 'robust', that is, they are stable to quite wide variations in input parameters.

24.12 In general the land would be colder than the sea. Any convection currents that existed would be over the sea, so that air would flow from land to sea. That, of course, means offshore winds.

24.13 Yes, because there would be no rainfall to wash the smoke down again and clear the skies. If the smoke were below the water vapour layer it would be fairly quickly washed away. It would not be too hard to find how high smoke rises after a massive forest fire, but those conditions are very different from those of a nuclear war. The problem is compounded because we do not know how the water vapour layer would behave in the days after a nuclear war. There could well be very little rain even if the smoke layer is low.

24.14 Initially more energy flows into the greenhouse than leaves it, but after equilibrium is set up the two quantities are the same. If this were not so, the temperature of the greenhouse would increase without limit.

24.15 The i.r. radiation falling on the greenhouse would be of shorter wavelength and thus the photons would have higher frequency and hence more energy per photon. The soil and plants absorb this energy and, because they are cooler than the original source, re-radiate it at longer wavelength (lower frequency).

24.16 It is suspected that a decrease in the ozone layer would allow more radioactive particles to reach ground level. Moreover, it would allow a greater intensity of ultra-violet light to reach the ground; this would probably cause an increase in the rates of skin cancer (already a serious problem) and also more mutations in animals and plants.

Answers to supplementary questions

Manipulation of numbers

S1.1 The mass to be cooked is proportional to r^3, the surface area through which the heat energy can enter is proportional to r^2, and the rate at which heat enters is proportional to the temperature gradient inside the egg, which is proportional to $1/r$. Hence the time taken to cook is proportional to r^2 or $m^{2/3}$. This gives a time of $5 \times 100^{2/3} \approx$ about 100 minutes. The same result can be found by the method of dimensions.

S1.2 There has to be an equal space between indentations, making $0.8 \ \mu m$ per bit. This gives 5.5×10^9 bits on the disc.

S1.3 Dinosaurs were so big that their skin surface area was quite small compared to their mass. So it would take a long time for a dinosaur to lose its body heat.

S1.4 From the graph shown, I find that the time is about 100 minutes and that $n = \frac{2}{7}$.

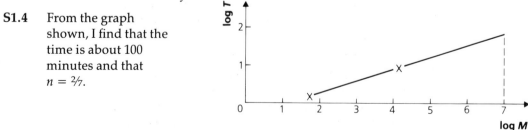

S1.5 The egg in the boiling water is heated from all sides but the dinosaur in the sunshine receives heat from one side only.

S1.6 The area is 4.6 km square.

S1.7 The graph is as shown. I have drawn it through the first three points, assuming some slowing at the end of 200 m. This shows that an athlete is going at full speed after 1 m and maintains that speed for 100 m.

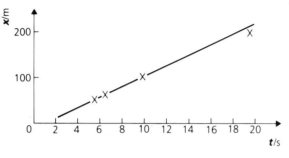

S1.8 When I plot the graph, I get a good enough straight line and find that the coefficient goes to zero at 80 m.p.h.

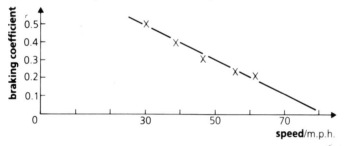

S1.9 If Africa and South America are separating at about 1.5 cm y^{-1}, then each is moving away from the Mid-Atlantic Ridge at half this figure, 0.75 cm y^{-1}. In 27 million years that makes about 20 million cm or about 200 km, which is about right. If ever there was a question where too much precision was unnecessary, this is it.

Straight line mechanics

S2.1 Using $d = \frac{1}{2}at^2$, we get $t = 2.7$ s and $v = 27$ m s^{-1} (100 km h^{-1}).

S2.2 Air friction would make the dive last longer and the final speed less. I watched a film of the event and estimated that the dive lasted about 3.5 s. I would not expect air friction to be very significant, the divers' bodies are perfectly straight for most of the path (although at night they dive carrying a flaming torch).

S2.3 The textbook answer is that the balloon appears to go forward. If you start to run holding a conker on a string, the conker seems to go backward (by Newton's first law). As helium is lighter than air it should move forward, but air resistance is very important for light balloons. You can get it to move forwards if you shield it by running backwards.

S2.4 Using $v^2 = 2ad$, we get 2.5 m.

S2.5 Modern parachutists land much slower, even standing up. I knew one parachutist who for a stunt used to get out of his parachute harness, holding on by one hand, when about 50 m up. Then just as he landed he would let go of the parachute and nonchalantly walk away.

S2.6 Using $d = \frac{1}{2}at^2$, we get $a = 24$ m s^{-2} and $v = 142$ m s^{-1}.

S2.7 The acceleration will be much greater at slower speeds, before air resistance becomes very significant. There is considerable discrepancy between the calculated and measured values; this must be due to increased friction at high speed.

S2.8 The brakes may be impaired by the rough treatment they get at the start of the run, when the cars are held on the brakes for some time – like airliners at the end of the runway before take-off.

S2.9 I find that the time to reach the greatest height is about 1.4 s, the total time of flight 2.8 s and the range 18 m.

S2.10 The discrepancy can be entirely accounted for by air friction (just to compare, a rugby ball goes about two-thirds as far when you kick it in a match as it would do in a vacuum). I expected that the fact that the seeds would not be shot out instantaneously would affect the issue, but it does not seem to.

S2.11 I make the total momentum to be about 560 kg m s^{-1} in a direction 22.5° north of east. Thus the speed after the tackle is $560/210 = 2.5$ m s^{-1}, direction 70° east of north.

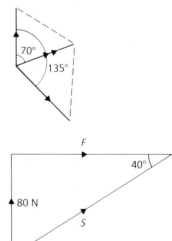

S2.12 We assume that the driving force is perpendicular to the sail and is not greatly affected by the speed of the boat. (This can be true in practice.) Then the force diagram is as shown. The force produced by the sail S is $80/\sin 40 = 125$ N, and the force of friction is $80/\tan 40 = 95$ N.

S2.13 The average speed is $18.4/0.51 = 37.6$ m s^{-1}. The final speed would then be 35.2 m s^{-1}. That figure of 90 m.p.h. looks mighty suspicious to me.

S2.14 The total work done is $43\,000 \times 9 = 387\,000$ J. The total power is this number divided by $3600 = 108$ W. Each man delivers 54 W.

A racing cyclist can work at more than twice this rate for this time, but many people in Malawi are greatly undernourished.

S2.15 The answer is (d). The only force is the weight, acting vertically downwards.

S2.16 The answer is (b). The weight is still vertical and the friction is in the direction opposite to the motion.

S2.17 The sacks move forward with the speed of the plane.

S2.18 It takes 3 s for the sacks to fall 50 m and so the vertical speed is 30 m s^{-1}. This is much less than the forward speed, so (d) is the better sketch.

S2.19 The sacks bounce along the ground – only rarely do they burst. You will have noticed that the villagers stand well back from the flight path. They know the damage that a 100 kg sack at the speed mentioned will inflict. You will have noticed, too, their quiet dignity. Although they possess nothing, they know their own worth.

S2.20 We assume that the air friction is proportional to the square of the speed. Thus the horizontal speed will be reduced 4 times as much as the vertical speed. Moreover the vertical speed is initially zero, with no air resistance. Thus, in reality, the path will be more like (d).

S2.21 The friction is given by $F = W \sin \theta$ and so here is $800 \times \sin 40 = 500$ N. At lower speeds, the friction is less, but the calculation cannot be made then because the skier is accelerating.

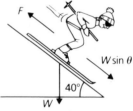

S2.22 For the hot-dogging skier, the necessary centripetal acceleration is provided by gravity, so $v^2/r = g$, giving a minimum speed of 5.5 m s^{-1}, much less than the downhill racer's speed of 30 m s^{-1}.

S2.23 The long-distance skier puts all his weight on one foot and then needs a large coefficient of friction so that the ski does not slide backwards. But when the other leg is slid forward a small coefficient of sliding friction is wanted.

S2.24 The ball takes 0.6 s to fall the 1.8 m from the top of the service stroke to the level of the net. In that time the ball travels the 8 m to the net, so its speed is 13 m s^{-1} – pretty feeble. Good players must hit the ball downwards slightly.

S2.25 The change in velocity is $13 - (-27) = 40$ m s^{-1}. The force is $60/1000 \times 40/0.03 = 80$ N. This is a reasonable figure, equivalent to the weight of a 8 kg mass.

S2.26 The contact time for a golf ball is less thhan for a tennis ball because the tennis ball is softer than a golf ball and the strings of a tennis racket have more give than the head of a golf club. The force is 100/1000 × 50/0.0005 = 10^4N. This is a very large force, but it only acts for a very short time.

S2.27 It takes 2 s for the car to fall 20 m. Hence the horizontal speed was 12 m s^{-1}, which is less than the speed limit of 50 km h^{-1}. The vertical speed on hitting the sand was 20 m s^{-1} and so the total speed (by Pythagoras) about 23 m s^{-1}. The car made a big hole in the beach.

S2.28 We want $v^2 = 2ad$, giving $a = 1.4$ m s^{-2}. For the time, we want $v = at$ or $t = v/a = 63$ s.

S2.29 Using $F = ma$, $a = F/m = 2.7$ m s^{-2}.

S2.30 At roll, $a = 1.7$ m s^{-2}; net thrust = 2.5 × 1.7 = 4.35 × 10^5 N. Hence air resistance = 6.72 − 4.35 = 2.37 × 10^5 N. At take-off, $a = 1.1$ m s^{-2}; net thrust = 2.5 × 1.1 = 2.75 × 10^5 N. Hence air resistance = 6.72 − 2.75 = 4.0 × 10^5 N.

S2.31 The air resistance increases with speed and will continue to do so until the maximum speed is reached. It will not rise proportionately, however, because the wing gets more efficient at higher speeds. It gives more lift for a smaller rise in drag.

S2.32 We have

$$work = force \times distance$$

Divide both sides by time. We have

$$\frac{work}{time} = power$$

and

$$\frac{distance}{time} = velocity$$

So

$$power = force\ (thrust) \times velocity$$

S2.33 Mach 0.8 = 0.8 × 320 = 256 m s^{-1}.

S2.34 The power developed at take-off = 6.72 × 10^5 × 90 = 60 MW. Cruise power = 2.9 × 10^5 × 256 = 74.2 MW.

S2.35 This is fishy. We know that the power at cruising is less than at take-off; certainly the engines make less noise then, they are throttled back. The reason can only be that the engines are more efficient at the higher altitudes and greater speed at cruise.

S2.36 The deceleration $a = v^2/2d = -1.6$ m s^{-2} and the total decelerating force as 1.6 × 0.18 × 10^6 = 0.29 MN.

S2.37 We note that this is a little more than the take-off force. We expect this because the air resistance will be about the same, the flaps are deployed again, the engines are still working but are now acting in reverse (you can see the 'buckets' extended) and also the brakes are applied.

S2.38 While gliding, engine off, the craft sinks 260 m for each forward 2000 m travelled. Hence the sink angle is about 8°. The weight of the plane is 1600 N and so the drag force is 1600 sin 8 = 250 N, a lift-to-drag ratio of 8:1. About right.

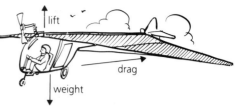

S2.39 If the air resistance is proportional to the square of the speed, then at 32 m.p.h. this equals $250 \times (32/22)^2$ = a little more than 500 N.

S2.40 At a speed of 32 m.p.h. (15 m s^{-1}) the power is $550 \times 15 = 7.5$ kW. This is a little more than the quoted value, but not too bad. I suspect that the discrepancy lies in the fact that the air resistance may increase more slowly than the square of the speed. At higher speeds, the sink angle would not be much greater than 8°, and so the drag not so much bigger.

S2.41 The weight of the plane is 720 000 N and the air resistance of the wings 90 000 N. This is much less than the total thrust of the engines of 220 000 N. The discrepancy arises because there is also the small extra air friction of the rest of the skin of the plane but, more important, the thrust quoted is the maximum, only needed at take-off. At take-off, the plane is going slowly so flaps are deployed to give extra lift at slow speed, and there is a penalty to pay in the form of extra drag.

S2.42 A thrust of 90 000 N exerted for 4500 km corresponds to work done of 4×10^{11} J. The energy content of the fuel is $2.3 \times 10^4 \times 10^8$ J. Thus the efficiency is about 20 per cent.
   This is a bit low, but then we did not take into account the thrust needed to overcome skin friction.

S2.43 The total weight is 14 400 N and the thrust is 2700 N, so the lift: drag ratio is only 5.3, rather low. Presumably this is because the wings have to fold away during the transit to launch height. The wings do look ridiculously small. They can be so small because the craft does not fly slowly during take-off from the ground but is launched from a fast-flying bomber (B52 or B1).

S2.44 The power developed is *thrust × velocity* = 700 kW, as much as a small hydroelectric generating station.

S2.45 Assume the car is approaching you and is turning to its right. There are two restoring torques, as shown in the drawing. That due to the weight of the sail is $200 \times 0.6 = 120$ N m. That due to aerodynamic forces is $5 \times 2 = 10$ N m. These torques would only be comparable if the speed were about 9 m s^{-1}, the forward speed of the car.

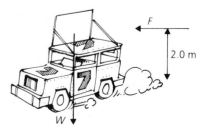

S2.46 I have not had the courage to tell my neighbour that I think the sail on his stock car is useless. That the weight is more important than the air friction is shown by the fact that the sail is put on the other side of the car if the track is left-handed, as opposed to the usual right-handed track. However, if the driver thinks that he can corner faster because of the sail, he probably does so.

S2.47 The acceleration $a = 2d/t^2 = 2 \times 400/(17.5)^2$, less than 3 m s^{-2}. The thrust is then 2200 N. The power of 76 h.p. is 55 kW and thus gives a maximum speed of 27 m s^{-1}. An acceleration of 2.7 m s^{-2} acting for 17.5 s gives a speed of 47 m s^{-1}, however. Clearly we have poor agreement. It is unrealistic to assume that the resistive force is independent of the speed.

S2.48 The total surface area of the eight slave pistons is twice the area of the master piston, so the force advantage is also twice, since *pressure = force/area*. The pressure in the brake fluid must be constant everywhere.

S2.49 The body of the car is attached to the wheels by springs and by the law of inertia will tend to keep moving when the wheels slow down. The difference in speed between body and wheels constitutes an acceleration and hence a force, and the torque exerted by this force turns the car into a nose-down position.

S2.50 I instinctively feel that applying the back brake would have less effect than if the front brakes were applied; however, the force must be the same in both cases and the torque also. Certainly you are more likely to go over the handle-bars of a bike when you pull hard on the front brake than when you apply the back brake. I cannot resolve this one.

S2.51 Some of the back-lean of a motor boat is due to its acceleration. A larger effect is due to aquaplaning; the boat rises out of the water due to a downward component of the thrust, and this makes it go much faster as there is then less water resistance.

S2.52 The k.e. of the motion is converted to heat energy and this is dissipated to the surrounding air. There is a better flow of air round a disc than inside an enclosed drum. As far as I know, this is the only advantage the ordinary motorist has gained from the millions spent on car racing.

S2.53 The k.e. = $\frac{1}{2} \times 800 \times (20)^2 = 1.6 \times 10^5$ J. The total mass of the discs is 8 kg, so it takes 4000 J to heat them by one degree. Thus in the absence of cooling, the discs would be heated to 40 °C. Most of the heat goes into the discs: the thermal conductivity of the brake pads is small and the heating usually takes place quickly so there is little time for loss of heat.

S2.54 The dancer raises his arms and legs until they are parallel with the ground (fore and aft) and this raises his centre of mass. (Old films of Nijinsky show him doing this.) Now the path of the centre of mass must be a parabola and we know and expect this. Thus raising the centre of mass will appear to make the jump lower and longer.

Rotational mechanics

S3.1 As the measured value is less than that for a uniform sphere, the centre of the Earth must contain matter of greater density. Any theory of the Earth must account for the measured value.

S3.2 The surface of a spinning liquid is a parabola. Consider a point on the surface, distance x from the axis. Then the slope at that point is $\tan \theta = \omega^2 x/g$, that is, the slope is proportional to x. If we differentiate $x^2 = 4ay$, we get $dy/dx = x/2a$, also proportional to x.

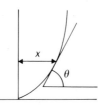

S3.3 For the particular mirror, $x = 1$ m and the focal length $a = 2$ m. Inserting in the formula, $\omega^2 x/g = x/2a$ yields $\omega^2 = g/4$ or $\omega = 1.6$ rad s^{-1}; this gives a frequency of about 4 Hz.

S3.4 If they were large they would tear themselves apart. Consider a point on the equator of the pulsar. Then $\omega^2 r = GM/r^2$. Putting the mass $= \frac{4}{3} \pi r^3 \rho$, we get $\omega^2 = G \times \frac{4}{3}\pi\rho$. Inserting the value for ω, this demands a density of the order of 10^{15} kg m^{-3}.

S3.5 Putting $\omega^2 r = g$, we get $\omega = 0.12$ rad s^{-1}, giving a period of about 45 s.

S3.6 They should stand on the inside of the larger radius, as at B. They must have something to give them an inward acceleration.

S3.7 The height of a human is of the same order as the radius of the torus. A human would have much greater g at his feet than at his head.

S3.8 By the conservation of angular momentum, the quantity L ($= mvr$) is constant. This yields a speed at ground level of 0.5 m s^{-1}.

S3.9 The centripetal force $= mv^2/r$ and we equate this to the force of gravitation $= GMm/r^2$. This yields $v^2 = GM/r$. If the Sun is a typical star, then the total mass of the galaxy M is $10^{11} \times 2 \times 10^{30}$ kg. Inserting these figures we find that the speed of the Sun round the galaxy is about 150 km s^{-1}. This compares with the value quoted of 250 km s^{-1}.

S3.10 If we neglect the stars in the spiral arms, then all the mass of the galaxy is in the central spherical part. We can then, courtesy of Newton, put all the mass of the galaxy at the centre.

S3.11 When the engine is idling, the clutch does not engage. But when the throttle is opened, the engine turns faster and the elements of the clutch are swung outwards radially because the retaining springs are not strong enough to provide the necessary centripetal force for circular motion of small radius. At high speed, the clutch engages.

S3.12 The chapatti is thinned out as it is given a circular motion. Again, the dough does not have enough cohesive force to supply the necessary centripetal force to maintain circular motion of small radius.

S3.13 This is the Law of conservation of angular momentum at work. The jet engines consist of rotating fans and compressors and so possess angular momentum. When the plane 'rotates', there is a change in the vector angular momentum and to conserve this the plane veers sideways (in fact, to the right though there is no value in knowing the rule). This is the 'gyroscope effect'. With propeller aircraft the effect is barely noticeable.

S3.14 If a jet engine jammed, then by the principle of conservation of angular momentum the whole plane would rotate about a horizontal fore-and-aft axis. The bolts holding an engine are made to shear off if the torque on them gets too big, and the engine then falls off. This has happened several times – quite recently, a DC9 (MD87) had to land with one engine.

S3.15 The angular momentum of an engine is the same wherever it is placed on the aircraft. In fact all jet engines rotate in the same sense; there would be no point in adding a further complication.

S3.16 The angular momentum of the l.p. rotor is $11.5 \times 880 = 10^4$ kg m^2 s^{-1}. For the h.p. rotor it is $7.2 \times 1290 = 9000$ in the same unite, giving a total of 1.9×10^4 units.

  The total rotational inertia of the wings is 2.7×10^6 kg m^2.

  The plane will begin to rotate with an angular velocity $\omega = 7 \times 10^{-3}$ rad s^{-1}, making a complete revolution in 1000 s (16 minutes). This could easily be corrected by use of the ailerons.

S3.17 The angular speed of the test tubes is $\omega = 2\pi/T = 11\pi$ rad s^{-1}. The linear speed is $v = \omega r = 11\pi \times 0.14 = 1.5\pi$ m s^{-1}. The inward acceleration is $v^2/r = 150$ m s$^{-2} = 15g$.

S3.18 Angular deceleration $= \alpha = d\omega/dt = -11\pi/2 = -5.5\pi$ rad s^{-2}.

S3.19 The speed of rotation is 500/6 rev s^{-1}. The angular velocity $\omega = 500$ rad s^{-1}. $v = \omega r = 500 \times 0.14 = 70$ m s^{-1}. The centripetal acceleration $= \omega^2 r = 3.5 \times 10^4$ m s$^{-2} = 3500\ g$.

S3.20 For the ultracentrifuge, $\omega = 200 \times 2\pi$ rad s^{-1}. The linear speed is 56π m s^{-1} and the centripetal acceleration $= 2.2 \times 10^6$ m s^{-2}. It is possible to get centrifuges which run ten times as fast, giving accelerations 100 times as big, and these will separate protein molecules.

S3.21   If the acceleration is $9g$ (90 m s^{-2}) and as $v^2 = ar$, then
$v^2 = 90 \times 5$ units and the speed is 21 m s^{-1}.

S3.22   If that speed is reached in 5.3 s (an increase from $1g$ to $9g$, which
is $8g$ at a rate of $1.5g \text{ s}^{-1}$), the linear acceleration is about
4 m s^{-2}.

S3.23   It is safer. As you go into the corner, as at A, you
must have an inward acceleration and this can
only come from the frictional force between the
tyres and the road. The faster you go, the greater
this friction must be. But when you enter the
curve you do not know if the state of the road
can provide that friction and often you do not
know if the curve will tighten, demanding even
more friction. When you come out of the curve,
as at B, you know the state of the road and can
safely accelerate out of the curve.

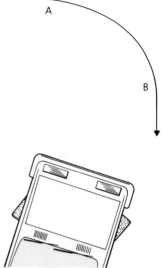

S3.24   Centripetal acceleration is given by $a = \omega^2 r$.
Both wheels have the same ω, but the outer
wheel has a bigger r and so needs a bigger
centripetal acceleration. This has to be supplied
by a greater frictional force at the inner wheel,
and this will straighten the car.

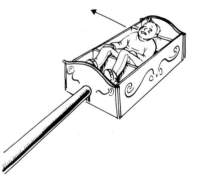

S3.25   The wretched pussycat will tend to go straight on (by Newton's
first law). As the car turns to the right, it will appear to swing to
the left.

S3.26   Physicists answer that if the man lies with his
feet towards the centre of rotation, there is
nothing to give the food an inward acceleration
and it will tend to move up his gullet. Biologists
say that being sick has nothing to do with the
forces on one's stomach – rather it is due to
one's perception of speed and acceleration.
With the man's feet towards the centre, his head
will experience a bigger acceleration than his
toes and so he will be more likely to be sick. So
perhaps the physicists' answer is right, but for
the wrong reason.

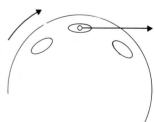

S3.27   The tyres, being on the rim of the wheel, will contribute most to
the rotational inertia of the cyclist and will demand a bigger
torque for a given angular acceleration.

S3.28   There is no such thing as centrifugal force. It is an obsolete
term known only to advertising copywriters. A drop of water
at a hole in the cylinder of a washing machine will have
nothing to give it an inward, centripetal acceleration and so
will fly out tangentially. The concept of centrifugal force is
dangerous because it encourages the idea that the water
drops are flung out radially, which is not so.

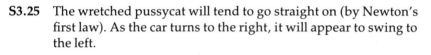

S3.29 If most of the mass is near the pivot (the hip joint), the rotational inertia will be small and less energy is expended in reaching a given speed. If you sit on a lab bench with one leg hanging over the edge, you will find that the natural period of your leg is about 1 second. This is also your natural speed of walking. If your shoes were very heavy, the natural period would be longer (a longer pendulum) and you would walk more slowly. This is why jogging is such an unnatural process; it's much better to go for a long walk (you can talk then, too).

S3.30 What happened occurred too quickly for me to be absolutely sure, and we badly need a slow-motion video film of the jump. It seemed that the gymnast made two distinct turns about two different axes, so that an increase in angular momentum in one turn was balanced by a decrease in angular momentum in the other. Unfortunately, the gymnast could not tell me precisely what she did.

In the same way, cats are able to turn in mid-air and land on their feet. When the great physicist James Clerk Maxwell was a boy he did a series of experiments with the family cat and found that the minimum height from which it could land upright was about one metre.

S3.31 This is not such an original idea after all. Farmers in Canada use this method for ploughing, harrowing and rolling, especially on those fields which are irrigated by rotating circular booms. It is fascinating to fly over parts of north-west Canada and see the circles of cultivated ground in large barren areas.

In this case the Law of conservation of angular momentum does not hold. By analogy with $F = \mathrm{d}(mv)/\mathrm{d}t$, we have $torque = \mathrm{d}(mvr)/\mathrm{d}t$, the rate of change of angular momentum. As the radius gets smaller the angular momentum gets less; to compensate, the mower exerts a tension in the rope and this tension exerts a torque on the pole.

S3.32 It increases your rotational inertia, I. As

$torque = rotational\ inertia \times angular\ acceleration$

the effect is to reduce your angular accleration and so give you more time to react to any sudden torque. Houdini was especially worried by the possibility of torques due to wind gusts down the valley of the Niagara river.

S3.33 In addition to the effect of the previous question, the umbrellas would tend to damp out oscillations by air friction. One of my students suggests that they would also act as parachutes if you got blown off the rope.

S3.34 The dancer begins the circular jump with arms and legs outstretched, then when in mid-air he drops his arm and legs to verticality. This minimises his rotational inertia about a vertical axes and so increases his speed of rotation.

S3.35 The angular velocity of the blade
$\omega = 17.5 \times 2\pi/60 = 1.8$ rad s^{-1}; the linear speed of the blade tip $v = \omega r = 50 \times 1.8 = 90$ m s^{-1} (comfortably less than the speed of sound) and the centripetal acceleration $a = \omega^2 r = 160$ m s^{-2}.

Properties of matter

S4.1 The work done in each heart beat is pV. Here $v = 70$ ml $= 70 \times 10^{-6}$ m^3, so the work done in each pulse is 0.84 J. The power developed is then $0.84 \times 72/60 = 1$ watt. This is a surprisingly small value, considering that the power developed by the whole body is about 100 watts.

S4.2 The excess pressure is 140 mm of mercury, which is equivalent to 140×13.6 mm $= 2$ m of water. Thus the head of the giraffe is 2 m above its heart, assuming that the relative density of blood is unity, and the giraffe is 3.8 m tall.

S4.3 The pressure exerted by a liquid does not depend on the area on which it acts. Presumably the blood pressure was measured at the level of the heart, which is why we are saying that the top of a giraffe is about 2 m above its heart. This is about right.

S4.4 $P = h\rho g = 1.2 \times 10^3 \times 10 = 1.2 \times 10^4$ Pa.
The area is 1.5 m^2, so the force is 1.8×10^4 N.

S4.5 At that depth, the pressure
$P = h\rho g = 90 \times 1000 \times 10 = 9 \times 10^5$ Pa. The area of the ear drum is 6×10^{-5} m^2 and so the force is 54 N. Clearly ear plugs were necessary.

S4.6 A single large jet of water has a smaller surface area than the three smaller jets that made it up. Hence the surface energy of the single jet is less, and this is a more stable system. After a while, the large jet sometimes breaks down into its three components. The temperature of the water should not affect the issue except that a thick cold jet should last longer than a hot one. I do not propose to have a cold shower just to find out.

S4.7 A domed head to the piston will cause better swirling of the mixture as the piston rises during the compression stroke. This will give a more complete and instantaneous combustion during the expansion stroke. The effective area of the piston will be the same in either case.

S4.8 Most of the coffee will stay stationary. A very thin layer will attach to the china of the cup and will move with it. A small air bubble attached to the cup will move with it.

S4.9 If we assume that the surface tension forces are vertical, we have:

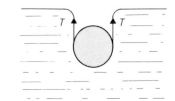

mass of needle = 10^{-4} kg;
weight of needle = 10^{-3} N;
surface tension force = $2 \times 0.07 \times 3.5 \times 10^{-2}$ N.

A needle easily floats on water. We can even float a razor blade.

S4.10 In practice, the surface tension forces are not vertical but act at such an angle as to balance the weight of the needle. In this case, $\cos \theta = \frac{1}{5} = 0.2$, and so $\theta = 80°$ approximately.

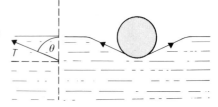

S4.11 In all three cases, the water will just not overflow. We can see this in the last two cases by manoeuvring the occlusion to the edge of the ice block.

S4.12 The volume of the gas increases as the pressure falls. The force of buoyancy is unchanged because the mass of the balloon does not change. The fall in temperature does not affect the issue for the same reason.

S4.13 The meaning of the book is quite clear but the author really should have said 'load' to spare the feelings of physicists.

S4.14 This is a fact of observation, but I do not have a convincing explanation. It cannot be a result of expansion, nor of surface tension. I can only suppose that the decreased viscosity of the water allows it to move faster. The faster the water goes, the thinner the jet – just as the jet gets thinner the greater the distance below the bottom of the tap.

S4.15 She arrived at the surface with her lungs full of air at double atmospheric pressure (how do you know it was double?). This could well tear her lungs apart or cause an embolism (air forced through the lungs into the bloodstream). These small air bubbles could join up into a larger one.

S4.16 Assuming that the westerner is not very adept at using chopsticks it will take him some time to eat the food. The thin noodles will cool more quickly than the fat ones as they have a larger surface:volume ratio. I have never understood why such a variety of noodles is offered, they all taste the same to me.

S4.17 The pressure across the spherical meniscus = $2T/r$. This equals the hydrostatic pressure at the bottom of the water column = $h\rho g$, and I find that the height is about 0.6 m.

S4.18 If a submarine is at a certain depth and some downdraught causes it to sink lower, then the increased pressure at the lower depth will cause the hull to decrease in volume. This will decrease the volume of water displaced and hence lower the buoyancy, so the submarine will sink further. Unless the submarine has a reserve of compressed air to blow its tanks or its hydroplanes can bring it up, it will sink more until its hull is crushed.

S4.19 The submarine could be made strong enough, but because plastic materials have such a low Young's modulus their hulls would deform greatly under pressure. They would be quite unstable.

S4.20 The stress is the same throughout short or long ropes. The long rope will extend more than the short one, however, and so will store more elastic energy ($E = \frac{1}{2}F \times d$).

S4.21 While the ball is skidding, all parts of it move with the same velocity. When it reaches the unoiled part, however, the force of friction is greater and this slows down the part of the ball in contact with the track until its velocity is zero.

S4.22 Backspin will only operate on the oiled part of the track, since during backspin the part of the ball in contact with the track must have a velocity greater than that of the centre of the ball.

Simple harmonic motion

S5.1 The intensity will consist of a constant component due to the light that is received directly and a sinusoidal component due to the reflecting mirror. During half the cycle, no light at all will be received.

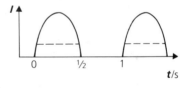

S5.2 Now, for one-third of the time both components are received, for one-third of the time only the constant component is received, and for the remaining one-third nothing is received at all.

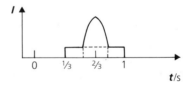

S5.3 We equate the p.e. lost by the jumper to the stored elastic energy in the rope; $mgh = \frac{1}{2}kx^2$, $80 \times 10 \times 50 = \frac{1}{2}k \times (20)^2$. This gives $k = 200$ N m^{-1}. Now use $\omega^2 = k/m$; this yields $\omega = 1.6$ rad s^{-1} and a period of about 4 s.

S5.4 We have the same value for k and use the same formula, with $m = 60$ kg. This yields $x = 17$ m, so a rope 33 m long is needed.

S5.5 We may not use $mg = kx$ because at the bottom of the fall the jumper is not in equilibrium; in fact, he is experiencing the maximum acceleration due to the s.h.m. That formula could only be used if the jumper were gently lowered on the end of the rope.

S5.6 We can use $mg = kx$ in this case, because the mother gently lowered the baby into the chair. Now $8.5 \times 10 = k \times 0.2$, yielding $k = 425$ N m^{-1}. This gives $\omega^2 = 50$, so $\omega = 7$ rad s^{-1} and the period is about 1 s.
The maximum speed is given by $v = \omega A = 0.1 \times 7 = 0.7$ m s^{-1}.

S5.7 In this case, the value of ω is the same and so is the period. The maximum speed is three times bigger $= 2.1$ m s^{-1}. The amplitude of the oscillation is now greater than the initial extension of the ropes, and hence the last part of the upward motion is without restraint – the child would be shot up towards the ceiling. Tears all round.

S5.8 The mother supports the infant while it is lowered into its seat and so the energy stored in the elastic is not mgh.

S5.9 The period $T = 0.45$ s, leading to $\omega = 13$ rad s^{-1}. The amplitude is 4 mm. The maximum speed is given by $v = \omega A = 5 \times 10$ m s^{-1}.

S5.10 In this case, $\omega = 160\pi$ rad s^{-1} and the amplitude $A = 6$ cm. This yields a maximum vertical speed of the piston of $v = \omega A = 1.6\pi \times 6 = 30$ m s^{-1}. The maximum vertical acceleration is given by $a = \omega^2 A$, and I make this about 1.5×10^4 m s^{-2}. This is $1500g$, an enormous value and a limiting factor in the design of internal-combustion engines.

S5.11 We want $f < 30$ Hz or $\omega < 5$ rad s^{-1} or $\omega^2 < 25$ rad^2 s^{-2}. To achieve this small number, then, we want a small value for k or a large value for m. There are certain tight constraints on both these quantities.

S5.12 It is essential that there be no resonance between the coolie's steps and the rate at which the load oscillates on the end of the pole. A coolie tends to walk at quite a quick pace, about 2 Hz. The frequency of oscillation of the load must be less than this, say ½ Hz. This means that $\omega = 4\pi$ rad s^{-1}. For a load of 20 kg, that requires the force constant of the pole to be about 3000 N m^{-1}.

S5.13 The displacement in the direction of blade travel is given by $y = A \sin \theta = A \sin \omega t$, the condition for an s.h.m.

S5.14 The rotational speed of the motor is $1600/60 = 26\frac{2}{3}$ rev s^{-1}, and the angular speed ω is this $\times 2\pi = 50\pi$ rad s^{-1}. Here the amplitude A is 1 cm, and so the maximum linear speed of the blade is $v = \omega A = \pi/2$ m s^{-1}. The maximum acceleration is $a = v\omega = 250$ m s^{-2}.

S5.15 Here $\omega = 2\pi f = 240$ rad s^{-1} and $A = 0.5$ mm. The maximum velocity is $v = \omega A = 12$ cm s^{-1}; the maximum acceleration is $\omega^2 A$ and I make that about $30g$. This is a very large figure. Perhaps it is only sustainable at these small amplitudes.

S5.16 For elastic ropes $\omega^2 = k/m$. For $\omega = 1.5$ rad s^{-1} and $m = 80$ kg, the force constant $k = 180$ N m^{-1}.

S5.17 We equate the loss in p.e. (mgh) with the work done in stretching the rope ($\frac{1}{2}kx^2$). Using the value of k from the previous question, I find that $x = 15$ m, giving an unstretched length of $23 - 15 = 8$ m.

S5.18 This should be called a 'pulse'. The wave rarely makes much more than one circuit. (It would *not* be a 'standing' wave!)

S5.19 When people stand up their heads rise about 40 cm, so the amplitude of the wave is 20 cm (0.2 m). The wavelength is 400 m, the frequency $\frac{1}{40}$ Hz and the speed 10 m s^{-1}.

Heat

S6.1 During the day, the top cork is removed; the air in the tank gets very hot and the residual water boils. At night, both corks are in place and as the tank cools the water vapour condenses, sucking water into the tank. In the morning, the tank is emptied, leaving a little water behind.

S6.2 The area of the collector is $\pi r^2 = 1.5$ m^2. Hence the total power is about 400 W. Not all of this will be absorbed, but it is still the same order of heating as an electric hot-plate.

S6.3 To heat $\frac{1}{2}$ kg of water by 40 °C requires 84 000 J of heat energy. At 500 J per second this is 168 seconds, or three minutes – not so much slower than an electric jug.

S6.4 In 8 hours the energy from the Sun is $250 \times 8 \times 8 \times 60 \times 60 = 50$ MJ. Heat energy delivered to incubators $= 2580 \times 4.2 \times 40 = 0.5$ MJ. The system is about 1.5 per cent efficient.

S6.5 In one sense the energy is free, but such an inefficient system is very wasteful of material. A better system might have needed only one solar panel, representing a lot of money to poor Zaïrese.

S6.6 The salt gradient prevents convection, as the salt water is too heavy to rise. Thus the water at the bottom absorbs solar heat energy throughout the day and the water gets comparatively hot.

S6.7 Short-wavelength rays such as those at A (blue light and ultra-violet rays) are little absorbed by the glass and pass straight through. These rays are absorbed by the plants and soil and the energy is re-radiated, but at a lower frequency (lower energy per photon). These rays, such as those at B, cannot pass through the glass and are absorbed in it. The glass gets hot and warms the greenhouse.

S6.8 The carbon dioxide in the upper atmosphere behaves like glass, absorbing long-wavelength radiation.

S6.9 More carbon dioxide is produced in cars, homes and factories. Besides, as the tropical rain forests (especially in the Amazon basin) are cut down, less carbon dioxide is being converted to oxygen.

S6.10 The sea levels worldwide would rise for two reasons. Much of the Antarctic ice cap would quickly melt and, more important, the sea water would expand.

S6.11 To heat 1 kg of water from 0 °C to body temperature (37 °C) needs 37 calories or 160 J of heat energy. To use up 2000 calories or 8400 J then needs about 50 kg of ice water. A water diet much favoured 80 years ago required people to drink 5 kg of water a day, but 50 kg is surely too much.

S6.12 We now have to include the heat energy needed to melt the ice, the latent heat energy of fusion of ice. To melt and heat 1 kg requires $37 + 80 = 117$ calories (or 500 J) of heat energy and so about 17 kg of ice would have to be eaten.

S6.13 The hot wind is cooled by the heat needed to vaporise the water in the tatti (the latent heat energy of vaporisation of water). The disadvantage of the method is that the cooled air would be saturated with water vapour; presumably it is worth making a tatti.

S6.14 As soon as the top layer of water gets hot, it evaporates and cools. It is now possible to buy a bottle of a special liquid with a very high specific heat and very high latent heat of vaporisation. Poured into a swimming pool, it forms a monomolecular layer which effectively prevents evaporation of water.

S6.15 The power station produces 3×10^9 J of waste heat energy, which is applied to 6×10^5 kg of water per second. This causes a temperature rise of about 1 °C.

S6.16 The power station must get rid of 6000 MJ of heat energy each second. It must therefore evaporate $6000/2.26 = 2240$ kg of water per second.

S6.17 The air is very dry (all the water vapour is blown away) and therefore there is nothing to retain the heat energy at night. The skies are clear and so the heat energy absorbed by the Earth during the day is re-radiated into space.

S6.18 To melt the ice block needs $0.05 \times 336 \times 10^3$ J. To heat the melted ice from 0 °C to 37 °C needs $0.05 \times 37 \times 4.19 \times 10^3$ J. So the total energy is $16.8 + 7.7 = 24.5$ kJ.

S6.19 Heat energy is absorbed only by the black print (especially if the ink is particularly absorbent in the u.v.). The paper is not heated. Thus the paper cools very quickly without having to be passed through cooling coils.

S6.20 The quartz–halogen lamps attain their full temperature very quickly and lose their heat similarly. They are safer.

S6.21 The glass top is a flat surface and so makes better contact with the flat bottoms of saucepans. There is better heat conduction. They are also much easier to clean than old-style hobs are.

S6.22 When the cooking is finished the outside and inside of the oven are cold. Also the food containers are not heated directly – they are only warmed by the hot food.

S6.23 The water is still in a liquid state because of the enormous pressure at that depth. A water molecule is travelling about four times as fast as it does at room temperature, but it cannot break away from the attraction of the rest of the molecules because of the great external pressure. As soon as it reaches the surface (atmospheric pressure) it turns to steam. It needs the latent heat of vaporisation to do this and some of the steam may revert to water. This is 'wet' steam. On other occasions the steam is 'dry'.

S6.24 Evaporating 1.5 kg of sweat uses up 3640 kJ in one hour (3600 s). This is equivalent to about 1 kW. One can only work at that rate for a very few minutes, such as when felling a tree.

S6.25 As the toast begins to go brown, it absorbs more of the radiant energy falling on it and thereafter rapidly goes black.

S6.26 (a) The polar bear would be almost invisible in a photograph taken with ordinary film (except for his snout and eyes) since his fur would reflect sunlight with almost the same efficiency as snow (in fact the processes are identical).
(b) The bear would also be almost invisible in i.r., since its insulation is so good that it emits very little heat energy.
(c) The bear would appear black in u.v., since it absorbs most of the u.v. whereas the surrounding snow reflects it.

Fields

S7.1 If the proton was stationary exactly at the centre of the circular electrode, it would stay at rest there. However, the slightest perturbation would cause it to move to the negative electrode while remaining in the median plane.

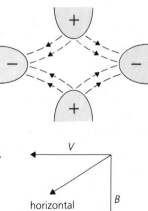

S7.2 The shape of the field is as shown above.

S7.3 The forces on the proton are as shown in the second diagram. The proton moves circumferentially, so it does not matter whether the magnetic field is up or down.

S7.4 Unfortunately that is impossible. The force on the proton due to the magnetic field is always perpendicular to its direction of motion.

S7.5 The paint particles must have a negative charge, picked up from the gun. The shape of the field is as shown.

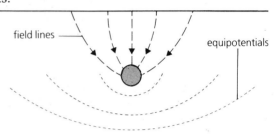

S7.6 The main advantage is that the paint gets round to the back of the object. It is also applied in a very even coat. The method is quick and there are no moving parts.

S7.7 The shape of the electric field in the dust precipitator is shown here. The field lines (dashed lines) must meet the plates perpendicularly because the plates are equipotentials. The bottom half of the sketch shows the equipotentials (dotted lines).

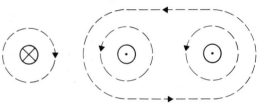

field lines

equipotentials

The intensity of the field is given by $E = V/d = 4.5 \times 10^3/0.15 = 3 \times 10^4$ V m^{-1}. (This assumes that the field lines are evenly distributed along the plate.)

S7.8 The magnetic field lines are shown in this sketch. The left-hand wire and the middle one will repel each other, and the middle one and the right-hand one will attract each other. Thus the centre one is, momentarily, attracted to the right. Because the currents are alternating, the wire will oscillate.

S7.9 The field is as shown. This system acts as a converging lens.

S7.10 The magnetic field is similar to that between the gaps of the Einzel lens; it too is converging.

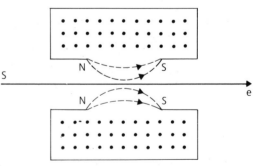

S7.11 The magnetic field method of focusing also rotates the beam. This is nothing more than the effect of the force on a conductor in a perpendicular magnetic field.

S7.12 It is a question of stability. Suppose the attractive system were chosen and that too many people got in the train. Then the carriage would be pulled down into a still weaker field and the carriage would drop off. With the repulsive system, if the same thing happened, the carriage would be pushed down into a stronger magnetic field, closer to the poles.

S7.13 The electric field is given by
$E = V/d = 2 \times 10^4/7 \times 10^{-4} = 3 \times 10^7 \text{ V m}^{-1}$.
The faces of the electrodes are bigger than the gap, so we may take this as a parallel-plate situation.

S7.14 Using the principle of conservation of angular momentum (mvr constant) we have $88 \times 10^9 \times 55 = 5.4 \times 10^{12} \times v$; this yields $v = 1 \text{ km s}^{-1}$.

S7.15 We have to assume that the mass of the comet does not change. In the case of the comet's last visitation we know this was very nearly true, because there was very little evidence of a tail.

S7.16 Using the same principle of momentum conservation,
$14.4 \times 10^{12} \times 7.5 = d \times 2.9$. This yields a greatest distance of 7.4×10^{12} km.

S7.17 The escape velocity of a particle is found by saying that the particle's k.e. must be greater than the work needed to take it right out of the sun's gravitational field. That is,
$\frac{1}{2}mv^2 > GMm/R$, or $v^2 > 2GM/R$, and this must be $> c$. Hence the condition is that $R < 2GM/c^2$, which I find comes to about 3 km. Black holes do have an enormous density.

S7.18 Presumably this was a publicity stunt as he would be weightless. He attached himself to a stout spring and measured the time of small oscillations, using $\omega^2 = k/m$. Although he was weightless, he still had inertia.

S7.19 The electric field is given by $E = dV/dr$. In this case, $E = V/r$ or $r = V/E$. Inserting the numbers, we find that the radius of the sphere is 0.3 μm.

S7.20 The flare constitutes a flow of positive charge emerging from and returning to the surface of the Sun. This forms a loop of current with a magnetic field passing through it, a north pole on one side and a south pole on the other. These magnetic disturbances can be detected on Earth.

Waves

S8.1 The layer of feathers, seen from the side, shows a series of ends – a serrated edge. Each of these acts as a light trap. The light is multiply reflected, and little is reflected back to the eye.

S8.2 A cylindrical convex mirror (the shape of a Roman soldier's shield) would be used. It would have to have a very long focal length not to be obvious.

S8.3 If the mirror were convex in the horizontal plane, then your apparent width would change as you approached the mirror. The change would not be great, however, because the image position does not change much for a big change in the object position. Most women stand at the same distance in front of the mirror and would not notice the cheat.

S8.4 (a) Most earthquakes are deeper than 10 km while few nuclear explosions are deeper than 2 km.
(b) A nuclear explosion usually sends out a compressive wave, whereas an earthquake, due to the sliding of two tectonic plates, emits shear waves.
(c) A nuclear explosion is a compact source and so emits high-frequency seismic waves, whereas an earthquake is an extended source (along the fault line) and so emits lower-frequency waves.

S8.5 The speed of sound in the helium mixture is greater than in air (why?). This does not alter the frequency of the sound produced by the vocal cords, but the resonant frequencies of the cavities of the larynx are increased; normal people sound like Donald Duck.

S8.6 The wavelength of dolphins' sounds is
$\lambda = 1.56/250$ m $= 0.6$ cm.

S8.7 If the dolphin's prey is 10 m away, then it will take $20/1560$ s for the sound to travel there and back. So that it does not confuse the emitted and reflected sounds, the dolphin emits sounds in millisecond bursts. These sound like 'clicks' to us.

S8.8 Water waves travel slower in shallow water. The submerged pile of sand will act as a converging lens and tend to focus the waves.

S8.9 The tube is open at one end and closed at the other, so constitutes a quarter of a wavelength. For the shortest length, 210 cm, the highest note is $340/0.84 = 400$ Hz. For the longest length, the frequency is $340/1200 = 280$ Hz.

S8.10 The fibres are half a wavelength long, since they are fixed at both ends, so $l = v/2f = 4$ cm.

S8.11 The opening to the ear is 2.5 cm long and this is a quarter of a wavelength. $\lambda = 0.1$ m, so the resonant frequency is about 3400 Hz.

S8.12 The wavelength of the radio waves is
$\lambda = 3 \times 10^8/10.2 \times 10^3 = 30$ km. Assuming that we may use the simple formula $\lambda = xd/D$, this yields $x = 1000$ km.

S8.13 A leaf appears green because the chlorophyll in it absorbs all of the light falling on it except the green, which is reflected to our eyes. This will not depend on the angles concerned. Interference effects are very dependent on the angle at which the light falls, and the colour seen changes as you move past the object in question.

S8.14 If there is a matrix of greater refractive index underneath, there is a phase change at both surfaces of the film. So $2t = \lambda$ is the required condition. The wavelength in the film is $580/1.4 = 414$ nm, and the film thickness is 212 nm.

S8.15 There is again a phase change at both surfaces, so the wavelength in the film is $500/1.38 = 362$ nm and the film thickness 90 nm.

S8.16 The beetle's grooves constitute a diffraction grating and the condition is $d \sin \theta = n\lambda$. We assume that $n = 1$ and so $\lambda = 1200 \sin 36 = 706$ nm – red light.

S8.17 Using the formula, I get $\Delta f = 8.8$ kHz. This is measured as the beat frequency, the difference between the emitted signal frequency and that of the reflected wave.

S8.18 As the temperature rises by 5 °C (2 per cent), the speed of sound increases by 1 per cent and so the frequency of wind instruments goes up by the same 1 per cent. This is a semitone at low frequencies, easily recognised. The length increase of the strings causes a decrease in pitch, but at 5×10^{-5} it would be too small to notice.

S8.19 This a real puzzle. We must accept that water globes were used since Balzac was a committed realist. When I used a 500 ml flask filled with water and a 24 W light bulb, I could not get a fine focus nor get greater illumination than without the flask.

S8.20 Newton's third law is at work here. As the pulse comes in it exerts a force on the support. The support exerts an equal and opposite force on the rope.

S8.21 This is a 'moving source' question and so basically a frequency effect. As the source is moving towards the prey, the frequency is increased and so the answer is $f = 60k \times 340/(340-10)$. The frequency will be increased by 3 per cent (2 kHz), so the reflected frequency is 62 kHz.

S8.22 The wavelength is given by $c = f\lambda$, and here is 0.75 mm. The smallest detail visible will be about a wavelength (1 mm) across. The speed of ultrasound in flesh must be slightly different from that in blood, otherwise they would not show up differently in scanning photographs.

S8.23 The wavelength is given by $\lambda = c/f$ and comes to 0.1 m (10 cm). There will be 3000 waves in the emitted pulse, and the extreme range at which a storm can be detected is 150 km (the waves have to go there and back). The energy in a pulse is 0.2 J.

S8.24 The base of a cumulonimbus thunder cloud may be about 2 km above the Earth's surface. It will take 6 s for sound to travel from the top of the strike to the ground and no time to travel from the bottom. You will know that the thunder is caused by the rapid expansion of the air as it is heated by an instantaneous current of the order of thousands of amps.

Current electricity

S9.1 The current through you would be too small ($I = V/R = 250/100\text{k} = 2.5$ mA).

S9.2 The shock would probably make you sweat, reducing your skin resistance to the order of 1 kΩ and increasing the current through you to 250 mA – lethal.

S9.3 Since the a.c. is an intermittent supply, it is more likely than the d.c. to upset the intermittent pulses to your heart muscles.

S9.4 The parachute was presumably made of nylon (an insulator), so there was no path through the man. Why he got burned is more difficult; in theory he should have been totally unharmed. However, he would have some capacitance and a charge would flow on to him every time the voltage went through its cycle. Presumably this flowing charge constituted a current sufficient to cause severe burns.

S9.5 The A.A. man connects the batteries in parallel (your drained battery has a large resistance). He connects + to +. If he connected them the wrong way round, he would attempt to drive the starter motor the wrong way and it certainly would not turn over your engine.

S9.6 The A.A. car supplies 50 A at 12 V for 5 s = 3 kJ of energy. A unit of electricity is 1 kW hour = 3.6 MJ of energy. You owe the A.A. about ½₀₀p.

S9.7 A 240 V, 60 W lamp also draws a current of 0.25 A. Therefore connect both lamps in series to the 240 V supply.

S9.8 Either connect two 16 Ω loudspeakers in parallel (the usual practice) or two 4 Ω speakers in series. (Why is the former preferred?)

S9.9 (a) Most ceramics are insulators (china and glass are used as such).
(b) Most metal oxides are insulators (rust, for instance).
(c) It will be very difficult to draw ceramics into fine wires.
(d) The limiting factor in the design of many compact computers is getting rid of the heat produced in chips. If the chips are too small (and we want them small for high speed), they get too hot. Superconducting chips will not get hot because they have no resistance.

S9.10 The total current is 1080 A at 3.5 V. The power is 3780 W.

S9.11 The power in each shock is $16 \times 60 = 960$ W. The energy delivered is this value times $0.005 = 5.8$ J. If this is administered 75 times per second, then the total work done is about 440 J. 700 cells in series would be needed to get the total potential at 60 V.

S9.12 The dielectric strength of snow must be greater than $750/0.05 = 15$ kV m^{-1}. In other words, snow can withstand an electric field of this magnitude without breaking down. Unfortunately, I cannot find the quoted value for this in any of my books.

S9.13 The total resistance per km is about 0.034 Ω (there are two driving rails in parallel to act as the return wire). Hence the total p.d. is $0.034 \times 3000 = 102$ V per km, and the total power loss is about 300 kW.

S9.14 When the train starts it draws a much larger current, about 5000 A. Hence the power losses would be trebled. In London's Underground network there is the same third rail system, but the power losses are not so great because it has been possible to arrange for each station to be at the top of a slight rise, with obvious advantages.

S9.15 The μ and M factors cancel, so the power is $15 \times 9 = 135$ W.

S9.16 The formula we want is $R = \rho l/A$. Inserting the figures, I get the enormous value of 250 MΩ.

S9.17 The switches are in series since both are needed, this is an AND statement.

S9.18 Surprisingly, the answer is (d). To see this we work out the resistance of each lamp. For the 15 W lamp it is about 3500 Ω and for the 150 W lamp it is about 350 Ω. With the two lamps in series, the total resistance is 3850 Ω and so the current is only enough to light the 15 W lamp dimly and the 150 W lamp not at all.

S9.19 Since the two blankets are on top of each other, this is a resistance-in-series problem, with the same current (or heat flow) through both. So the order of the blankets does not matter. The best solution to the problem is to get married.

S9.20 We have 40 lamps in series to give a total voltage of 240 V. The current through each is $12/6 = 2$ A and the total power is $40 \times 12 = 480$ W. They look horrible, totally artificial.

S9.21 In order of increasing heat output, we have two resistors in series, one alone and two resistors in parallel.

S9.22 For two resistors in series, the total resistance $= 960$ Ω, current $= \frac{1}{4}$ A and power $= 60$ W. For the single resistor of 480 Ω, current $= \frac{1}{2}$ A, power $= 120$ W. For the two in parallel, resistance $= 240$ Ω, current $= 1$ A, power $= 240$ W. This question is somewhat artificial in that the two elements do not need to have the same resistance and thus do not give such a wide difference in power output. That problem is very tricky, however; in science we only tackle those problems we can solve. In Sir Peter Medawar's words, 'Science is the art of the soluble.'

S9.23 You wait until the junkie is in a drugged stupor and then push the two needles into separate nerves. Connect them to the battery and the victim is electrocuted. No one will suspect you; the needle marks will not show in the junkie's body, and because of the absence of cars there are no high-tension batteries for miles. This question does have a serious point, though. Anyone undergoing a surgical operation is open (literally!) to a lethal shock from a low voltage through exposed nerves. That is why great care is taken to ensure that there are no stray potentials about, and why the floors of operating theatres are covered in conducting tiles.

S9.24 Strictly speaking all electric heaters are 100 per cent efficient, but not all are equally useful. A 1 kW heater that delivers its energy at a temperature 1 °C above ambient is useless.

S9.25 As there are 2 V to spare with ¼ Ω resistance, the current is 8 A.

S9.26 As both lamps draw the same current, they will both be at nearly full brightness.

S9.27 My friend is quite wrong and I have told him so. The flow of heat from a room is analogous to the flow of electric current in parallel resistors. The insulation is analogous to the electrical resistance, and the temperature difference to the potential difference (voltage). The total heat flux is the sum of the separate heat flows. Any insulated wall will reduce the total heat loss.

S9.28 They are in parallel because you can have the heater and fan on separately. Actually, it is a bit more complicated, because you cannot have the heater on without the fan (otherwise the heater would burn out). So the switch is arranged so that the fan is always on and the heater may be added, in parallel.

S9.29 They are wired in parallel. The interior light and the warning light come on when any door is opened. This is an OR statement in logic, as the lights go on when any switch is closed.

S9.30 The connection is made through the chassis of the car. This is also joined to the (usually) negative side of the battery and generator.

S9.31 Each set of four resistive elements has a resistance of 1½ Ω. Two of these sets in series have a resistance of 3 Ω.

S9.32 With 12 V p.d. and total current of 4 A, the total power is 48 W.

S9.33 The total power and resistance are fixed. Because glass is such a poor conductor of heat we want the resistors to cover as much of the window as possible. If all the resistors were connected in series they would have to have sixteen times the resistance of a single one and so would have to be sixteen times as wide (the resistors are in the form of a ribbon). This would obscure too much of the view through the window.

S9.34 The fuses should be in parallel, so that each will carry 5 A; currents in parallel add.

S9.35 The two 5 A wires will tend to carry more than a single 10 A fuse because they have a bigger surface area and will be able to dissipate heat better. In any case, in my experience, fuses can carry a bigger current than they are rated for, especially if the current is increased slowly.

S9.36 This is called a 'fools' circuit'. The cell will be rapidly drained because of the short-circuit across it.

S9.37 When a bird sits on a high-tension wire its claws are of the order of a few centimetres apart, with a p.d. between them of, say, 10^{-5} V. As the resistance of the bird's claws is of the order of 10^{+5} Ω, the current through the bird is very small – not enough to be felt. If the bird spans two overhead wires, with a p.d. of 11 000 V, the resistance in its feathers may not be big enough to prevent electrocution, or the tripping of the cut-outs at the power station. Generally, the closest wires are in parallel, with the same potential, and so present no danger to birds.

S9.38 The high-tension wires carried by pylons are about 1 metre apart, so the wing span of a bird is not the limiting factor. The danger arises from the possibility of two adjacent wires being blown together, with a p.d. between phases of the order of 200 000 V.

S9.39 By Ohm's law, we get the current as 1500 A and the power generated as 450 MW. There are about 750 thunderstorms occurring at any time, somewhere on Earth, most in the warmth and humidity of the tropics. The ionosphere presumably has a high concentration of free ions and these are conductors of electricity.

Capacitors

S10.1 The rules for adding capacitors are the opposite to those for resistors. Thus we need two capacitors in series to give ½ μF, with another capacitor in parallel to these two.

S10.2 The capacitance is $C = A\varepsilon/d = 6.5 \times 10^{-10}$ F, $\varepsilon = 8.9 \times 10^{-12}$ F m^{-1}. The voltage on the plane is then $V = Q/C = 1.6$ kV.

    Before a plane is refuelled, great care is taken to ensure that it is earthed, that is, that any charge it has acquired is allowed to leak away. Otherwise, this kind of voltage could easily cause the jet fuel to explode.

S10.3 We have two capacitors in parallel, so the total capacitance
$= 2A\varepsilon/d = 2 \times 0.48 \times 9/7.5 \times 10^{-9}$ F $= 1.15 \times 10^{-9}$ F.
The charge is then $Q = VC = 1.15 \times 10^{-6}$ coulomb.
The energy stored $E = \frac{1}{2}QV = 5.75 \times 10^{-4}$ J.
A mesh is used because a solid plate would prevent the central electrode moving by air friction; more importantly, it is acoustically transparent.

S10.4 A man totally enclosed in a metal can would be safe, because there is no electric field inside a hollow container. In practice a suit with a closely wound wire mesh is used and this totally encloses the worker. It is much better to effect a repair without having to shut down the supply.

S10.5 The capacitance $C = A\varepsilon/d = 1.8 \times 10^{-10}$ F. The charge on the electret is $4 \times 20 = 80$ nC. The voltage, then, is $800/1.8 = 440$ V.

S10.6 The energy stored in a capacitor is $E = \frac{1}{2}QV$; as $V = 336$ V, the charge $Q = 5000/336 = 15$ coulomb, and the total capacitance $C = Q/V = 15/336 = 0.045$ F. The answer is between 4 and 5. We settle for 5 because the capacitors may not be completely discharged by the welding machines. The value 336 V comes from the fact that 240 V is the r.m.s. value and $336 = 240 \times 2^{\frac{1}{2}}$. The capacitors take an appreciable time to recharge, but that will be used by the operator putting the next piece of work between the jaws of the welding machine.

S10.7 The formula for the capacitance is $C = A\varepsilon_r\varepsilon/d$; remembering that $A = 10^{-4}$ m^2, we find that $C = 0.7$ μF (a very large figure).

S10.8 The energy required to be stored is 20 J. The energy stored is $E = \frac{1}{2}QV$ or $\frac{1}{2}CV^2$. Inserting the figures gives $V = 900$ V and $Q = 4.5$ mC.

S10.9 We have to assume that the flash gun totally discharges the capacitor. In practice, this will not happen precisely, but the error will not be large. This is why the flash gun does not use a much larger capacitor at a lower voltage to store the same energy.

Electromagnetism

S11.1 The work done by the falling water per second
$= 58 \times 10 \times 50 = 29$ kW. The efficiency is $20/29 = 60$ per cent. This is very high for such a small system. China has pioneered the use of these small hydro schemes.

S11.2 The total length of wire $= 200 \times 2\pi \times 3$ cm $= 12\pi$ m. The total force is given by
$F = BIl = 0.6 \times 12\pi \times 2 \times 10^{-3} = 4.4 \times 10^{-4}$ N.

S11.3 Such a loudspeaker would work as a microphone but very inefficiently, because the diameter of a loudspeaker is up to

20 cm (compare with the diameter of the human mouth). Loudspeakers were used to 'bug' rooms in the infancy of the trade.

S11.4 The formula here is $F = BIl = 0.02 \times 1000 \times 0.08 = 1.6$ N.

S11.5 If a conductor is caused to move in a magnetic field, an e.m.f. is induced in the conductor. This will cause a larger current and so a larger magnetic field and so on. The system behaves like a self-exciting dynamo.

S11.6 This is an inductive effect. The voltage induced in the metal in the crucible is given by $E = -M\,dI/dt$. Not much can be done with M, but the current can be large – hence the thick wires – and dt can be small – hence the high frequency.
   The alternator would spin faster than those for 50 Hz supply. Alternatively (sorry!) it could have more coils.

S11.7 The force is given by $F = BIl = 5 \times 150\,000 \times 1 = 750\,000$ N.

S11.8 Here the force is $f = k \times I \times I \times l/d = 4.5 \times 10^6$ N, using $k = 2 \times 10^{-7}$ units.

S11.9 We equate the loss in electrical p.e. (eV) to the gain in k.e. ($\frac{1}{2}mv^2$). This gives a speed of about 8×10^7 m s^{-1}, about one-quarter of the speed of light.

S11.10 This would be the speed of undeflected electrons as they hit the screen. Deflected electrons would have the same forward component of velocity, but a changed speed.

S11.11 The formula here is $F = Bev = 8 \times 10^{-16}$ N.

S11.12 The deflected acceleration is given by $a = F/m$ where m is the mass of an electron, giving $a = 5 \times 10^{14}$ m s^{-2}. The time for the electron to travel the 0.2 m to the screen is given by $t = d/v = 2.5 \times 10^{-9}$ s. Finally, we use $d = \frac{1}{2}at^2$ to get a deflection of about 3 mm.

S11.13 Some of the electrons would be deflected upwards (or downwards) and so would be more nearly parallel to the magnetic field. These would experience less deflection, causing distortion of the television picture; for a lot of programmes, this can only be an improvement.

S11.14 We equate the applied magnetic force, $F = Bev$, with the centripetal force, $F = mv^2/r$. Simplifying, this gives $r = mv/eB$. The difference in deflection after a semicircle will be $2\,\Delta r = 2\,\Delta m\,v/eB$. Here $\Delta m = 2u = 2 \times 1.66 \times 10^{-27}$ kg. I make this yield $2\,\Delta r =$ about 5 mm.

S11.15 The induced e.m.f. is given by $E = d\phi/dt = -M\,dI/dt$, where M is the mutual inductance of the coil and the object if $I = I_0 \sin \omega t$ then $dI/dt = I_0\,\omega \cos \omega t$, so the bigger ω is, the bigger the induced e.m.f.

S11.16 Nothing can be done to minimise the induced e.m.f. but if the resistance is large the induced current can be smaller. Thin insulated strips have a larger resistance than a thick solid.

S11.17 I think that the shape of the field is as shown. If an electron gets off-centre, as at point P, then the force on it is in the upward direction, returning it to the centre.

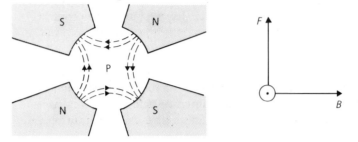

S11.18 I think that the polarity is as shown. (Remember that these are electrons.)

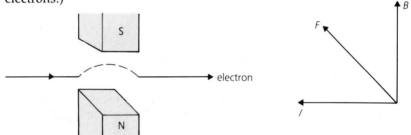

S11.19 Electromagnetic waves are emitted whenever an electron is accelerated. During a lightning discharge, the electrons are subject to large accelerations as they change their direction (I presume that they travel at constant speed). In fact sferics are of much greater intensity than any radio broadcast and cover a frequency range from A.M. up to many MHz.

Alternating current

S12.1 The vector diagram is as shown. The voltage then (by Pythagoras) is 69 V. The load resistance is $40/300 = 0.13 \ \Omega$. The reactance is $69/300 = 0.23 \ \Omega$ and this $= \omega L$, so $L = 0.23/100\pi = 0.7$ mH.

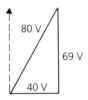

To make the power factor unity, we want a capacitor to balance the inductive load, that is, $1/\omega C = 0.23 \ \Omega$ or $C = 1/0.23 \times 100\pi$. So $C = 0.013$ F. Presumably there is no attempt at achieving resonance in this case because such an enormous capacitor would be needed.

S12.2 Although the two surfaces of the metal may seem to be absolutely smooth there are always very small pits and hills, called asperities. Where these are in contact, the area of metal actually touching is very small and so there is a very high resistance at these points.

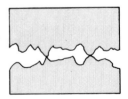

S12.3 The power is 10^5 W and the energy supplied is 5×10^4 J. This amount of energy would heat 0.1 kg by $0.1 \times 420 = 1200$ °C.

S12.4 For resonance, we put the reactances equal: $\omega L = 1/\omega C$ or $\omega^2 = 1/LC$. Thus $C = 1/L\omega^2$. Inserting $\omega = 2\pi \times 1.5 \times 10^6$, we get $C = 10\ \mu F$.

S12.5 A discharge tube, such as a fluorescent lamp, has a negative resistance characteristic. Unless an inductor is used to control the current the lamp would pass such a large current it would burn out.

S12.6 For unit power factor we want resonance, $\omega L = 1/\omega C$. Here $\omega = 100\pi$ and I find that the capacitor must be $2\ \mu F$ in value. This is a large value, as we cannot use an electrolytic capacitor (why?). Some systems do not attempt to get the power factor to unity.

Modern physics

S13.1 The centripetal force on the protons mv^2/r is provided by the magnetic force Bev. Hence $B = mv/er$; at this relativistic energy E the momentum mv is equal to E/C, so that $B = E/Cer$. Putting in the figures gives $B = 4.8$ T.

S13.2 Again we equate Bev with mv^2/r. Transposing gives $v = Ber/m$, and inserting the numbers gives 9.5×10^5 m s^{-1}. This problem is non-relativistic.

S13.3 The frequency is $f = c/\lambda = 3 \times 10^8/6.94 \times 10^{-7} = 4 \times 10^{14}$ Hz. The energy $E = hf = 4 \times 10^{14} \times 6.6 \times 10^{-34} = 2.88 \times 10^{-19}$ J. Or $2.88 \times 10^{-19}/1.6 \times 10^{-19} = 1.8$ eV.

S13.4 If n is the number of β-particles per second, then $n \times 1.6 \times 10^{-19} = 2 \times 10^{-6}$. This gives n as 1.25×10^{13} counts per s.

The voltage measures the energy with which the β-particles are emitted. A slow-moving β-particle would be repelled by the charge built up by the other β-particles already arrived.

This battery could be used to power fluorescent lamps.

S13.5 The mass defect is 0.005 23 u = 4.87 MeV.

Consider the recoil of the Rn nucleus and the α-particle. Since momentum is conserved, $Mv = mV$. The ratio of the kinetic energies = $\frac{1}{2}MV/\frac{1}{2}mv = m/M = 1/55$. Thus the α-particle carries off almost all the k.e., leaving the Rn nucleus only one part in 50.

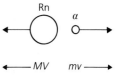

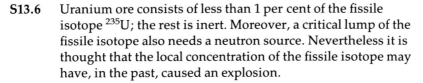

S13.6 Uranium ore consists of less than 1 per cent of the fissile isotope ^{235}U; the rest is inert. Moreover, a critical lump of the fissile isotope also needs a neutron source. Nevertheless it is thought that the local concentration of the fissile isotope may have, in the past, caused an explosion.

S13.7 As the star was very hot, it burnt its hydrogen fuel in a very short time. As it was massive, when the pressure imbalance did come, there was a big explosion – a supernova.

S13.8 The wavelength is $3 \times 10^8/2.45 \times 10^9 = 10$ cm. As this is the same order as the size of the oven, standing waves would be possible; but as the photons are sent in all directions by the rotating fan, I do not foresee many standing waves. (In any case, what would be the point?)
The energy of one photon is given by
$E = hf = 6.6 \times 10^{-34} \times 2.45 \times 10^9 = 1.6 \times 10^{-24}$ J.
The number of photons per s is $500/1.6 \times 10^{-24} = 3.1 \times 10^{26}$.

S13.9 The Earth is very old. Presumably nuclides with shorter half-lives were formed when the Earth was born, but these have long since decayed to near nothing.

S13.10 If the activity has declined to one-eighth, that is three half-lives, the age is $3 \times 5760 = 17\ 000$ years. (But were there people about making wooden bowls that long ago? Probably there were.)

S13.11 We have to find the number of atoms in 10 kg of uranium-235. Avogadro's law tells us that there are 6×10^{23} particles per mole (i.e. 235 g of this isotope), hence there are 6×10^{26} atoms in 235 kg. Thus I find the energy released to be 8×10^{14} J.

S13.12 The energies are: for the γ-ray, 0.0040 u; for the first β-particle 0.0014 u; for the second β-particle, 0.0008 u. In fact, the γ-ray will carry off more energy, as fast neutrons are needed for the first reaction.

S13.13 I find that the Q value is 0.000 514 u, equivalent to 8.3×10^{-30} kg and, using $E = mc^2$, this comes to 7.5×10^{-13} J.

S13.14 The rate at which the Sun is converting hydrogen to helium is inferred from the amount of radiation it emits. On the Earth we receive about 1 kW per square metre, as the Sun is 1.5×10^{11} m away. The Sun emits about $4\pi \times (1.5 \times 10^{11})^2$ kW, or about 3×10^{26} W, and this is equivalent to about 3 million tonnes. The Sun also emits other kinds of radiation not taken into account here.

Index

Answers to questions are indexed only where they contain information not mentioned in the corresponding question.